Wali

The Other Side of the Lens

Volume 1

A Sniper's Photographic Adventure in Afghanistan

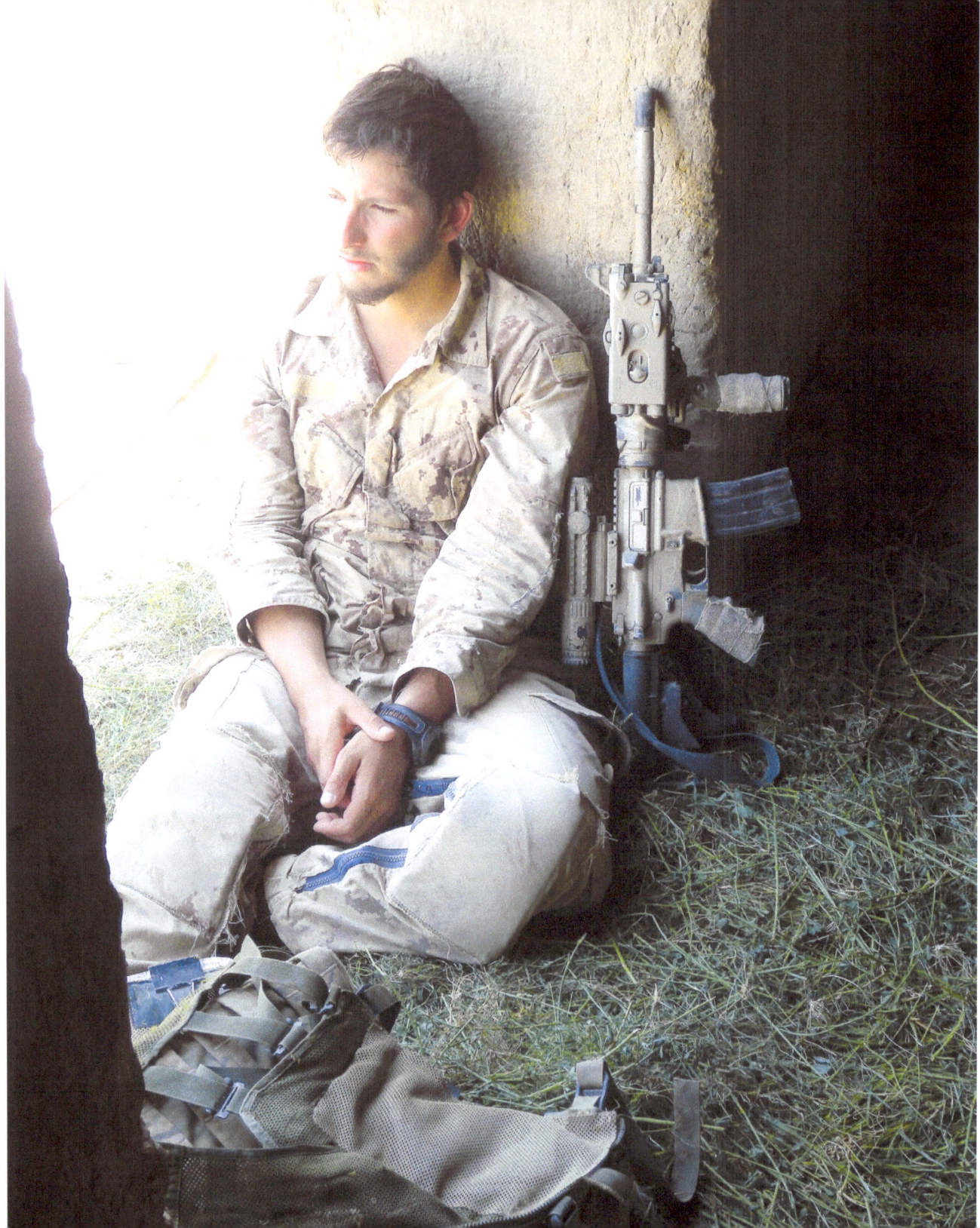

To those women whom we almost never see. To those women who are both everywhere and nowhere. To this beauty that is hidden from the eye and the photographer's lens. To those women whom no sniper would dare aim at. To the Afghan women.

From the same author:

The Nameless Traveller, a philosophical tale

Author's website:

www.wali-auteur.com

Translated from the French by Elizabeth S. Yellen (esyellen@acotranslations.com)

ISBN 978-2-9812324-3-4

Dépôt légal — Bibliothèque et Archives nationales du Québec, 2014
Dépôt légal — Bibliothèque et Archives Canada, 2014

© OLOrtiz.com, 2014

Acknowledgments

I would like to thank my family, my friends, and especially my mother, who for more than a year and a half expected uniformed soldiers to show up at any moment to announce the death of her son in Afghanistan.

I would also like to thank Michelle Lapointe and her sister Marie-Josée, who were quick to believe in my projects.

The same goes for Michel Létourneau, who is currently the president of the Régie du Cinéma du Québec and who introduced me to leading cultural figures.

I would like to recognize the producer Michel Gauthier and his wife, Nicole Magny. Their smiles alone would be enough to make anyone want to enter the world of cinema and television.

Thank you also to Nicole-Marie Rhéault, writer and editor, for her advice on the French language. She wields a pen as adeptly as a musketeer wields a sword.

Thank you to Zoé Lavigne, professional artist and graphic designer, for her help with design and layout.

Kudos to Anaïs Barbeau-Lavalette, talented filmmaker, and her husband, Émile Proulx-Cloutier, actor and creator, for their gracious welcome. They are living proof that those who succeed often have lovely personalities.

Finally, I warmly thank the soldiers and employees of the National Defence, who supported me as I went through the publishing process.

Preface

War, although it is sometimes necessary, is always a failure of mankind. The biggest military victories are also the biggest human defeats. War is like a poker game, but in this case, even the winner loses something. In war, it is impossible to win one's money back. Participants do not take back what they have lost. Mothers will never again see their sons. Sisters will never again embrace their brothers. The winners' families, like the losers' families, will live forever with this painful memory of the grand departure for the kingdom of death.

I got to know Afghanistan. I loved the country, its culture, its people. I chose to savor its beauty—despite the war, and despite my job as a soldier. For this beautiful region is much more than bulletproof vehicles and helmeted soldiers. It is much more than explosions and bloody corpses. The dark smoke of explosions always ends up dissipating, and light always manages to break through.

I was first deployed in 2009, as a sniper in the Royal 22nd Regiment. I returned in 2010 with a group of trusted advisers to train the Afghan police force. I spent a total of sixteen months there. I would not have hesitated to stay twice as long.

Afghanistan is a country of contrasts. On the one hand, there are bombs and ambushes. There is fanaticism. There is the enemy. On the other, there are children who play and shepherds who lead their animals to the pastures. Beauty can be found even in a country at war. Even in the darkest sky, the starts still shine. And delicate roses grow underneath the coarse stones of a fortress.

In Afghanistan, between the lens of my weapon and that of my camera, there is the soldier and the photographer. There is the warrior and the artist. I knew my weapon's ballistics intimately. I carried my weapon like a man; I played with my camera like a child.

Photography is a perpetual battle against laziness. How many times did I find myself hesitating between my camera and a few extra bottles of water before embarking on a patrol in the mountains? With the temperature at fifty degrees Celsius in the shade, I often would have left my camera at the military camp. How many times did I think, "It will be small patrol of no interest. I don't need my camera," only to then congratulate myself for changing my mind at the last second? For although I was looking for the enemy, I was above all hunting for beauty. My main weapon was not my assault rifle, but the innocuous lens of my camera.

It is hard to simultaneously be a soldier and a photographer. The camera strap would cross the weapon strap. They would get caught and irritate my neck under a layer of sand, dust, and sweat. After several hours in the heat, I would find a scene worthy of being photographed. As in an ambush, I would have only a few seconds to take aim and "hit the clay pigeon," which was fleeing for good. At that moment I would exchange the lens of my weapon for that of my camera. I would exchange the trigger of a gun for a flurry of photos.

When I was a vehicle gunner, I would have even less time. After grabbing my image machine, I would blow on the dusty lens. I would then do my best to offset the strong vibrations of the vehicle. Having done my work, all I could do was hope that of the burst of photos, at least one clear picture would come out.

As soldiers, we knew that when there were hardly any journalists and photographers left, the sector was dangerous. Conversely, an abundance of cameras reassured us that a region was stabilized and safe. It was rare for journalists to want to embed themselves in truly dangerous patrols.

I will bring you to these places where the lenses that are seen are those that are attached to a weapon. I welcome you to what is more than a combat mission—it is a guided tour that is protected by an infallible paper window. Welcome to a patrol that alternates between winter and summer, that is close to what some people call hell, but above all is close to beauty. Welcome to one of the world's most dangerous regions. I present to you not images of a beautiful war, but beautiful images of a war.

The one whom the Afghans called Wali, May 2014

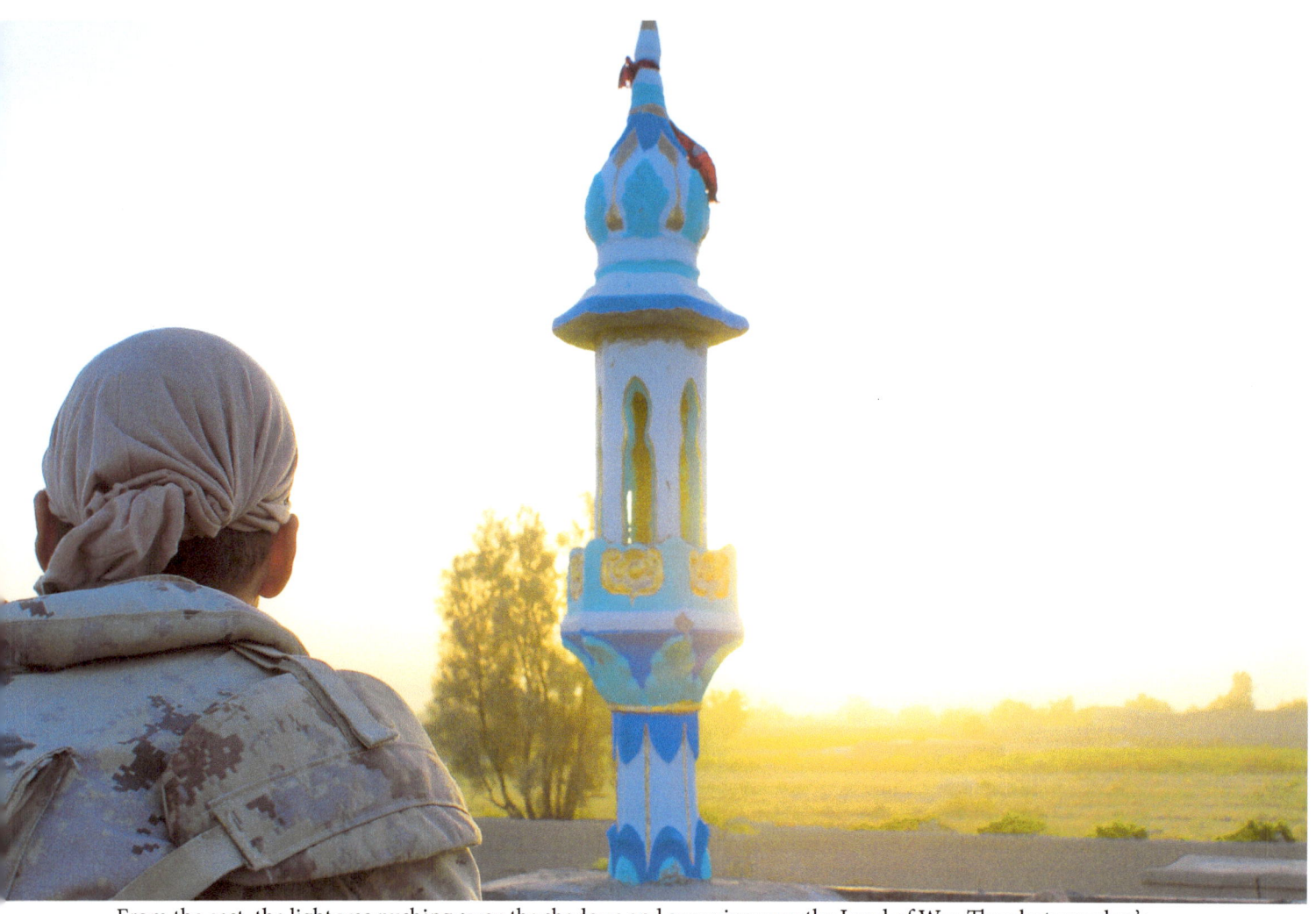

From the east, the light was pushing away the shadows and sweeping over the Land of War. The photographer's adventure was beginning. The soldier's work was, alas, continuing.

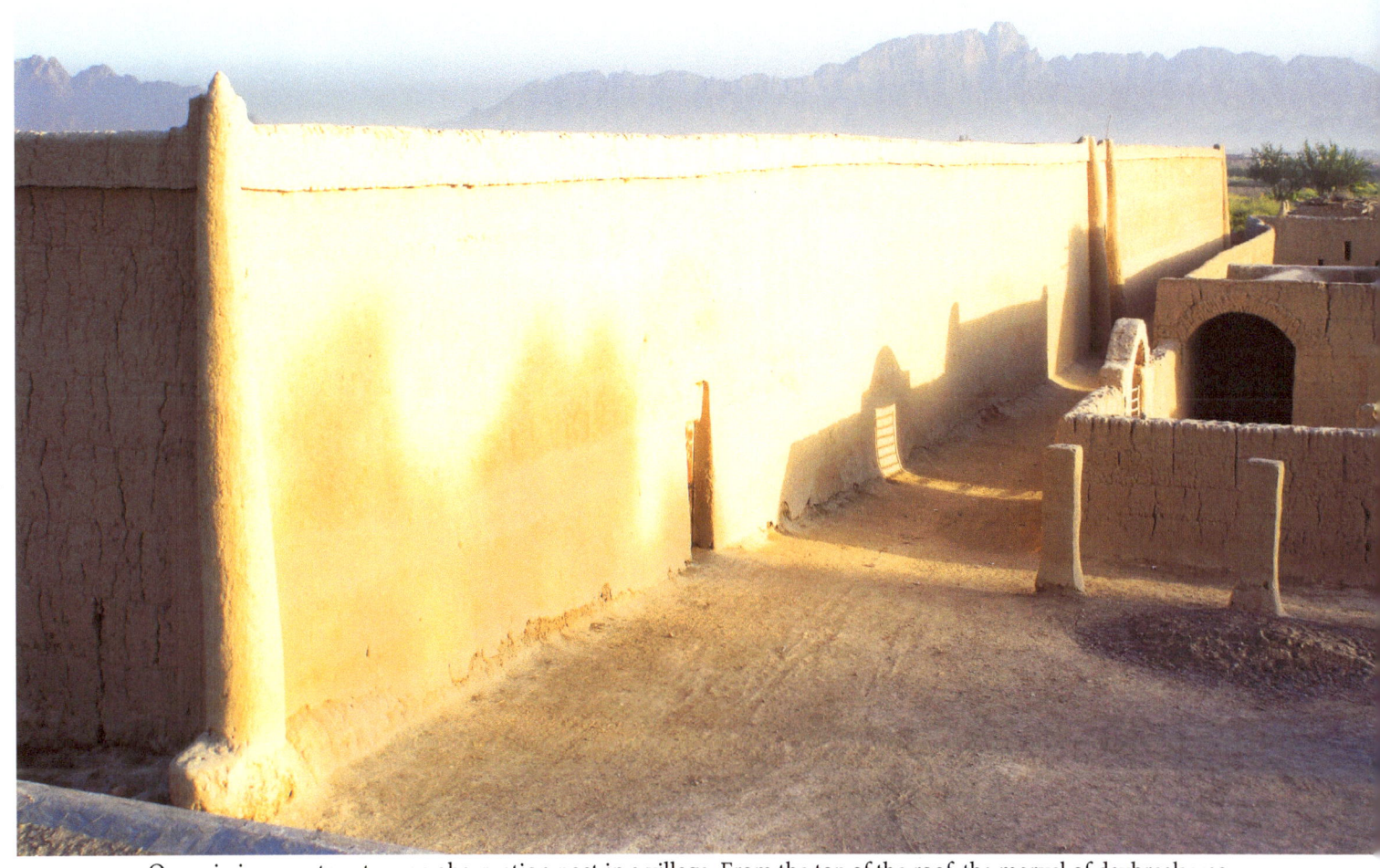

Our mission was to set up an observation post in a village. From the top of the roof, the marvel of daybreak was unfolding before our eyes.

On the horizon, an ancient fortress was hidden in the hollow of the mountains. Its walls had watched the soldiers of Alexander the Great and Genghis Khan march by. These walls still stand, witnesses to the precariousness of civilizations.

A bit closer, the religious chief of the village, the mullah, lived in the building on the right. Seconds after I took this photo, the clay roof gave way under my feet. Fortunately, I avoided what could have been an unfortunate fall. I found myself sitting astride a metal bar, my feet dangling in the air, and for a moment I felt like Indiana Jones in a temple of doom!

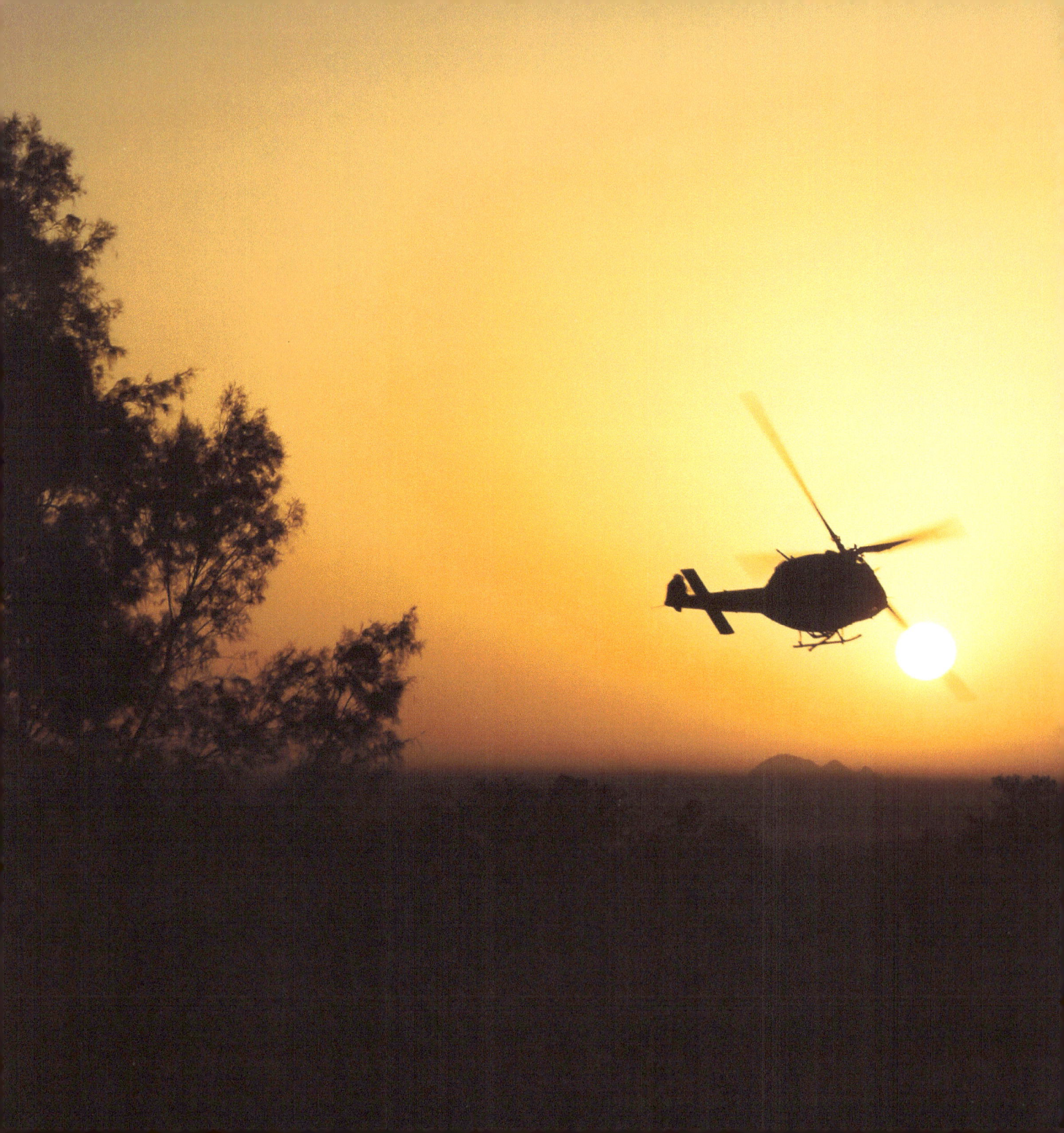

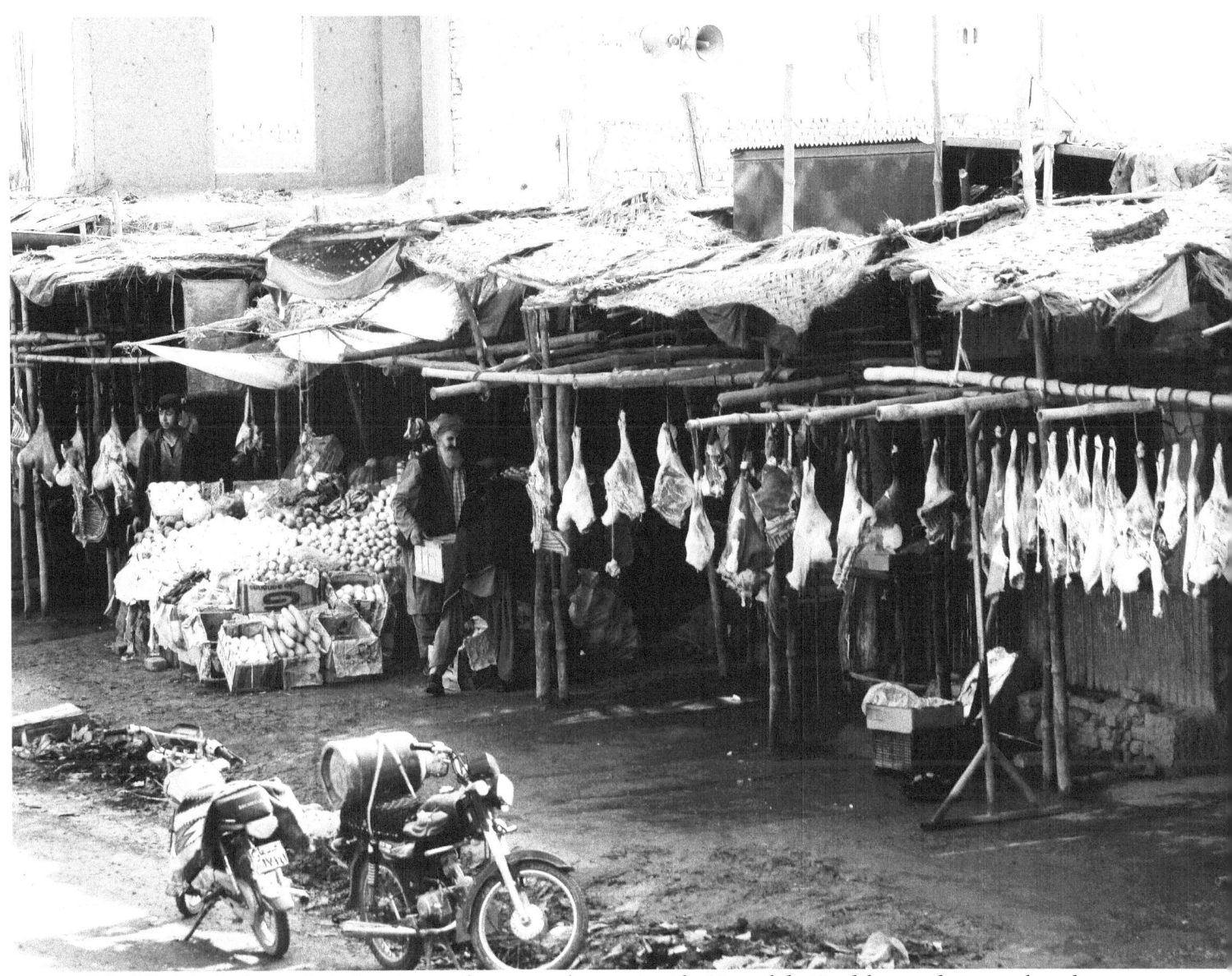
Like a bird of prey, the helicopter was flying over the countryside. Meanwhile, Kandahar was being awakened in the calm. A mosque's loudspeakers (top of photo) were already filling the air with a voice that seemed to come from the heavens. It was the call to prayer, immutable for centuries, like the succession of the days and nights.

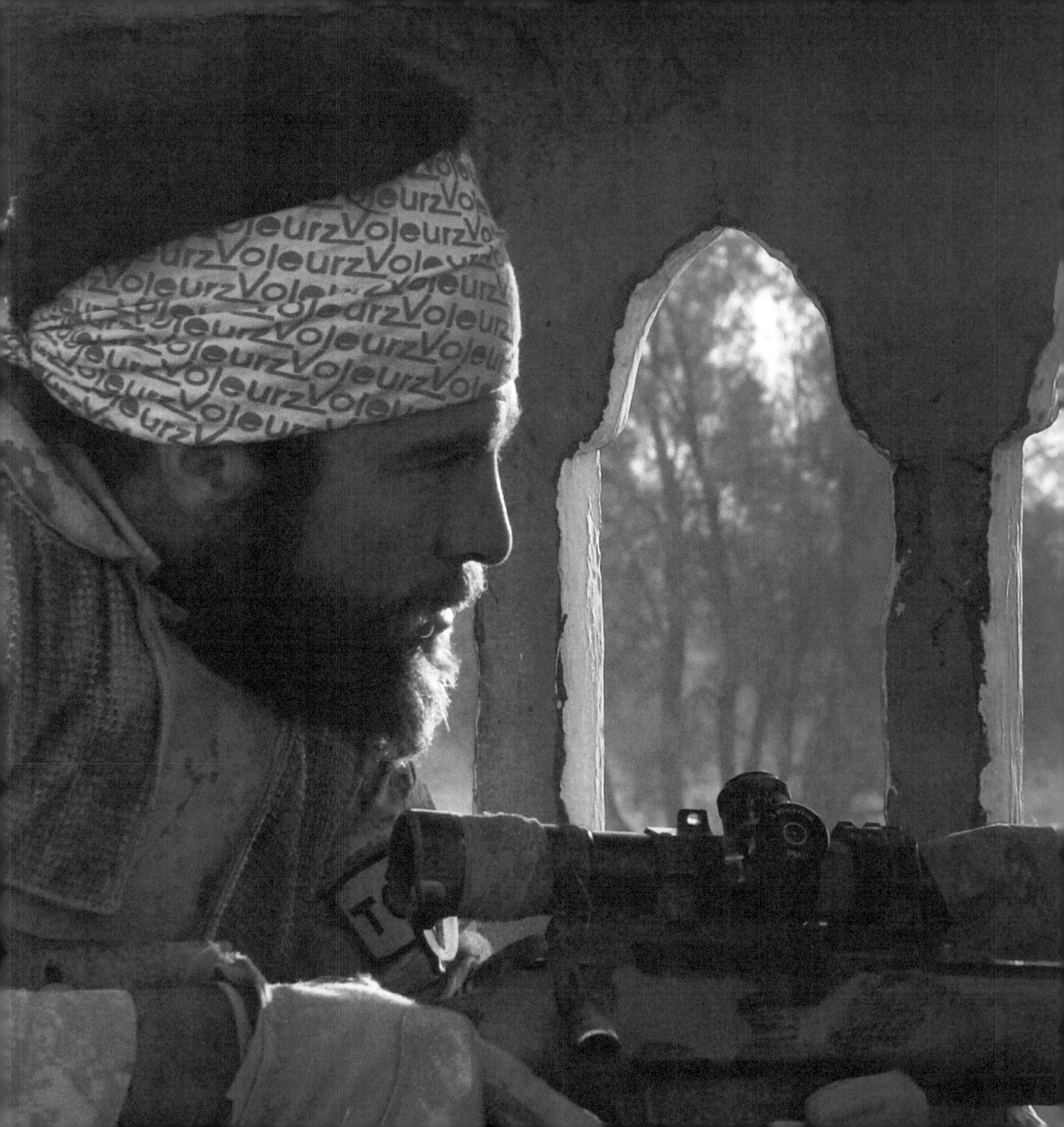

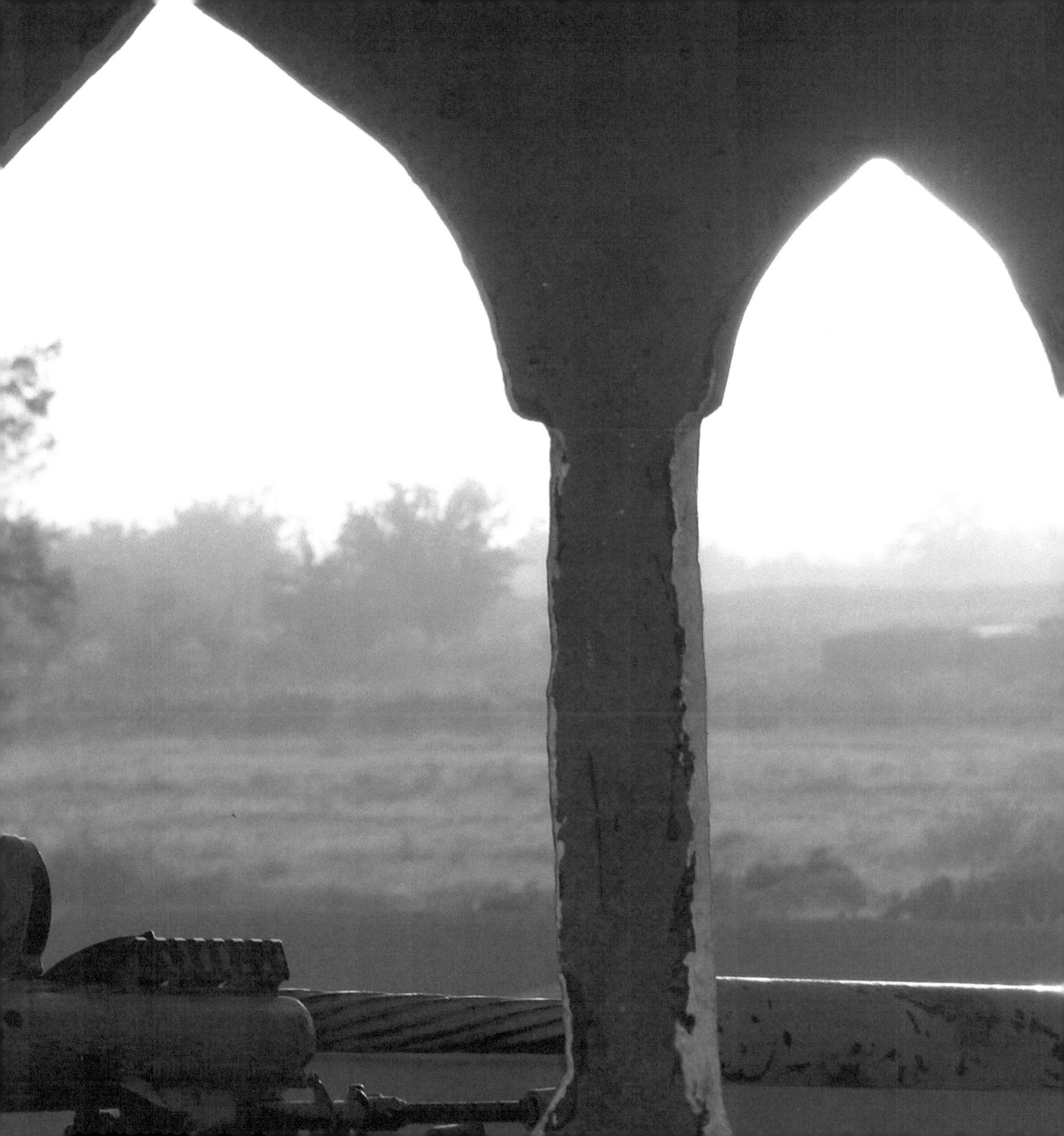

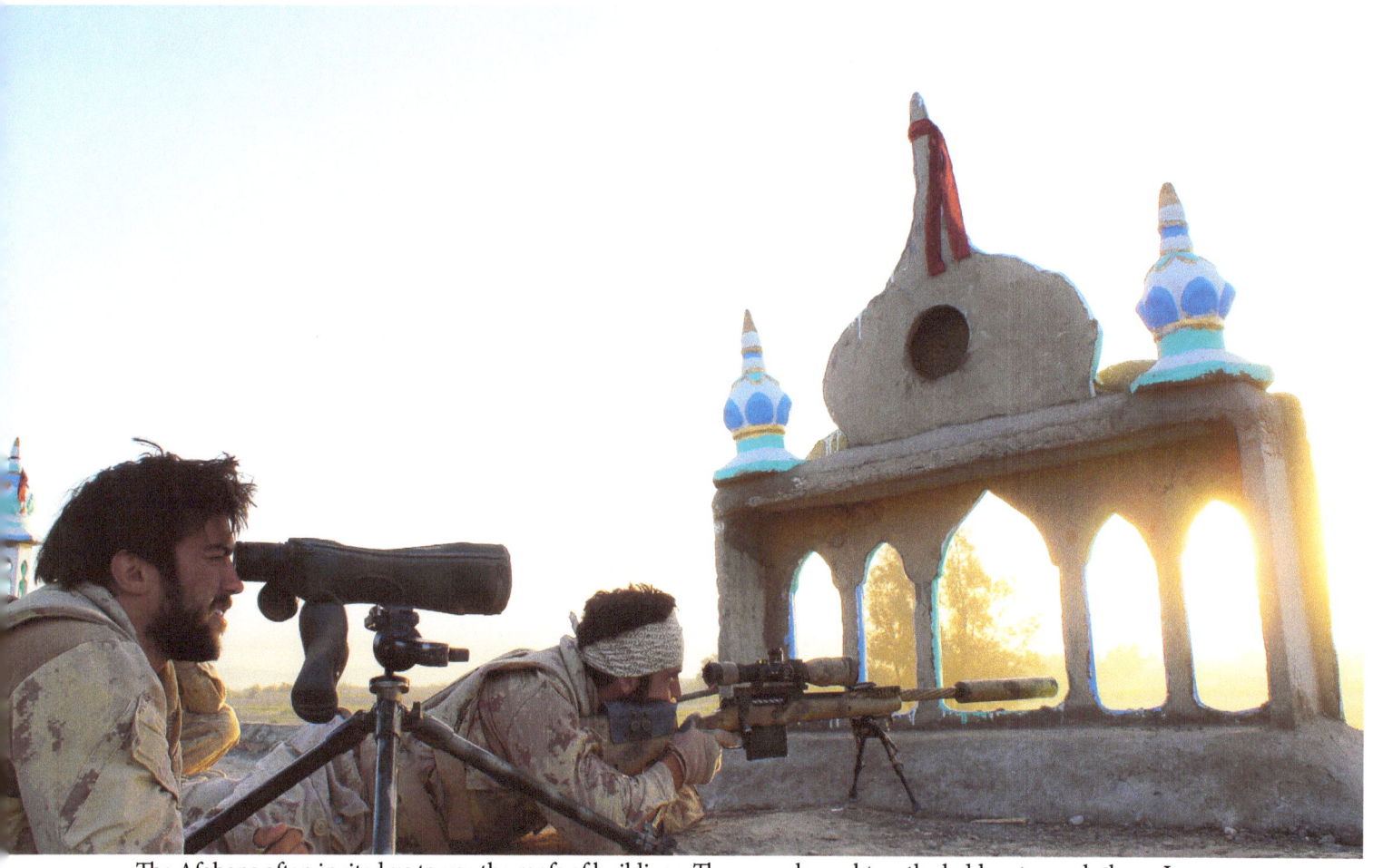

The Afghans often invited us to use the roofs of buildings. They even brought us the ladders to reach them. I remember one particular time when a father and his children climbed up with us. They kept pointing at us and smiling. They stayed a long time, as if we had become their new pastime. I would have done the same thing if people from another world had descended on my home with bizarre gadgets.

During one patrol, we intercepted a message between enemy insurgents. The tone of the exchanges was feverish and their origin was unknown. The exchanges discussed setting off a bomb as our soldiers, who were patrolling in the village, passed. The atmosphere was strained and electric. The danger was palpable. The residents, perhaps acting on a premonition, all shut themselves in their houses.

A radio communication from one of our soldiers soon alerted us about an armed man who was watching our soldiers from a hiding place. We immediately trained our sights and adjusted our weapons' ballistics in order to compensate for the wind, distance, temperature, and air density.

My weapon's mechanism was tense and activated. The compressed springs were on the verge of causing death! A few pounds of pressure exerted by the finger were all that postponed the ending of a life, of a world. A cartridge was waiting in the darkness of the barrel. I imagined it cold and terrifying. It was waiting to emerge into daylight. It would then race pitilessly toward this life and drive it away to an endless night.

The light was going through the optical sight. The focus was blurred and the target was obscured. It looked more like mist dancing in front of an indistinct shape. Was it a mirage? I adjusted the image. The fuzziness dissipated and a face appeared. The enemy to shoot down had been transformed. Now I saw a face with definite contours under a colored veil floating in the wind. It was a living symbol of innocence! It was the face not of an insurgent, but of a little girl with angel-white skin. She was so pretty and looked so happy that I would have adopted her forever!

I removed the cartridge from my gun.

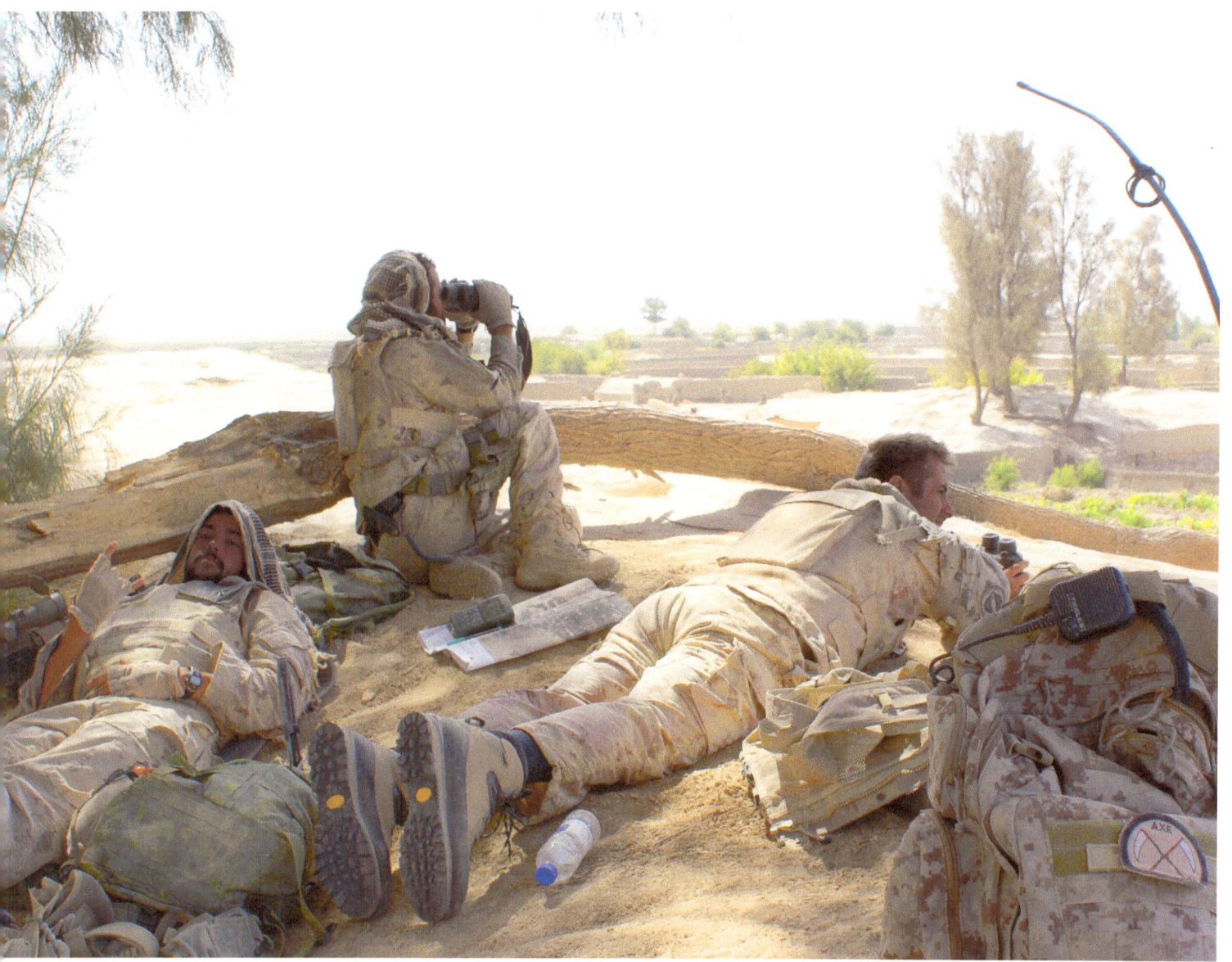

An observation post overlooked squads of infantry that were being drilled in interminable labyrinths of earth and dust. During lulls, the soldiers rested. Then they took turns keeping watch.

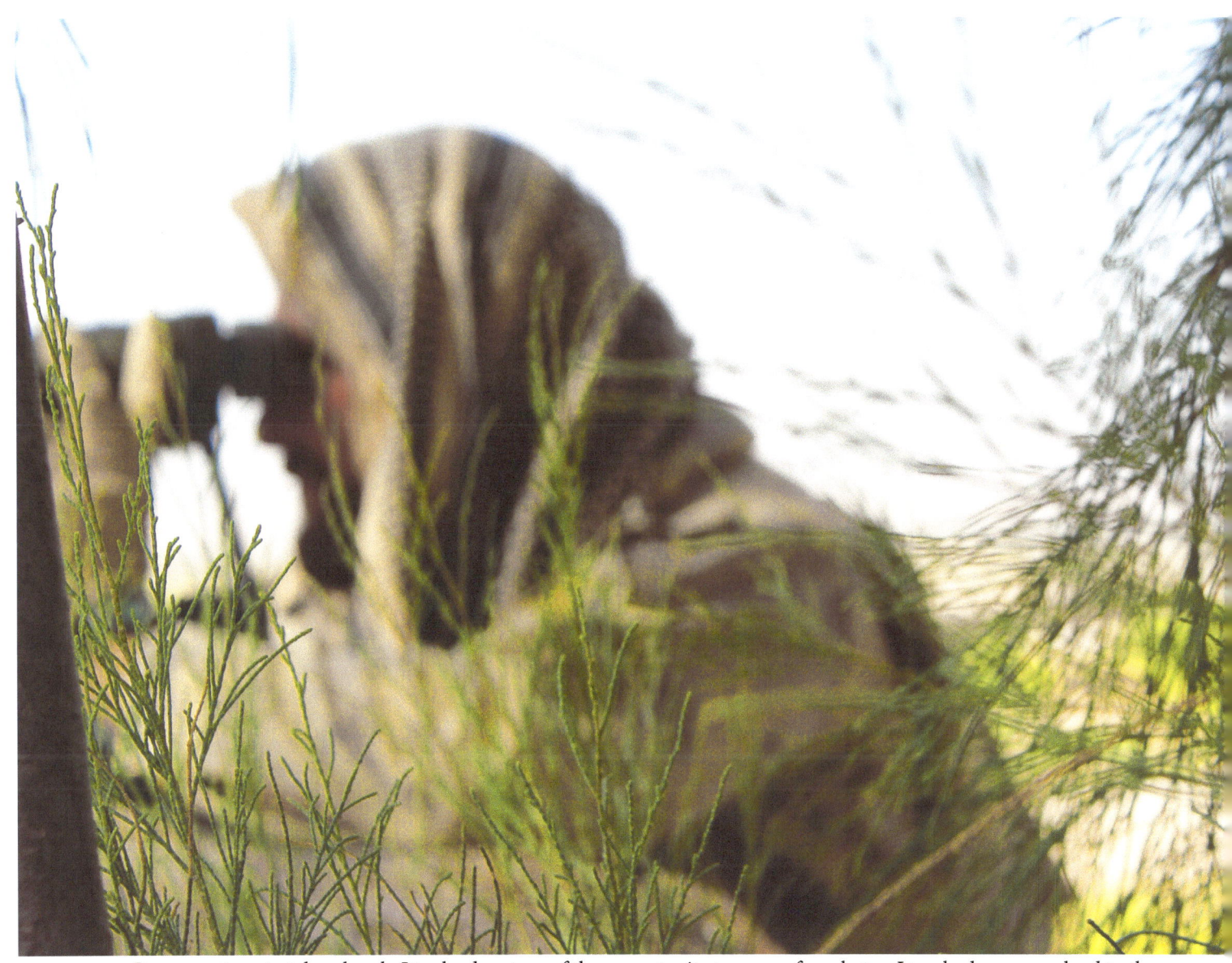

It was my turn to take a break. I took advantage of the opportunity to snap a few photos. I too had my eyes glued to the lens of a sight. But instead of looking at a distant enemy, I was looking at my friend, who was watching the village under the horizon of the burning stretches of desert.

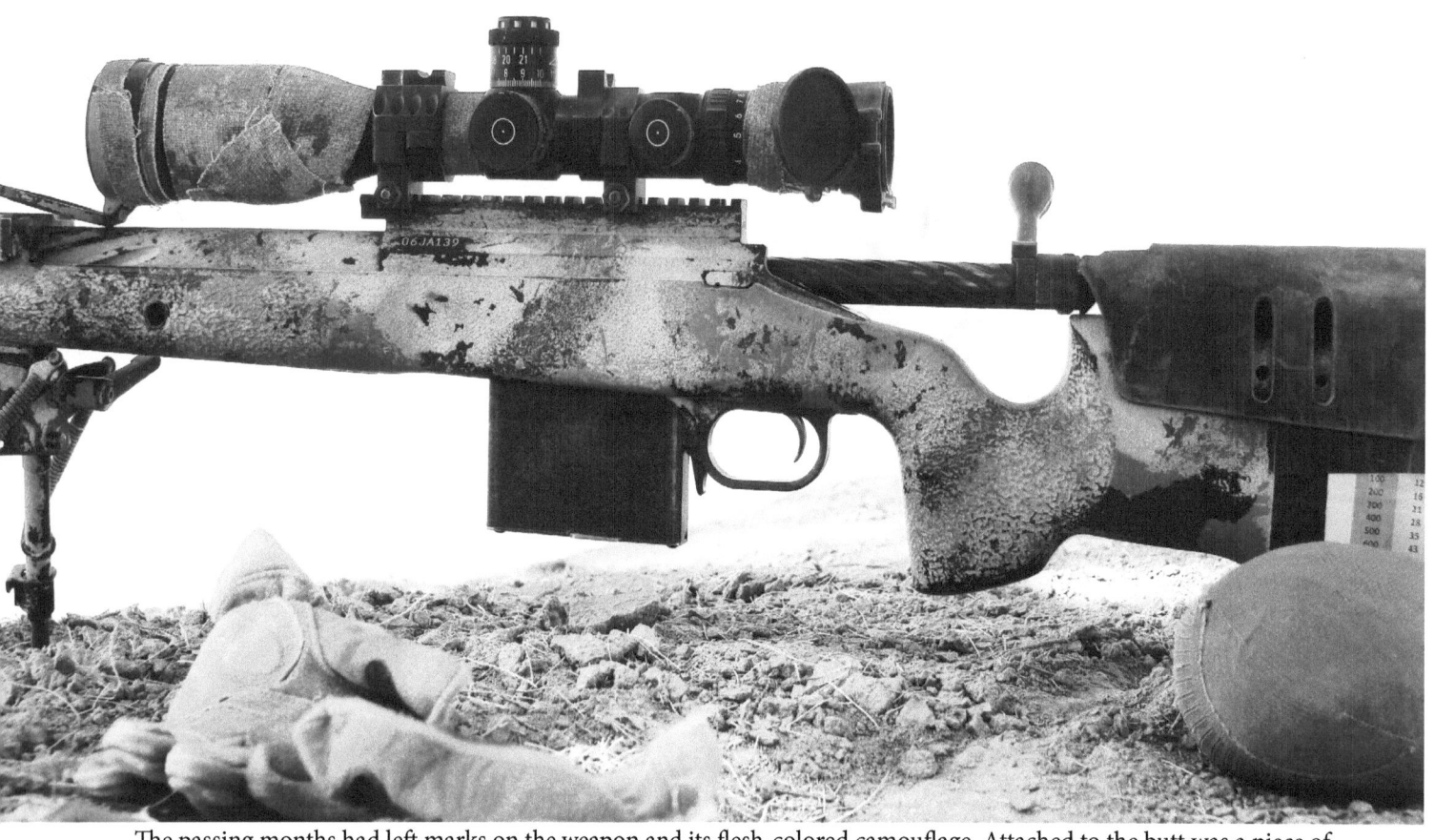

The passing months had left marks on the weapon and its flesh-colored camouflage. Attached to the butt was a piece of paper with firing data. The shooter could access it at a glance. Most often, the confrontations occurred too quickly to allow for complicated ballistic calculations.

Over the months , the soldier's body and soul also end up marked. I got out with just a few scratches. War had not changed me much. It had simply confirmed what I had always been at my core: a soldier. When people ask me what my experience in Afghanistan was like, I can see that they are expecting a sad, negative answer. They are surprised and smile when I answer that Afghanistan was the most wonderful experience of my life.

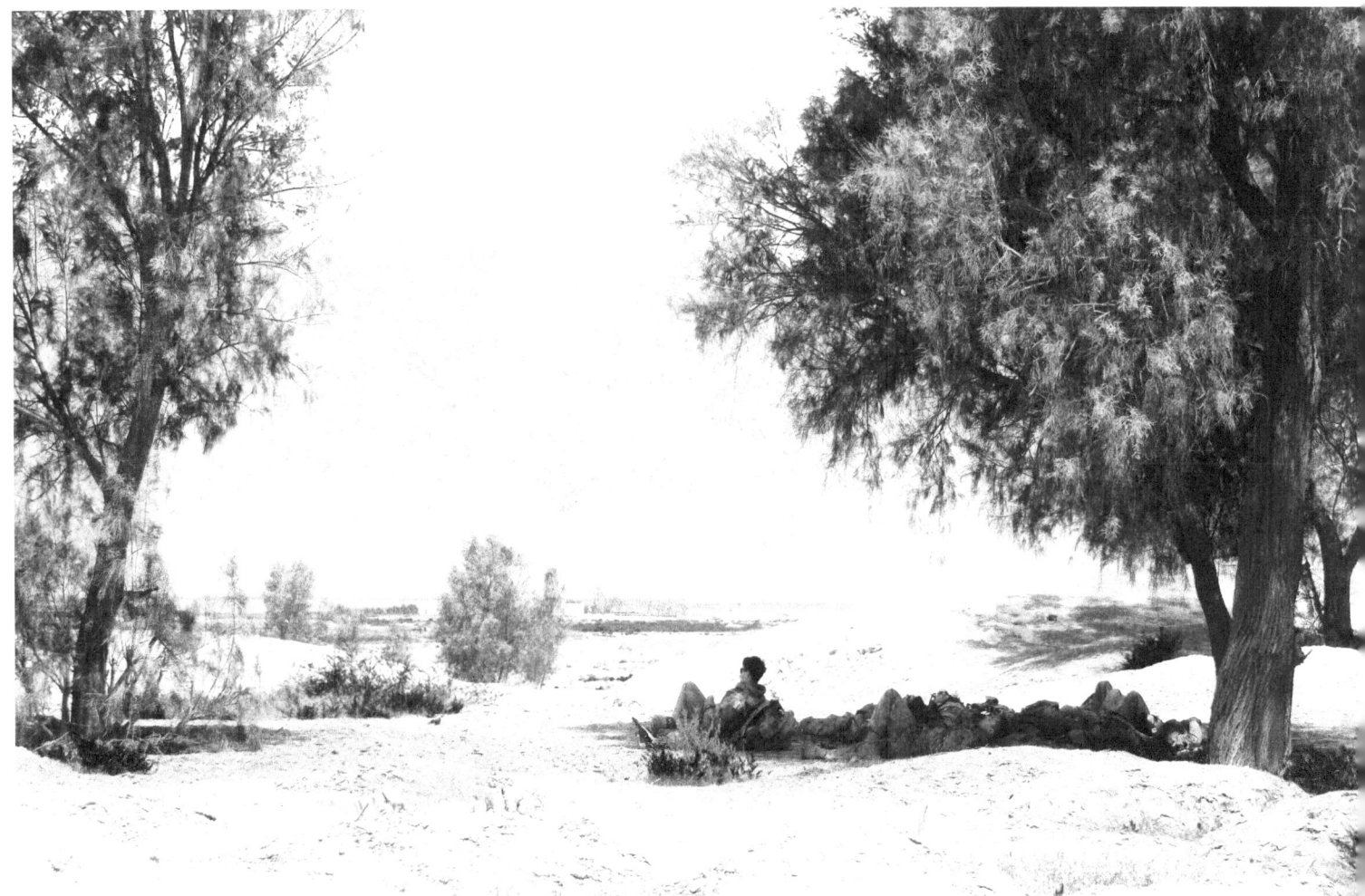

Another mission was nearly over. The soldiers would soon return to the vehicles and then to the base. While they waited, they rested in the shade, between the graves of a cemetery. I noticed that nearly all the cemeteries in the region are raised. Is this due to the accumulation of graves over the course of centuries? In Afghanistan, as in many countries around the world, if all the war casualties were gathered, every village would have its own small mountain.

These places that shelter death were often those that were most resplendent in life and colors. They abounded in lush trees that were visible from kilometers away in all directions. I often used them as markers for navigation, a bit like a lighthouse for a ship, but there was no ocean. In Kandahar, a soldier quickly loses the need for a compass, map, or GPS. He recognizes the shape of the mountains so well that a mere photo can indicate the place and angle where it was taken. The soldier can point out where he walked, the village where he patrolled, the place where he saw a friend die.

The convoy had stopped in the middle of a park. Some of the soldiers set out on foot to meet an important person from the area. The other half guarded the vehicles.

In the park, the iron of weapons mingled with the iron of innocent swings and slides. There were young Afghans there. Against the ruins of past battles, two distant civilizations were meeting, but not to wage war!

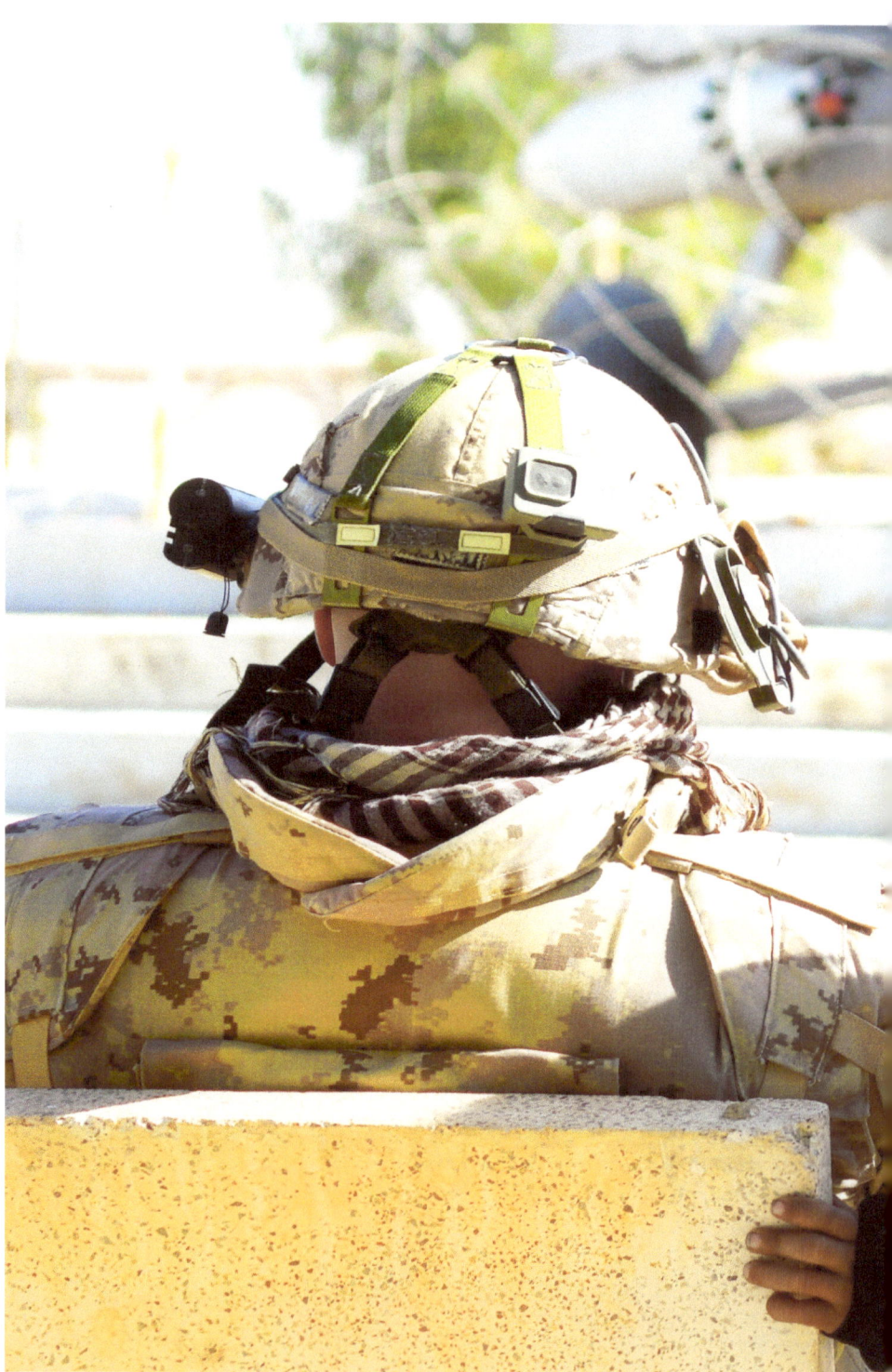

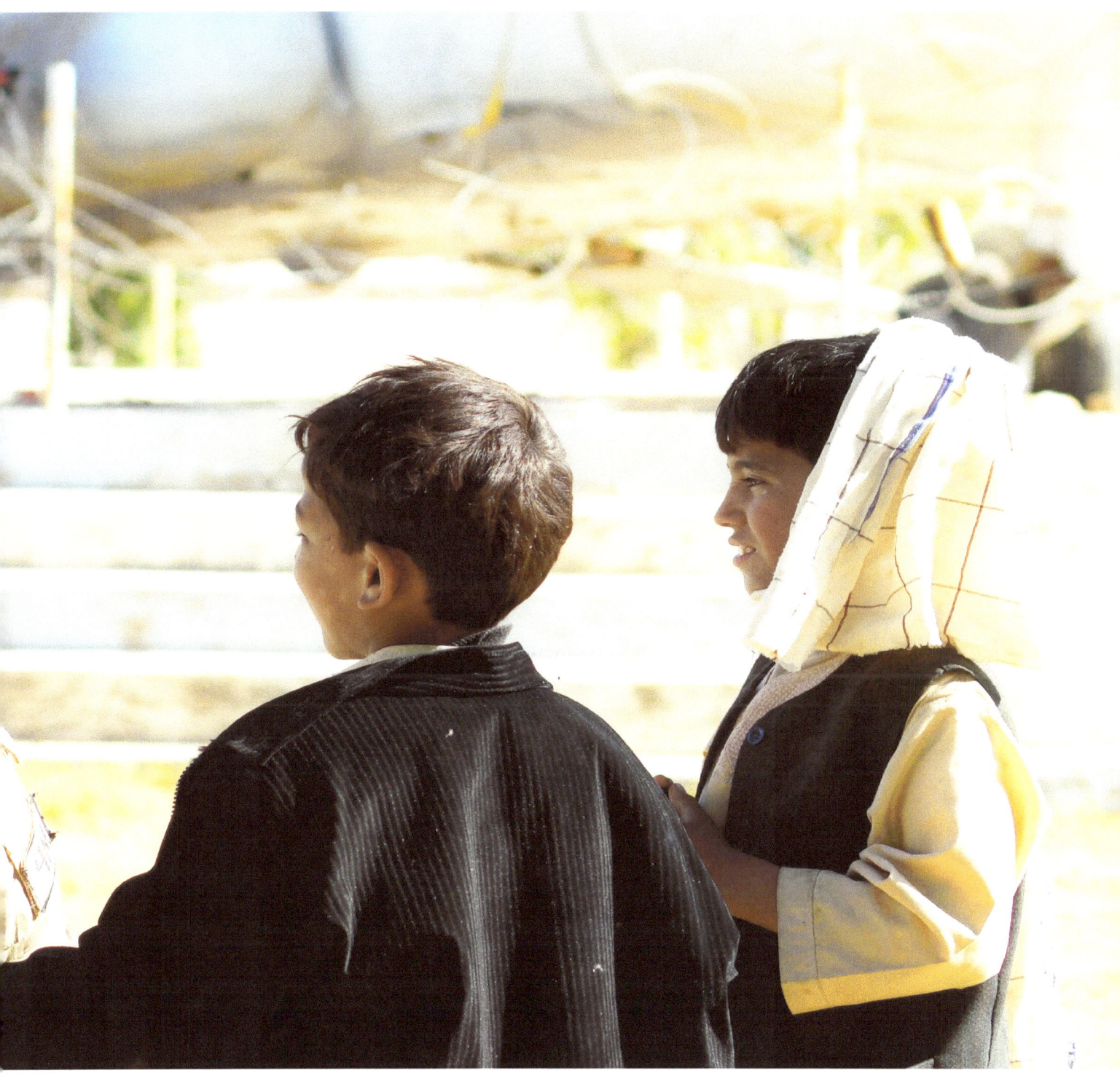

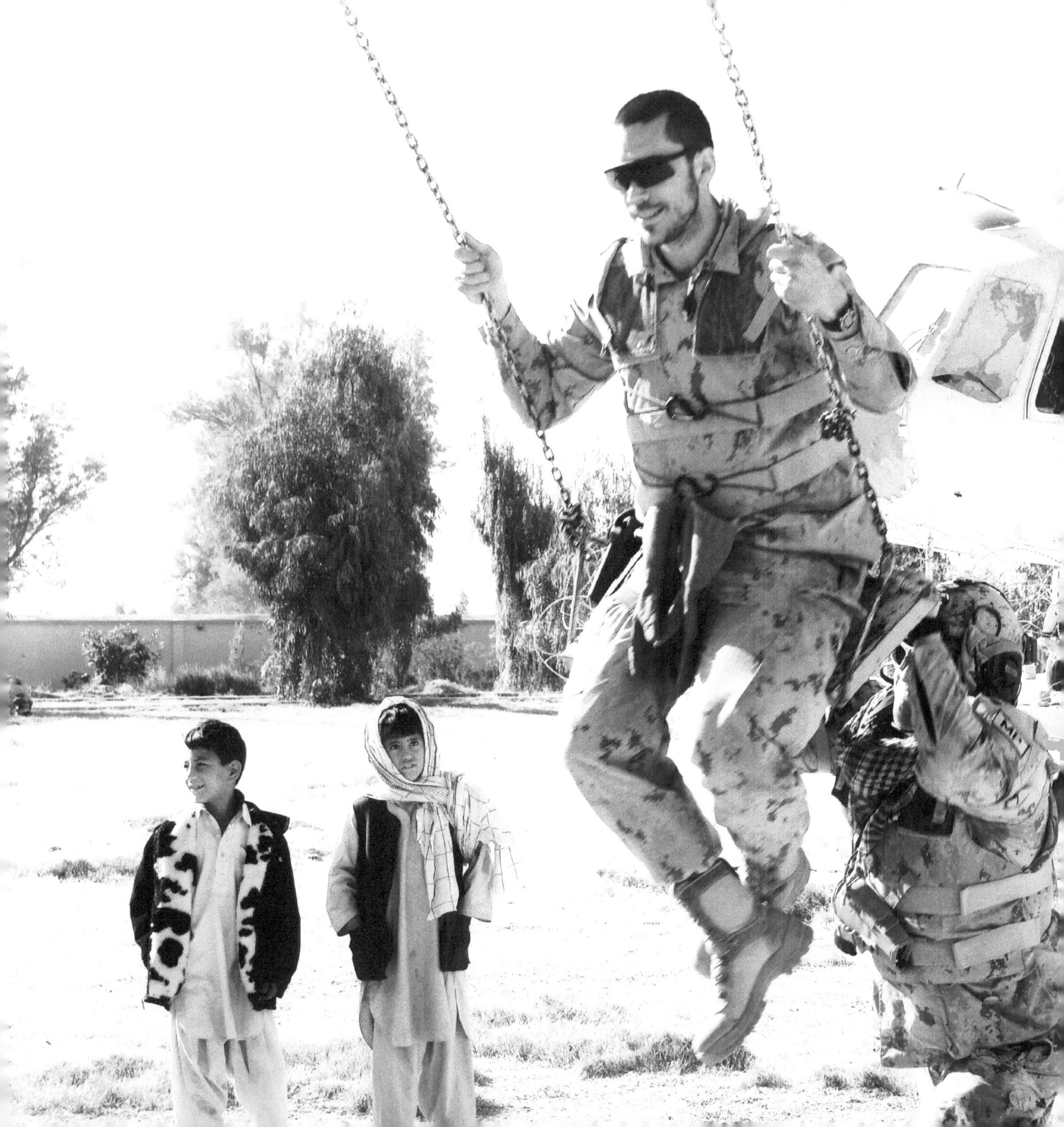

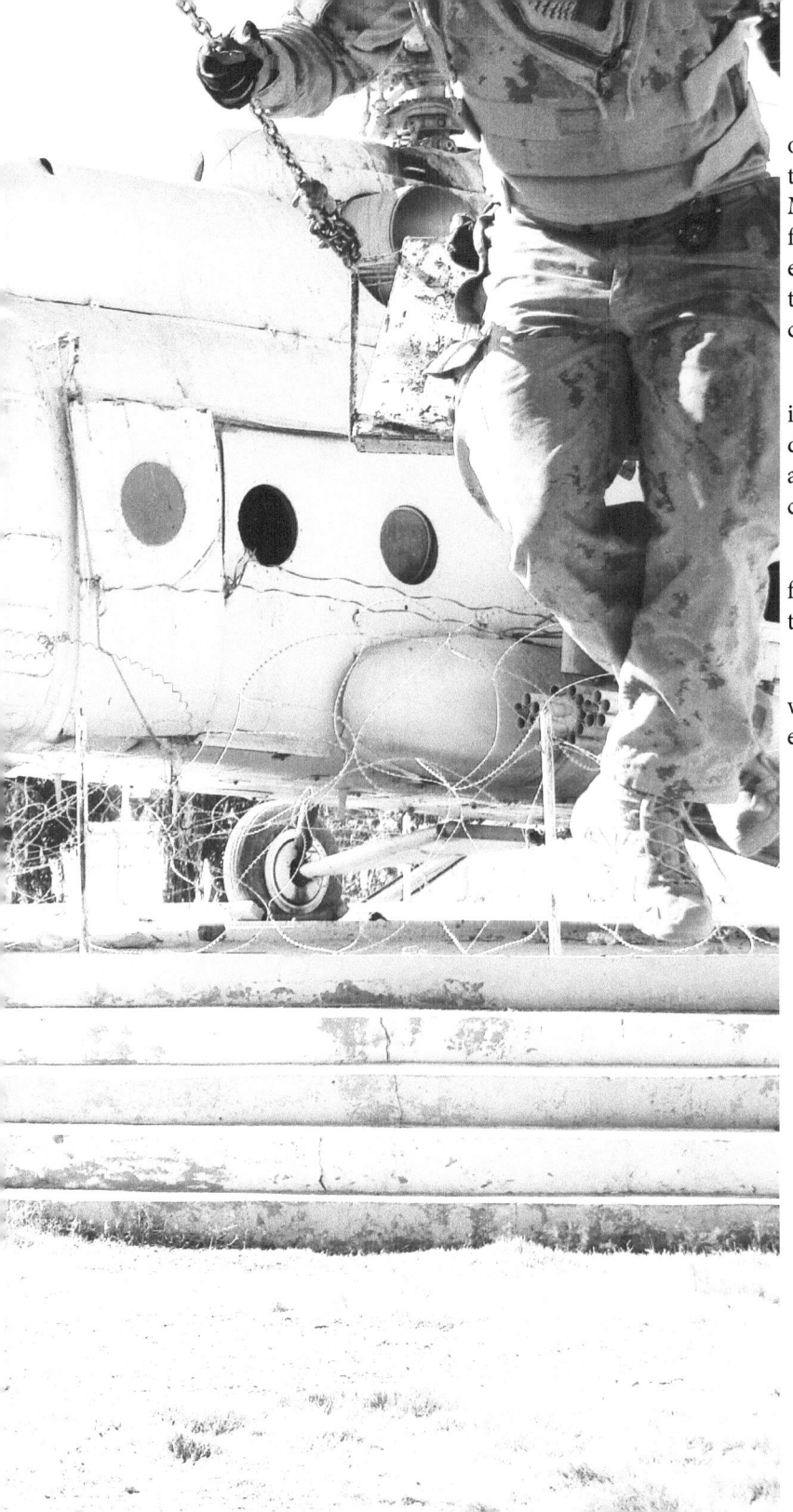

While some soldiers secured the premises, others let off some steam! Setting down our weapons and protective gear, we bravely launched an assault on the park. Mission accomplished! The slides and swings quickly fell under our command—to the delight of everyone, even these two young Afghans. It was as if I had heard them utter Obelix's famous phrase: "These Canadians are crazy!"

Yes, one needs to be crazy in order to still find joy in the middle of a land of sadness and misery. A certain dose of madness and recklessness may be necessary after all! I have always liked to think that someone who is not crazy is not living.

I have heard that forcing oneself to smile, even falsely, makes one happier. "If you're not happy, pretend to be!"

Life itself is a battle that is lost in advance to death. A war where regardless of the victories, the winners always end up losing. What can we do if not smile?

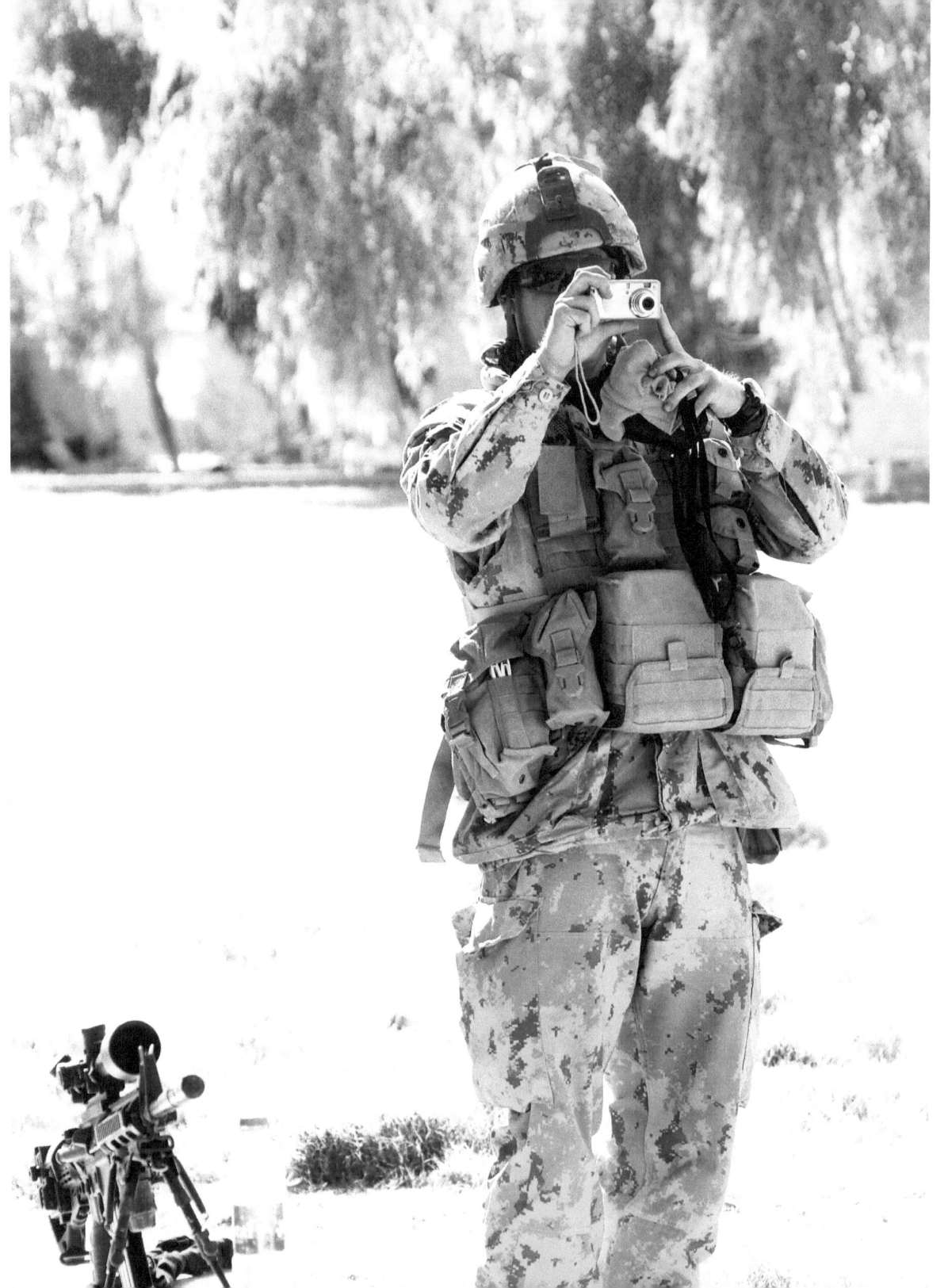

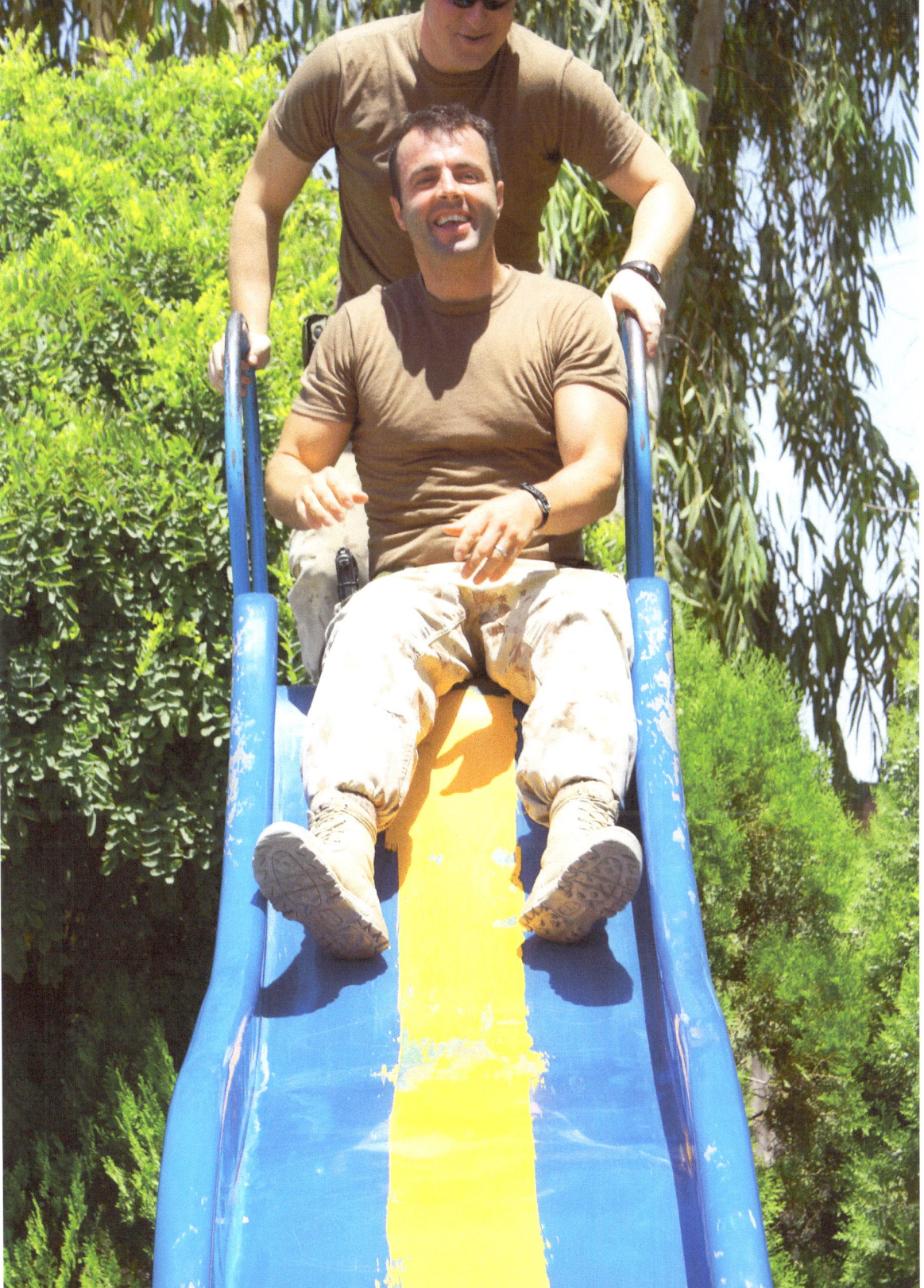

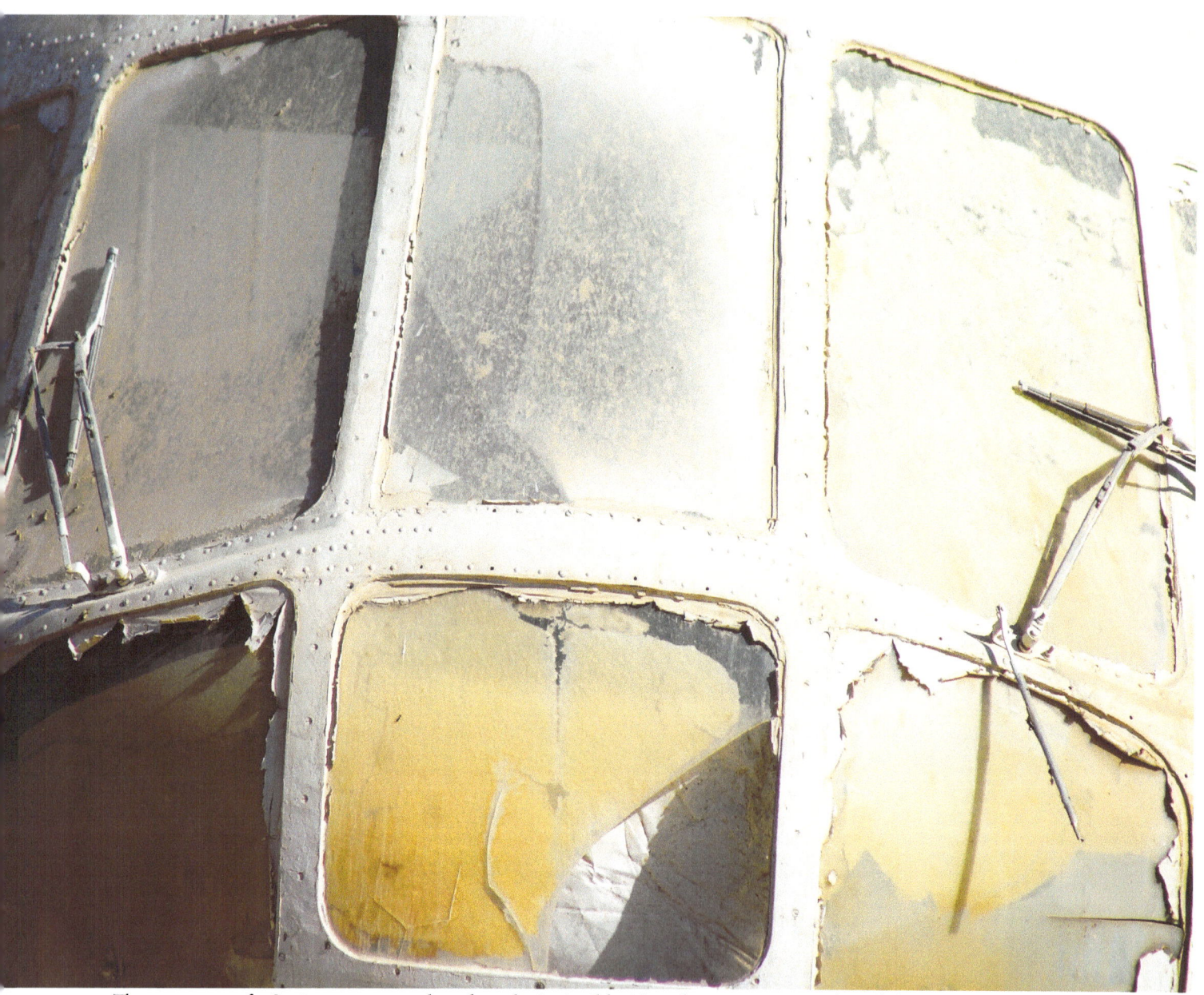

The remnants of a Soviet army once thought to be invincible. Now they are a war trophy exhibited in a park on a pedestal of barbed wire and cement.

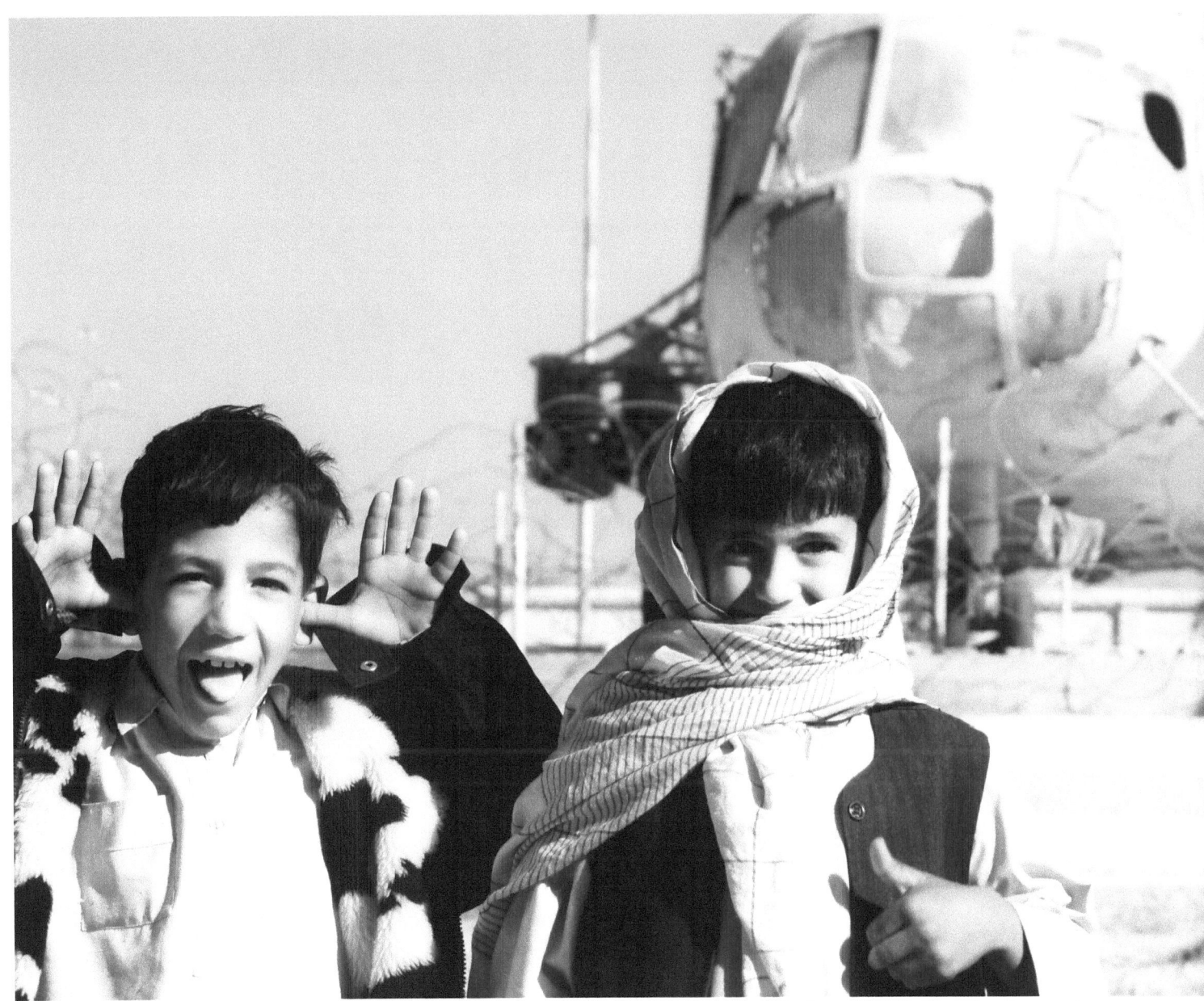

The conclusion of the war against the Soviets: a young Afghan making faces in front of the helicopter of an ancient empire. The Afghan, who is unarmed, is still standing. The empire has been reduced to powerlessness.

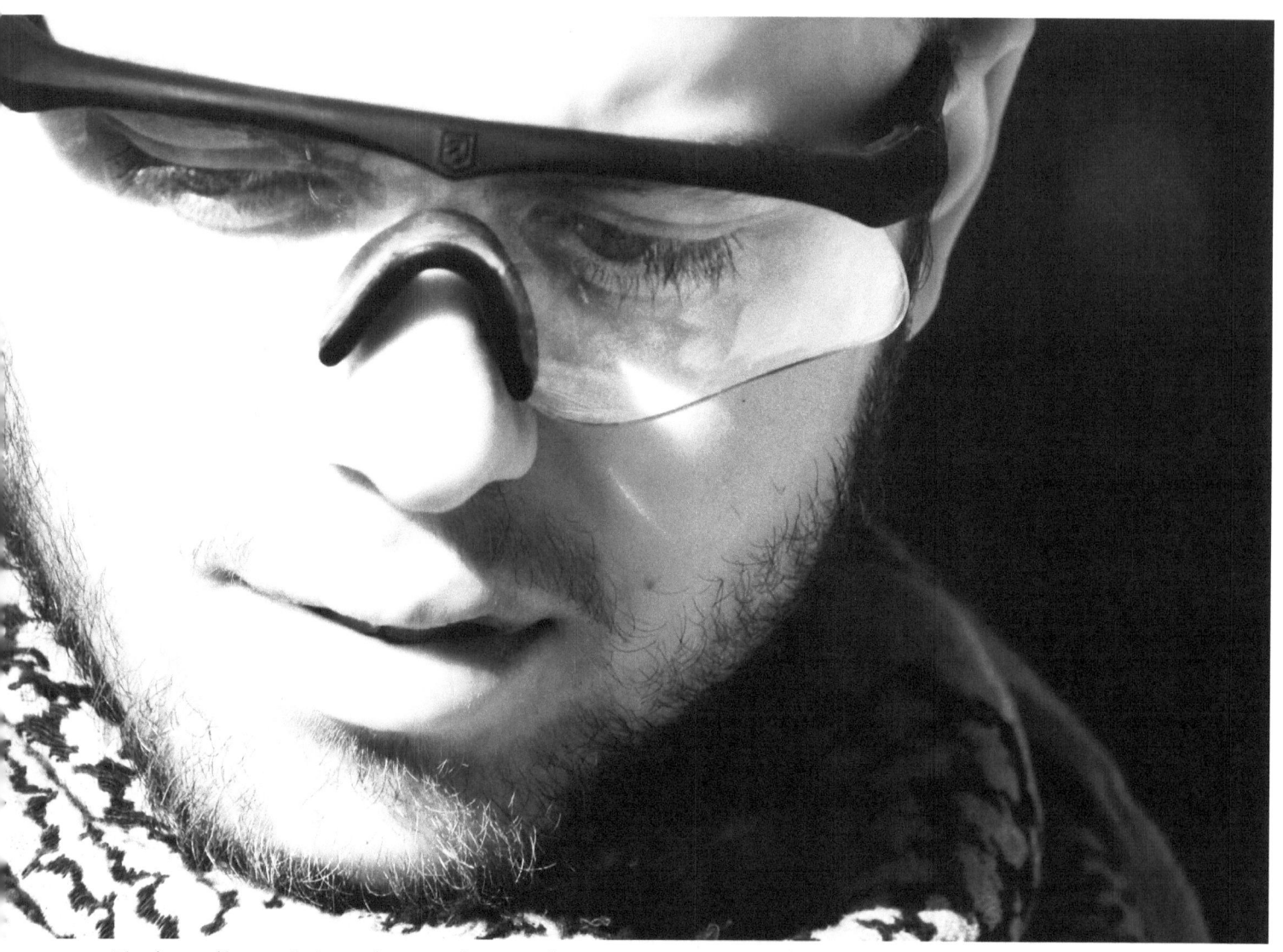

The faces of human beings who come from two distant countries. A young bearded soldier and an Afghan child playing. They hail from two completely different civilizations. And yet each of them has two eyes, a nose, a mouth, two ears. But above all, each of them has a heart. Unlike us, the camera lens does not make a distinction. We are all human beings before being citizens. Humanity transcends nationality.

Except for some groups such as the snipers, Western soldiers must shave every day. For many Afghans, the beard is what makes the difference between a boy and a man.

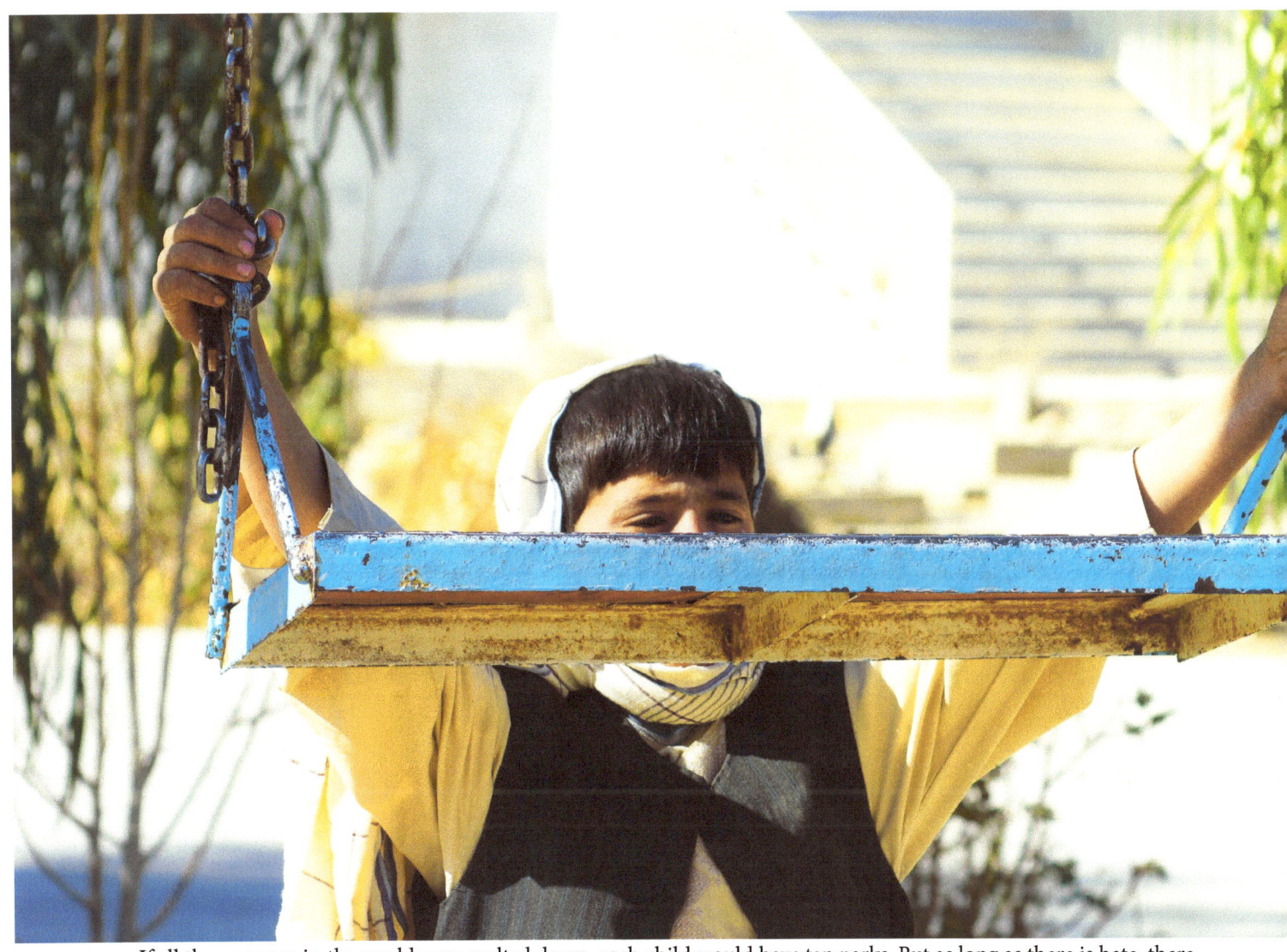

If all the weapons in the world were melted down, each child would have ten parks. But as long as there is hate, there will be weapons to spread it or defend against it.

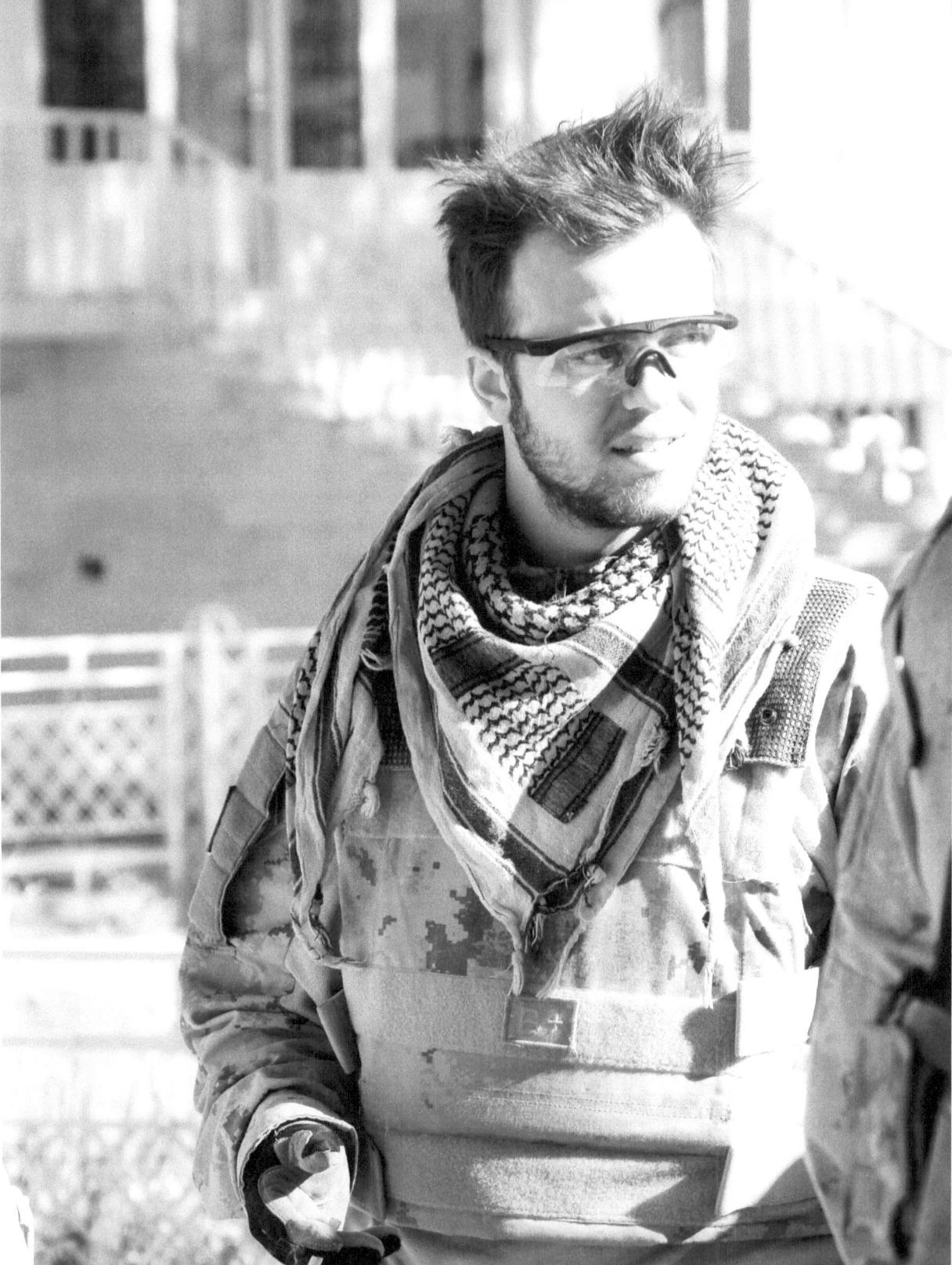

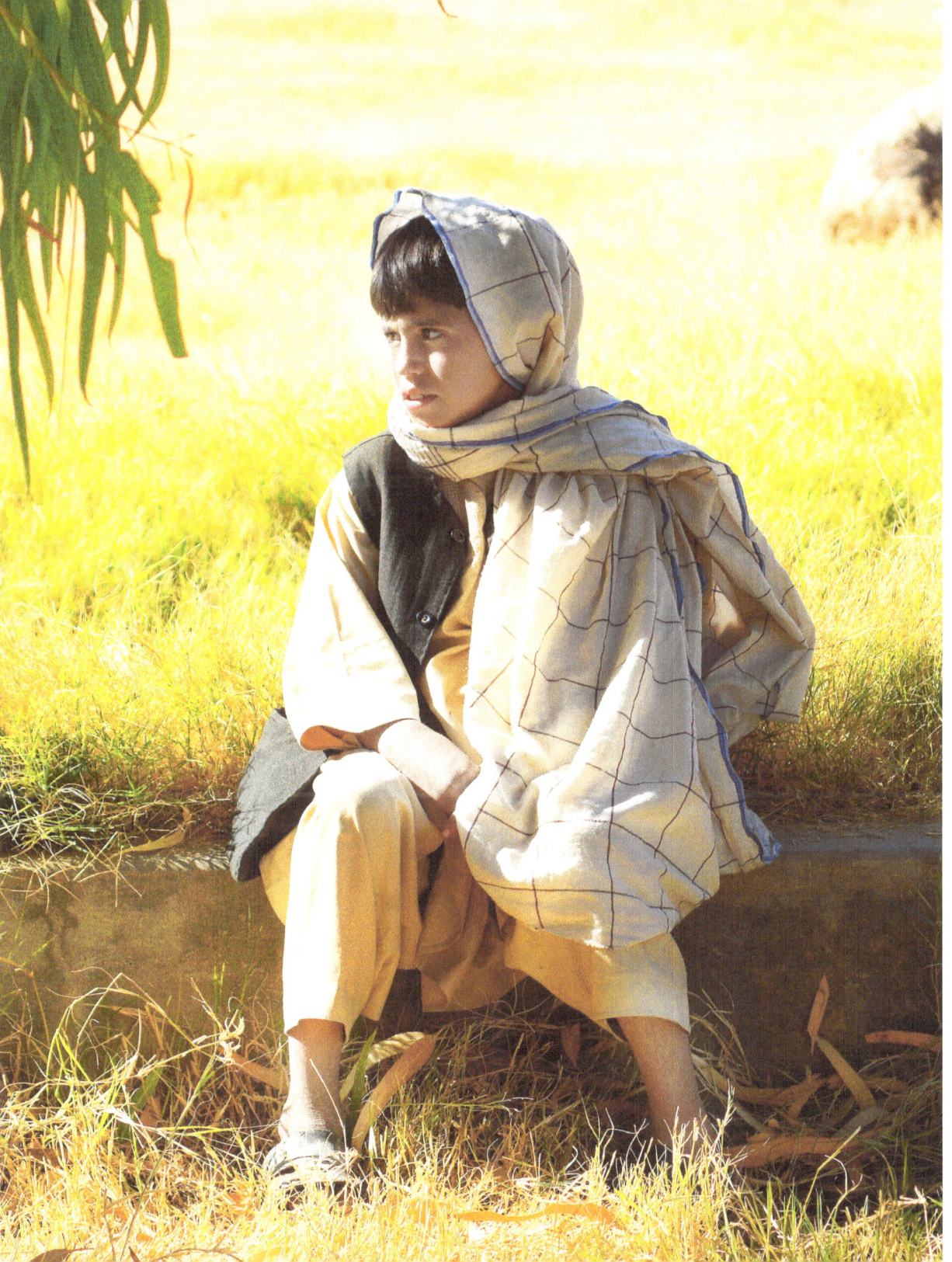

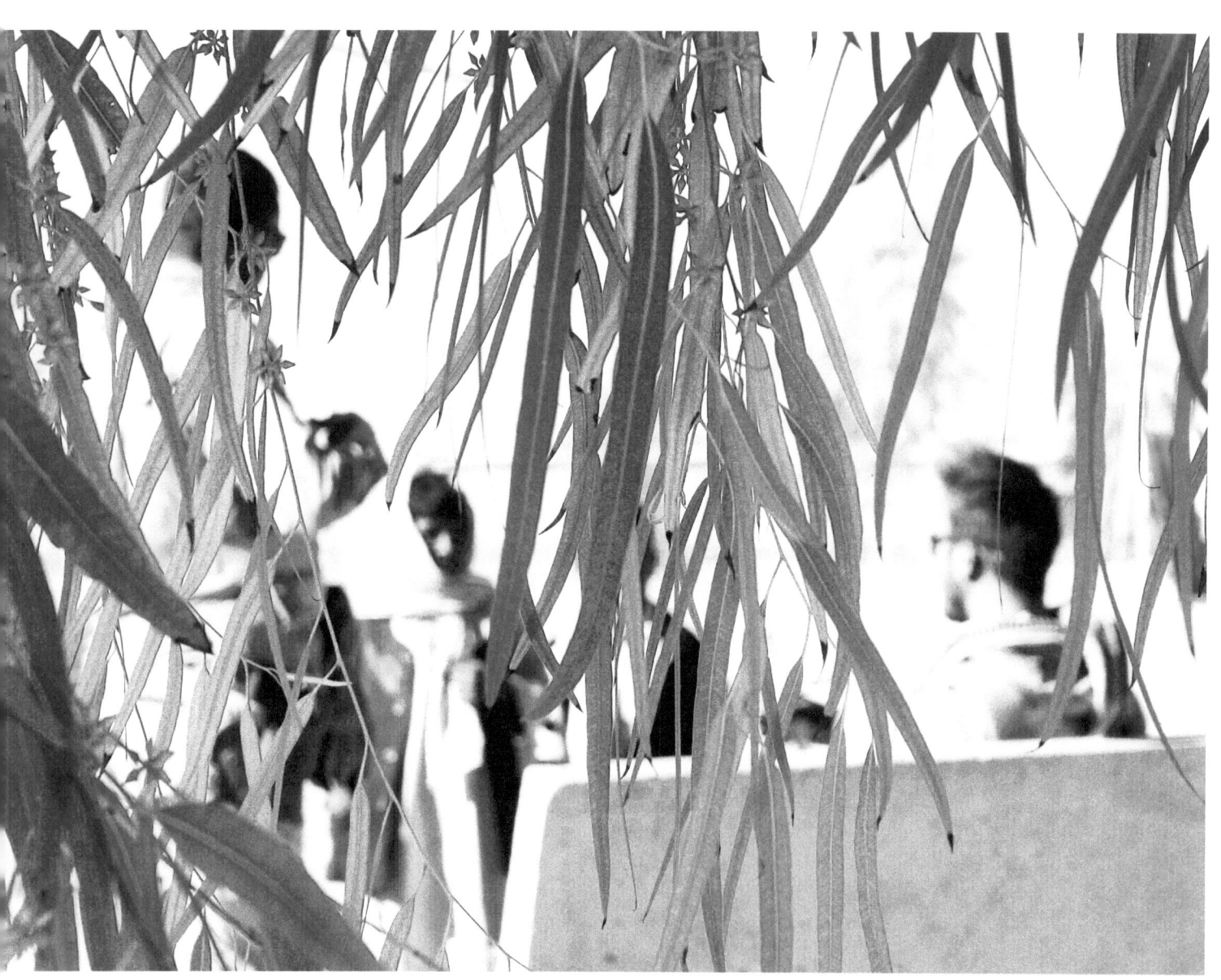

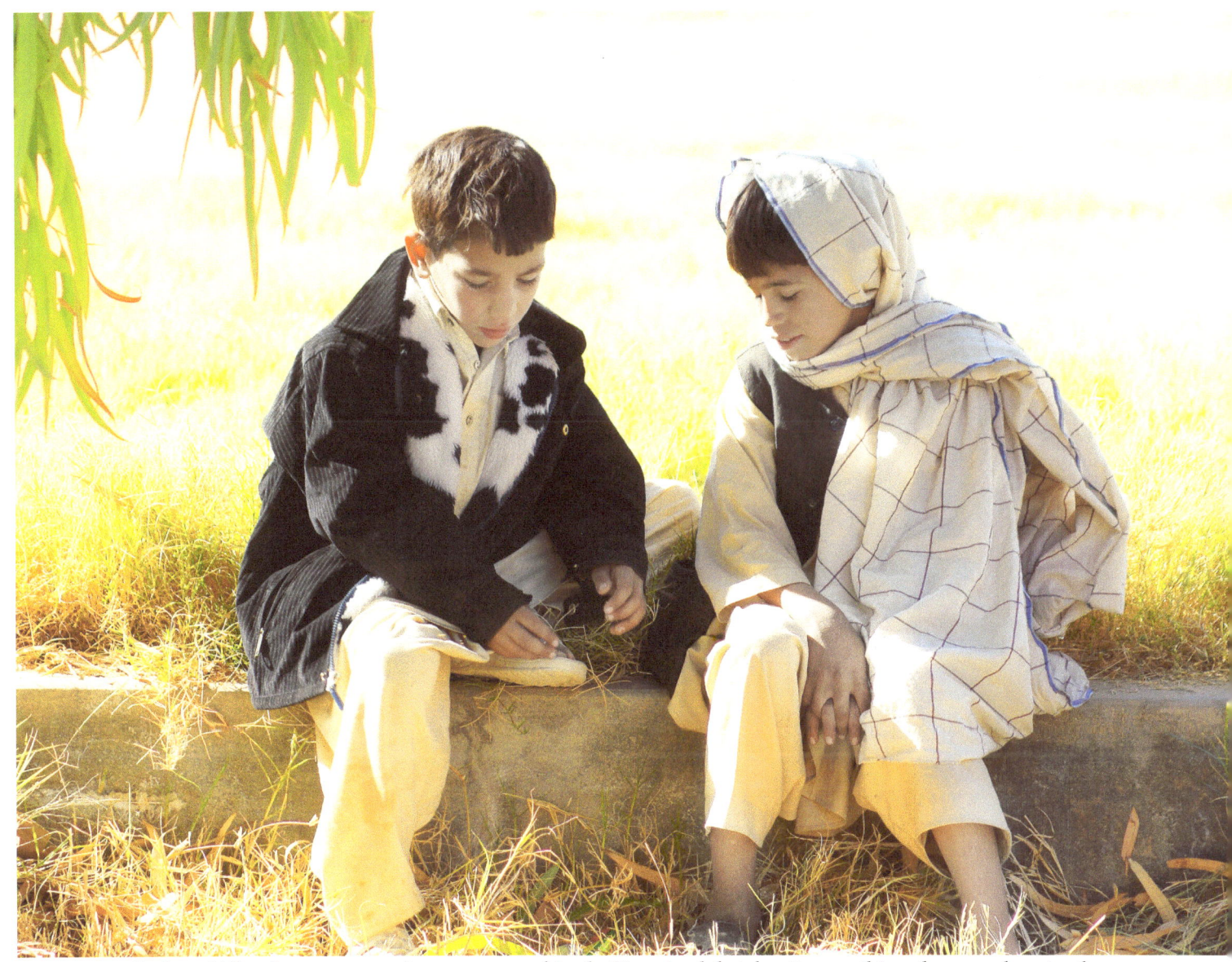

In the middle of a war-torn region, two young friends. I imagined that despite everything, they were happier than many children in large Western cities, far from the culture of consumption and performance. In Afghanistan, life is often hard. But at least it is simple.

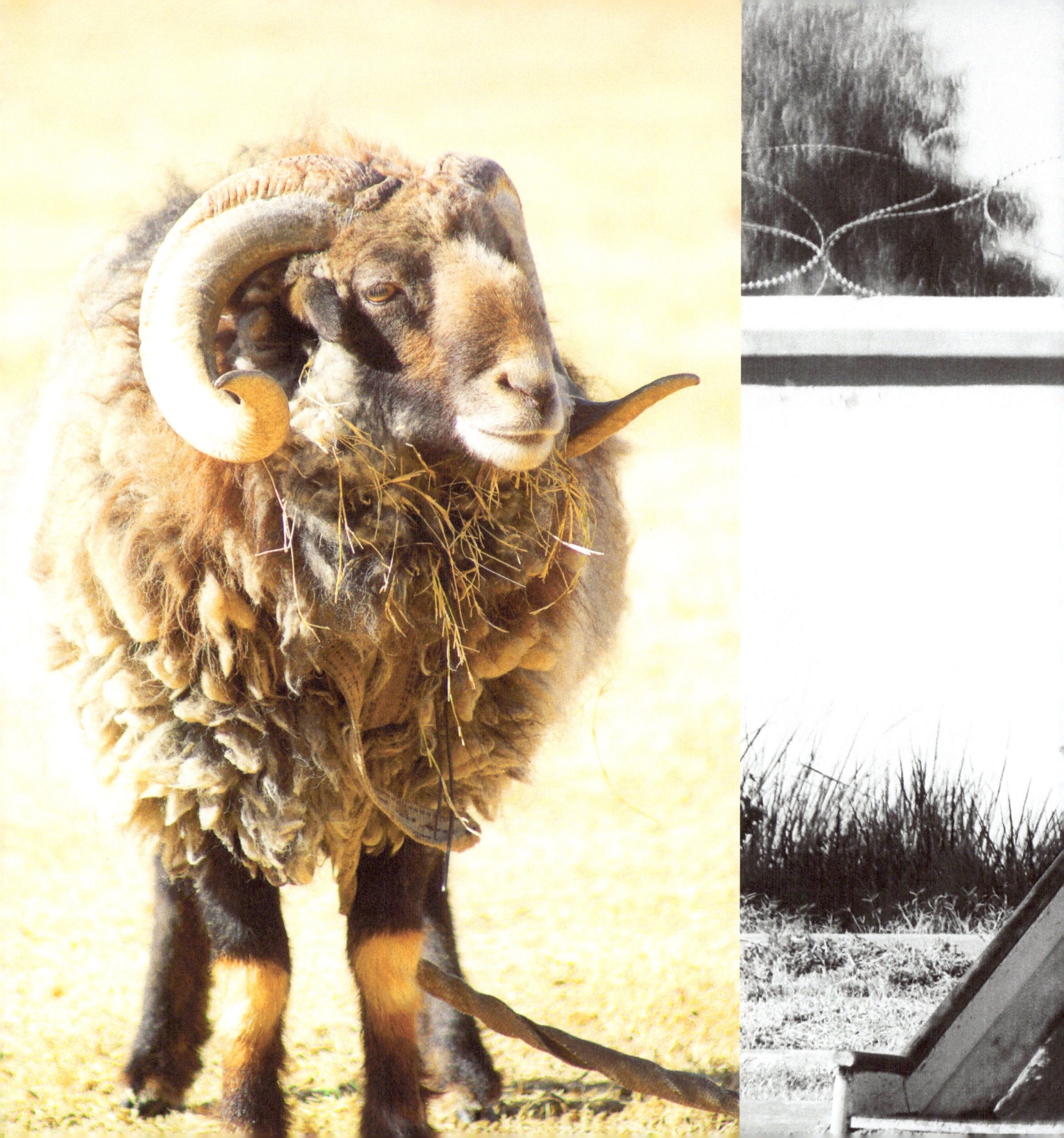

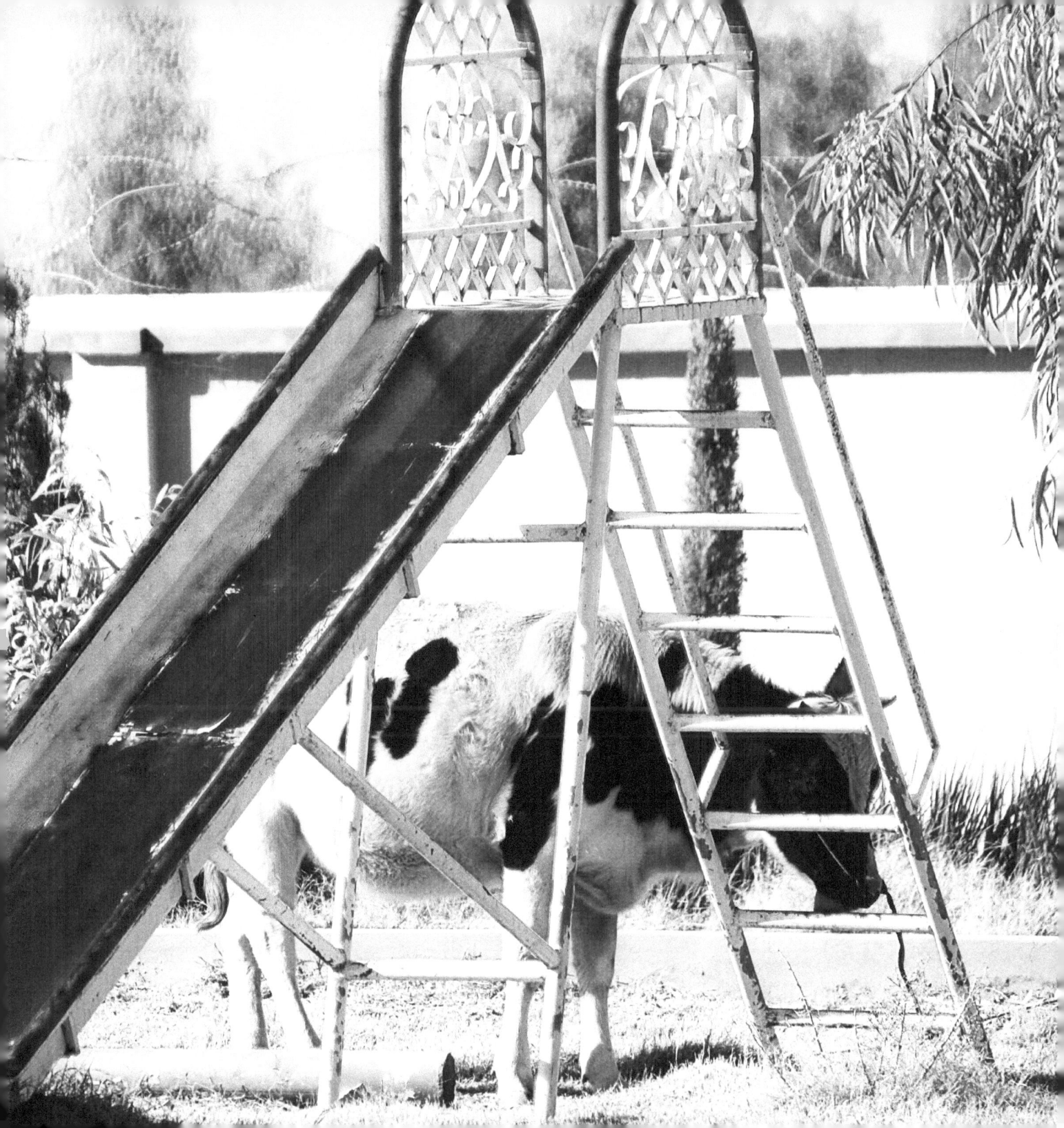

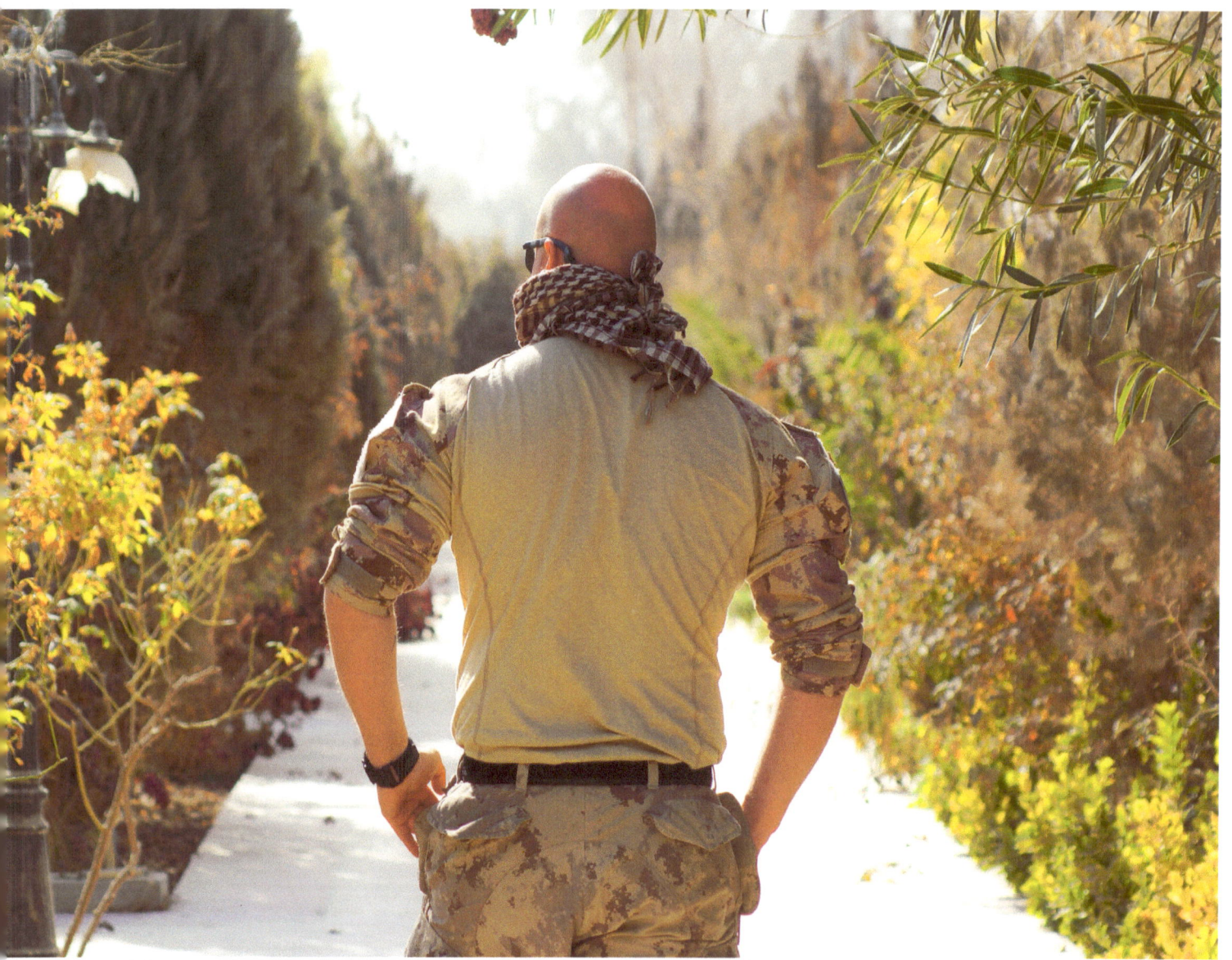

While some soldiers walked through the autumn-colored garden, others climbed the steps of a large, abandoned swimming pool. I pray that one day this pool will be filled again and that after strolling through the blossoming gardens, families will be able to go cool off and swim.

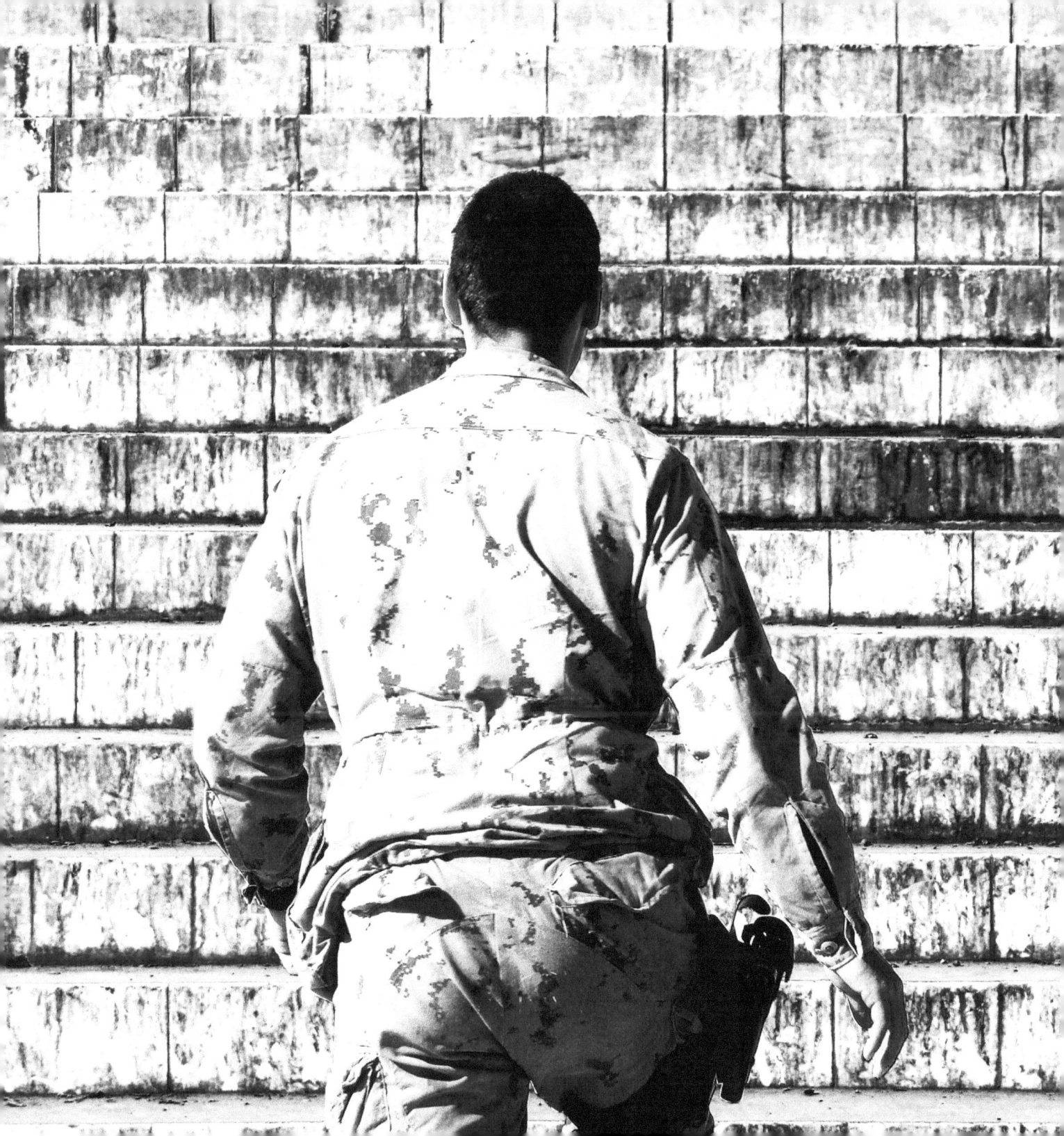

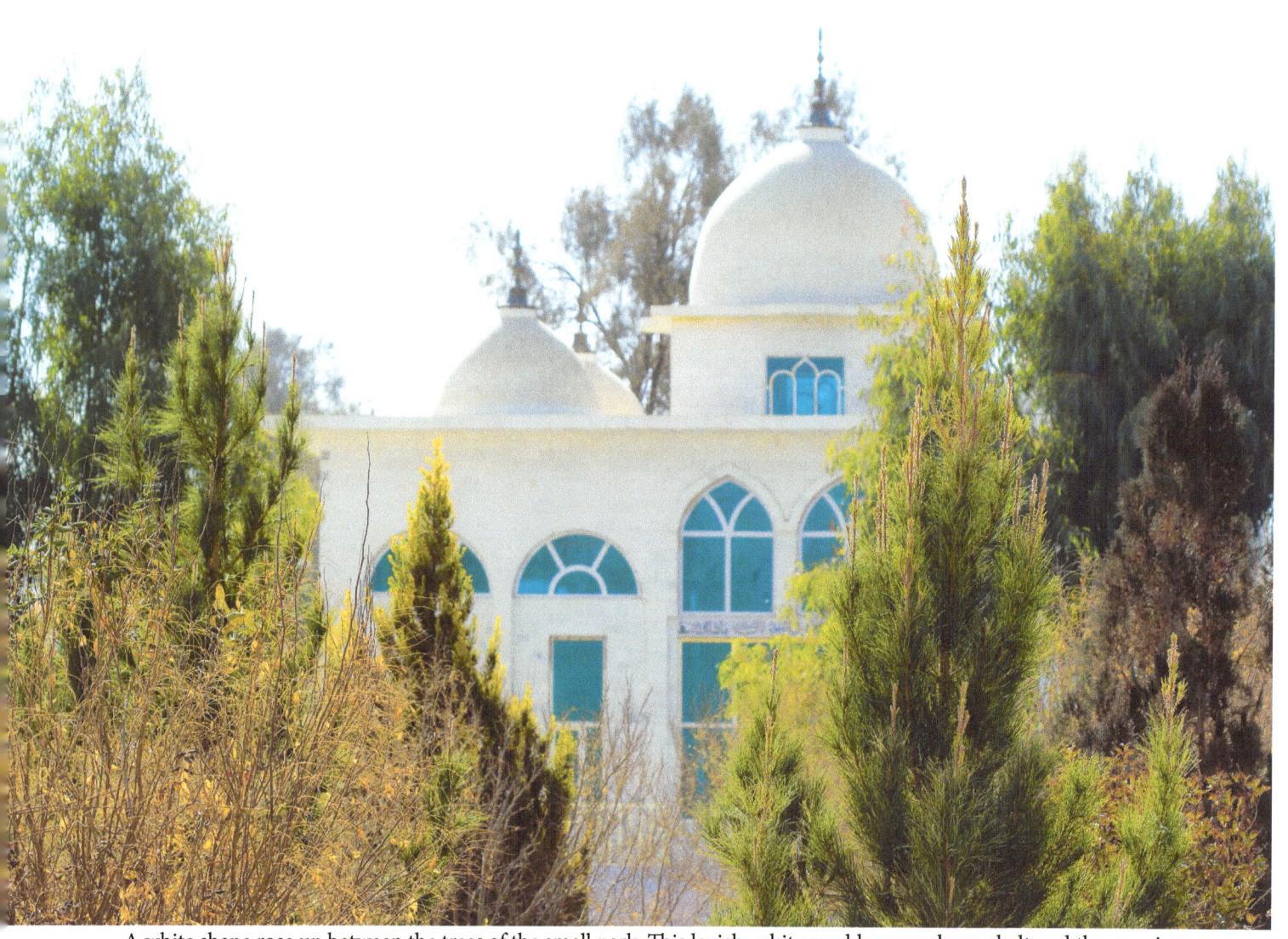

A white shape rose up between the trees of the small park. This lavish, white marble mausoleum sheltered the remains of an important person. Inside the snow-white structure, a corpse was bathed in a light that was blue like heaven.

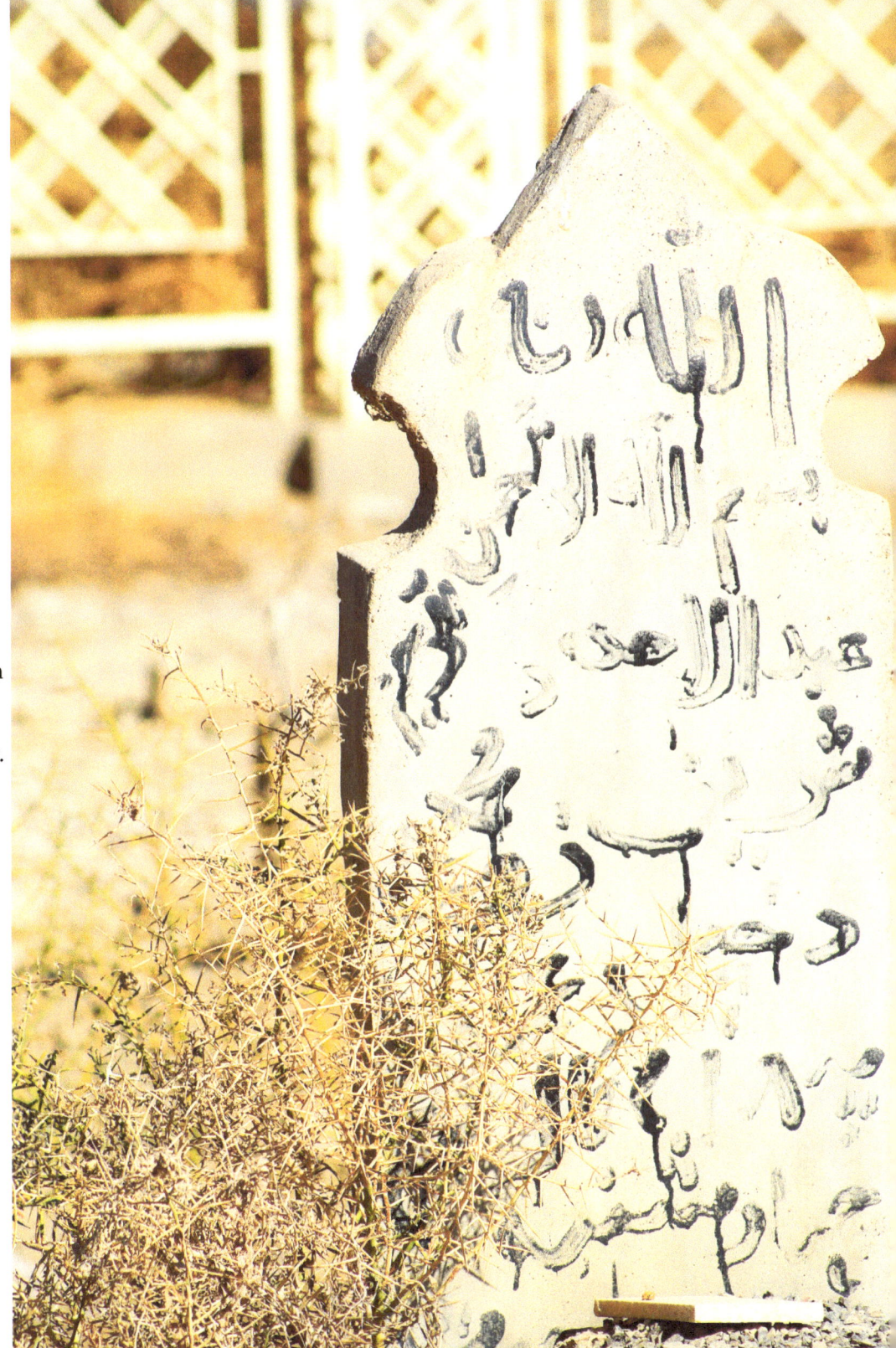

Near the large mausoleum, a humble grave was covered with thorns, dust, and burning rocks. Despite this, the gravestone was still shrouded in a heavenly light.

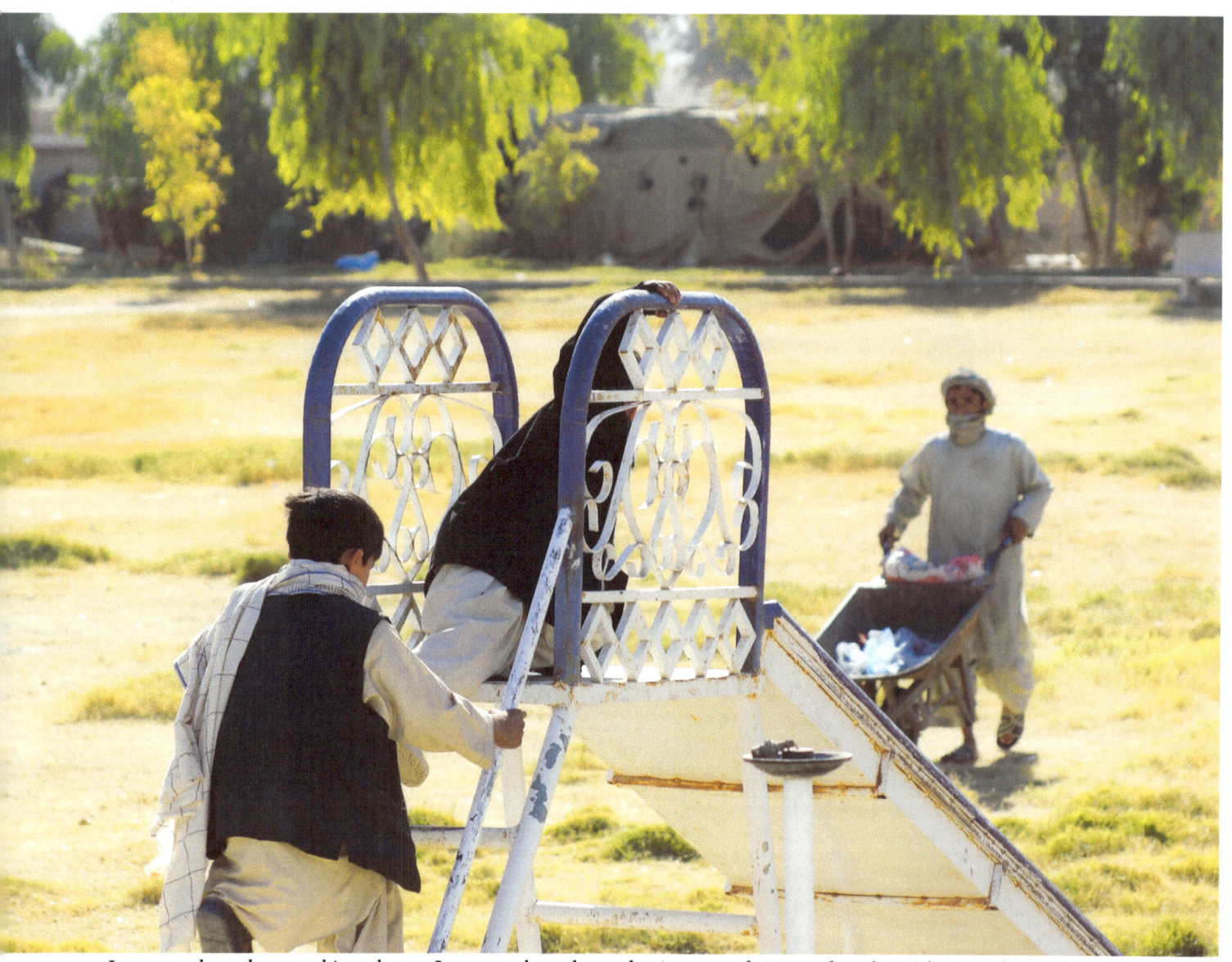

I was not the only one taking photos. I was not the only one having a good time and smiling. This metal would typically have been used for something other than to build games for children, and this grassy area should have been used for something other than a park. Most metal in Afghanistan is found in weapons.

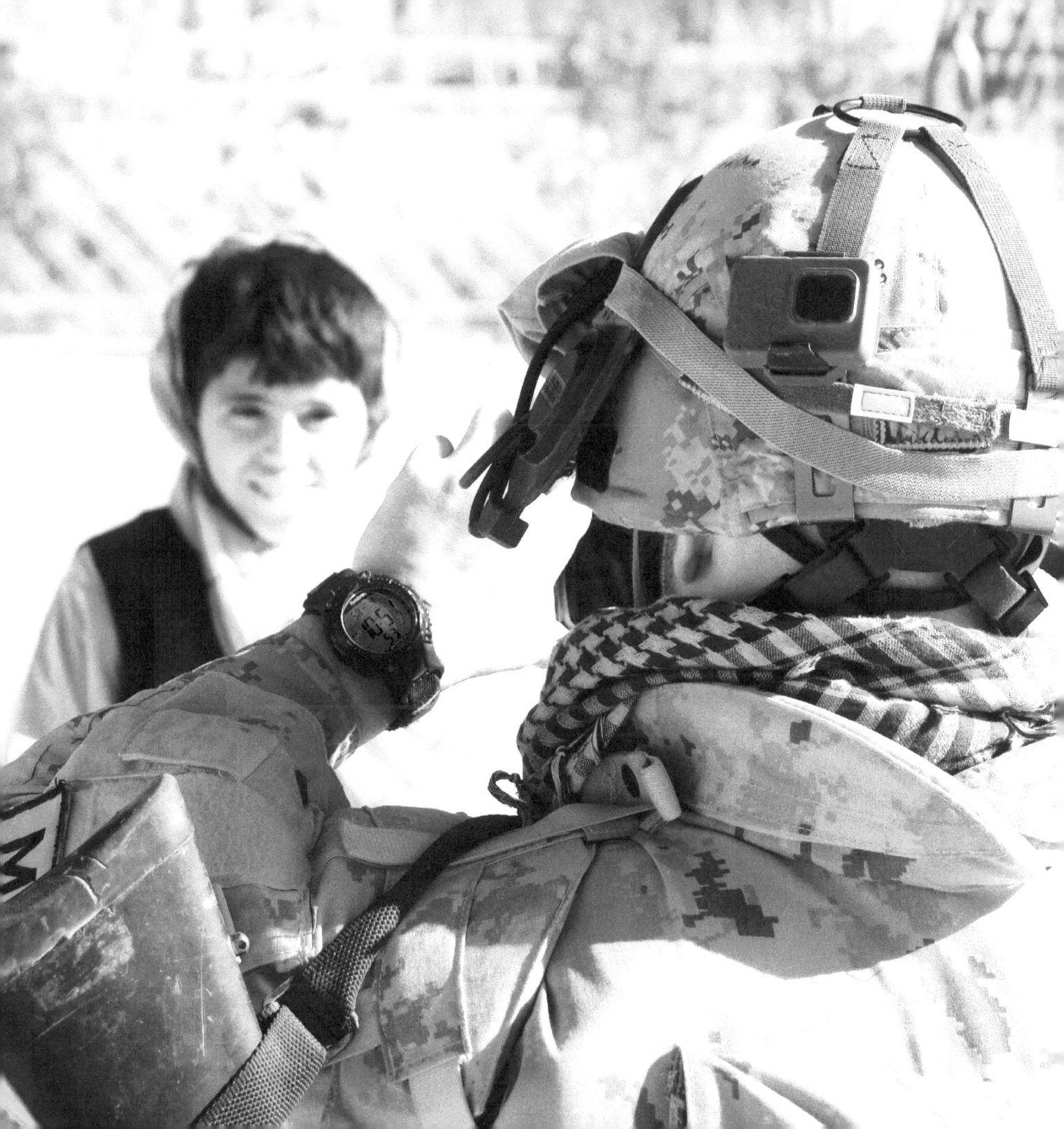

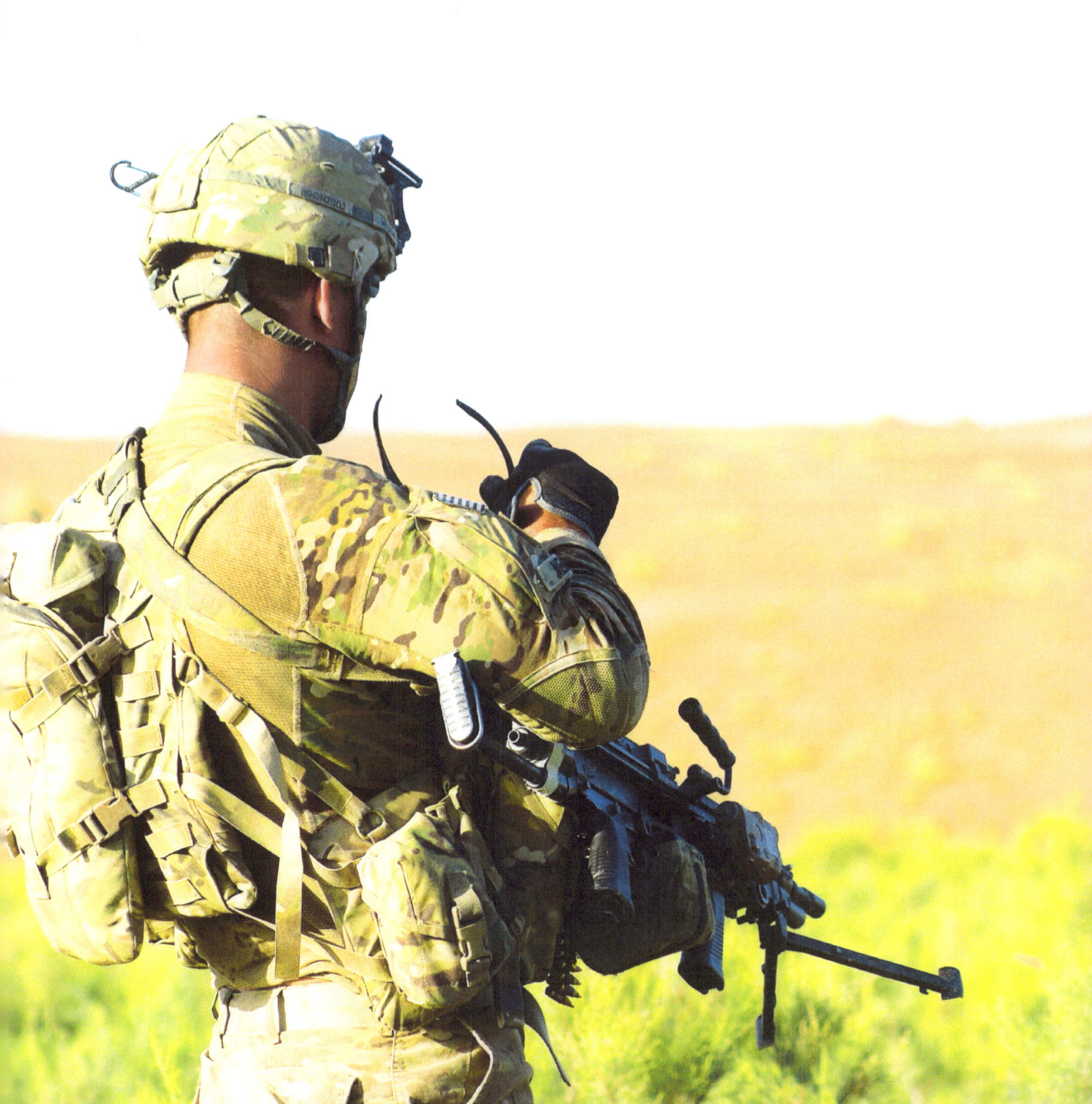

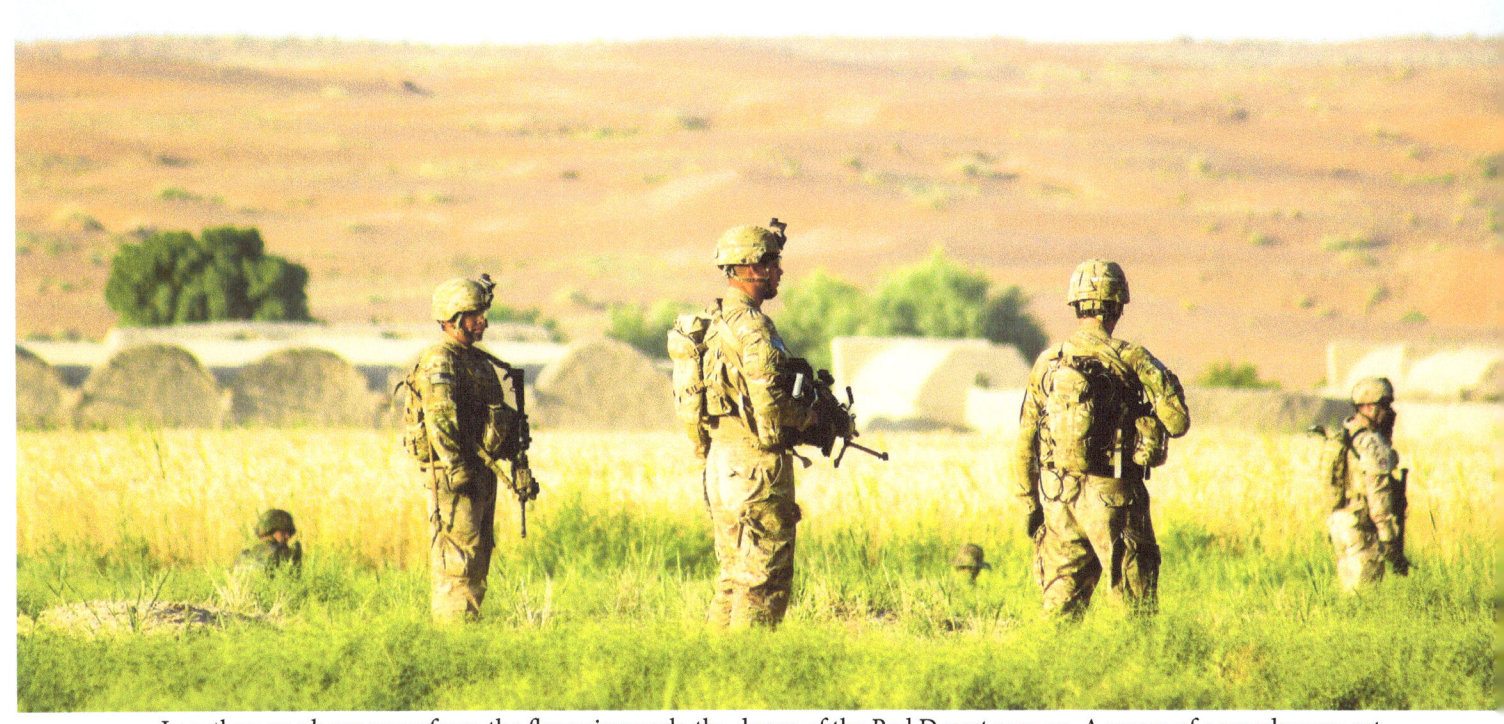

Less than one hour away from the flowering park, the dunes of the Red Desert rose up. A group of nomads were getting ready to cross it. They had only camels and rudimentary gear. The vehicles of our convoy, the fruit of several millennia of technological development, did not dare to venture into this austere environment. We had to get out and continue on foot. American soldiers were beside us. Noise coming out of several radios scattered among the rows of infantrymen could be heard. Meanwhile, the sound of the engines was receding into the distance.

Through my lenses, I watched the nomads draw away toward the emptiness of the desert. They were advancing quickly. They seemed comfortable in their loose garments. In contrast, the patrol was moving slowly. Each soldier was hauling thousands of dollars' worth of equipment distributed over his body, not to mention the tens of thousands of dollars that had been spent on transporting him and training him for his deployment to Afghanistan. Under the bulk and weight of our gear, the simple act of walking was burdensome. On some missions in the mountains, I would carry 150 pounds.

The nomads did not have powerful lenses through which to watch us. For them, something that is not close enough to be seen or heard is something that does not warrant stopping for.

Our patrol continued its march. The nomads vanished in the steam of the mirages. They are probably still in the desert to this day. But I have already disappeared, like an ephemeral vision.

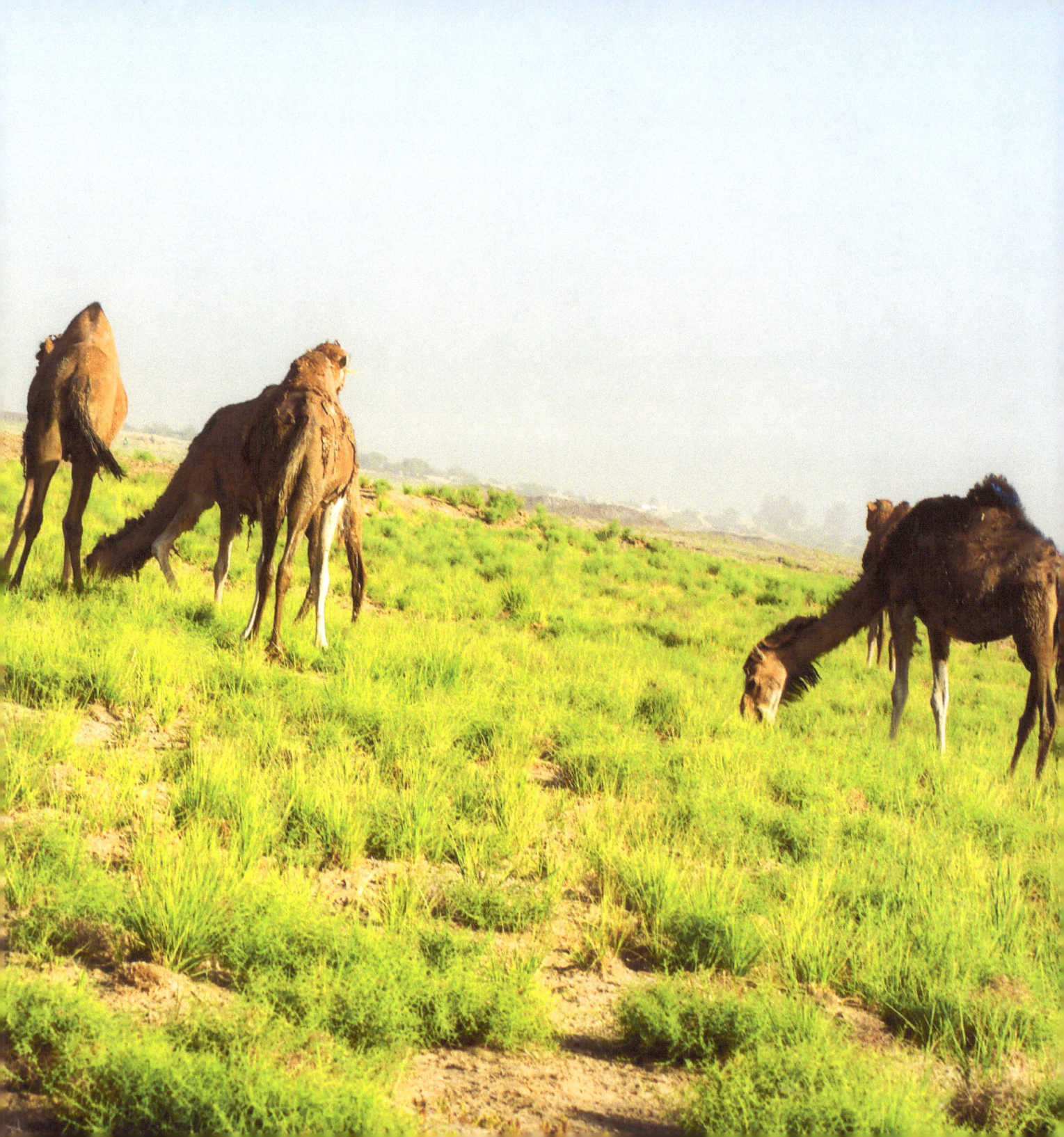

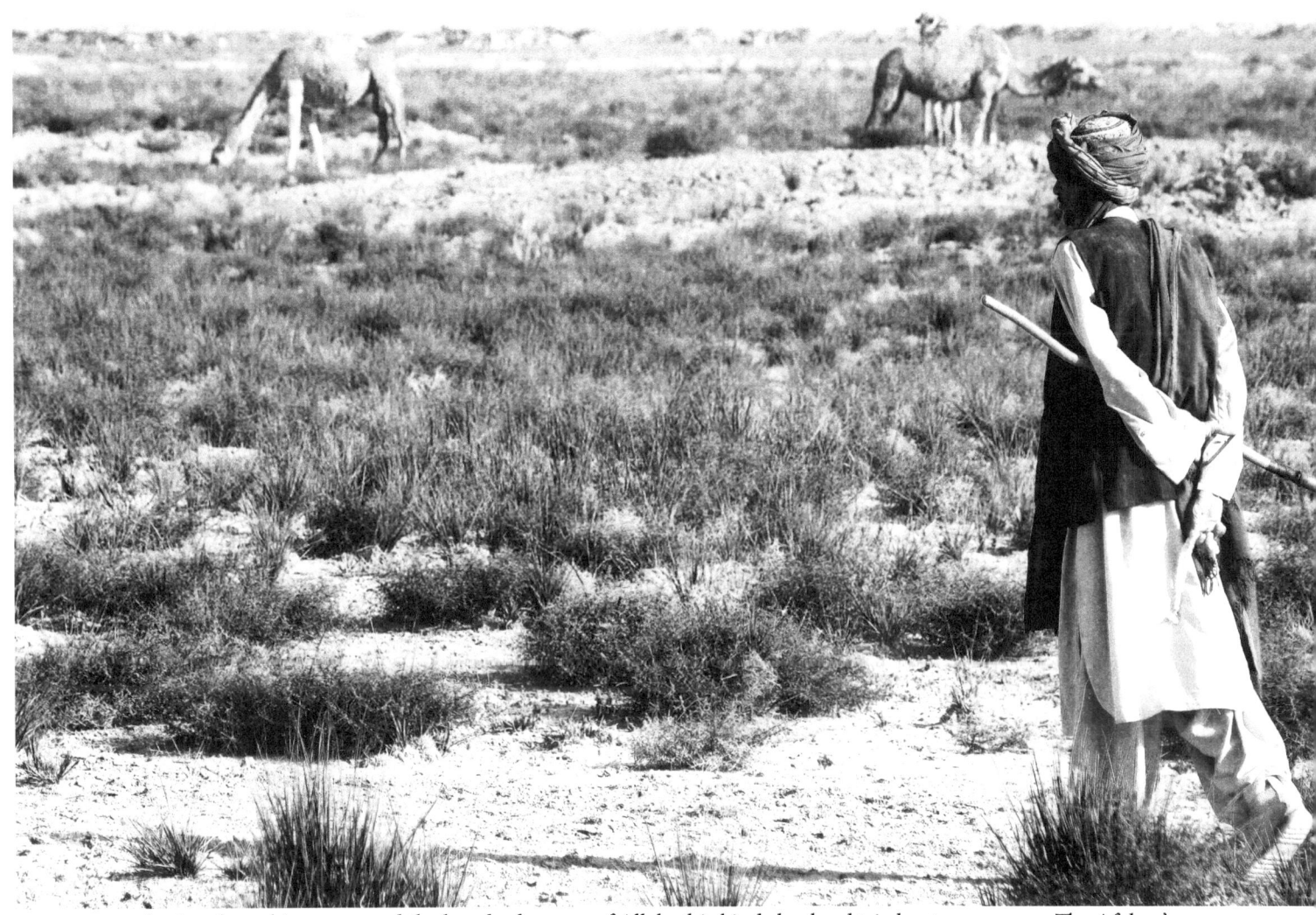

Setting down his rosary and the hundred names of Allah, this kind shepherd tried out my camera. The Afghan's dust-tattooed fingers, although darkened, looked white against the black plastic of the case. He trained the lens on his family, who lived in tents nearby, and he took a series of blurry and crooked shots. Then he directed his attention to the appearance of the object he was holding. He shook his head in surprise. I think I would have witnessed the same display if I had shown a futuristic rifle to a peasant who had stepped straight out of the Middle Ages.

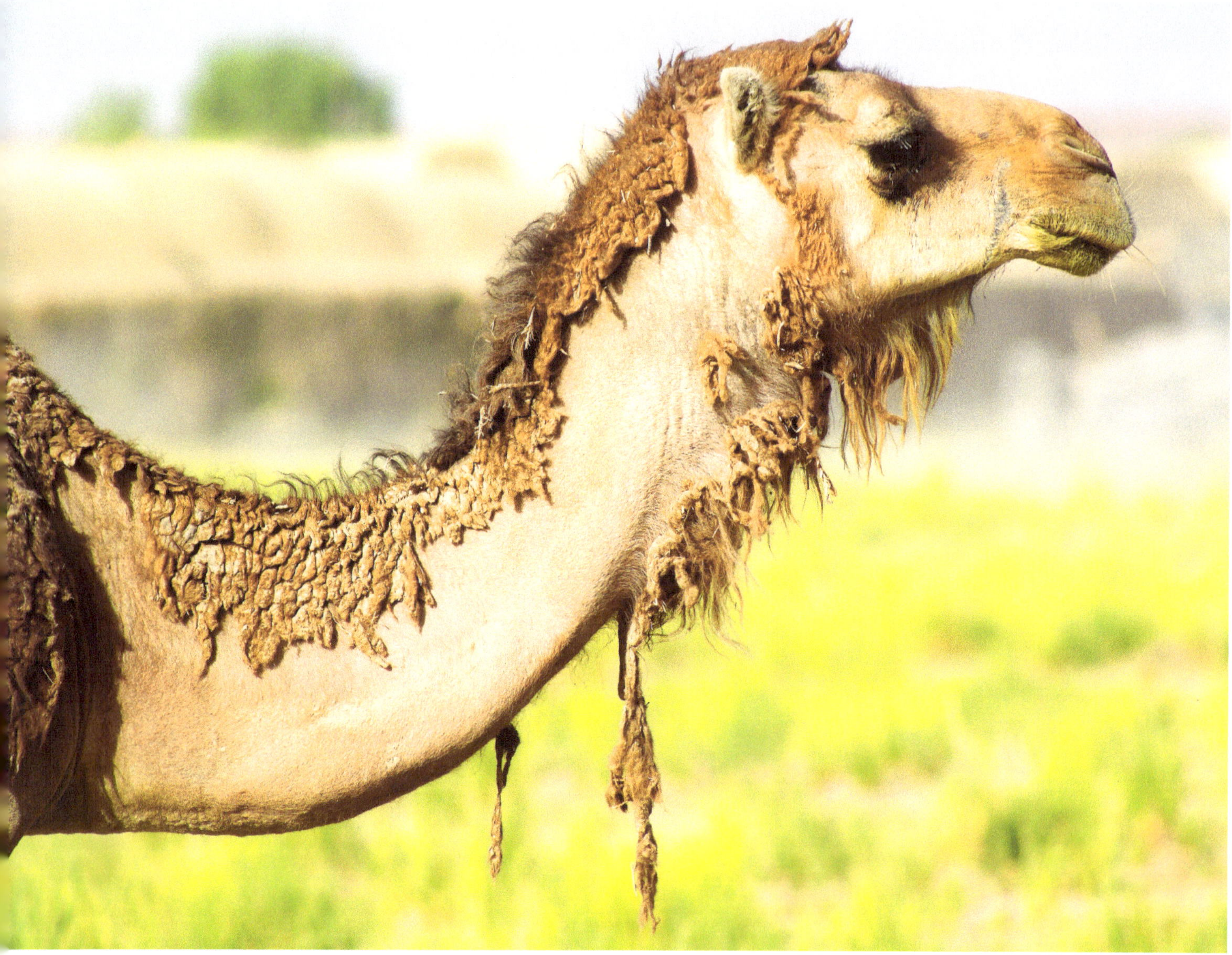

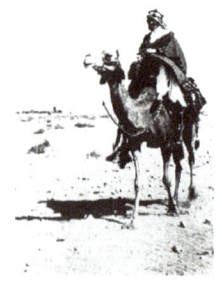 These camels were taking their time shedding the last layers of their winter coats. In the photo on the right, the black and white bring to mind the old documentaries about Lawrence of Arabia (left) setting off on a camel to fight the enemy. It was the era when war could still seem romantic, an era when the black and white of the faraway images made it possible to imagine all the exoticism of the distant regions. Like me, Lawrence of Arabia loved the foreign people he fought with.

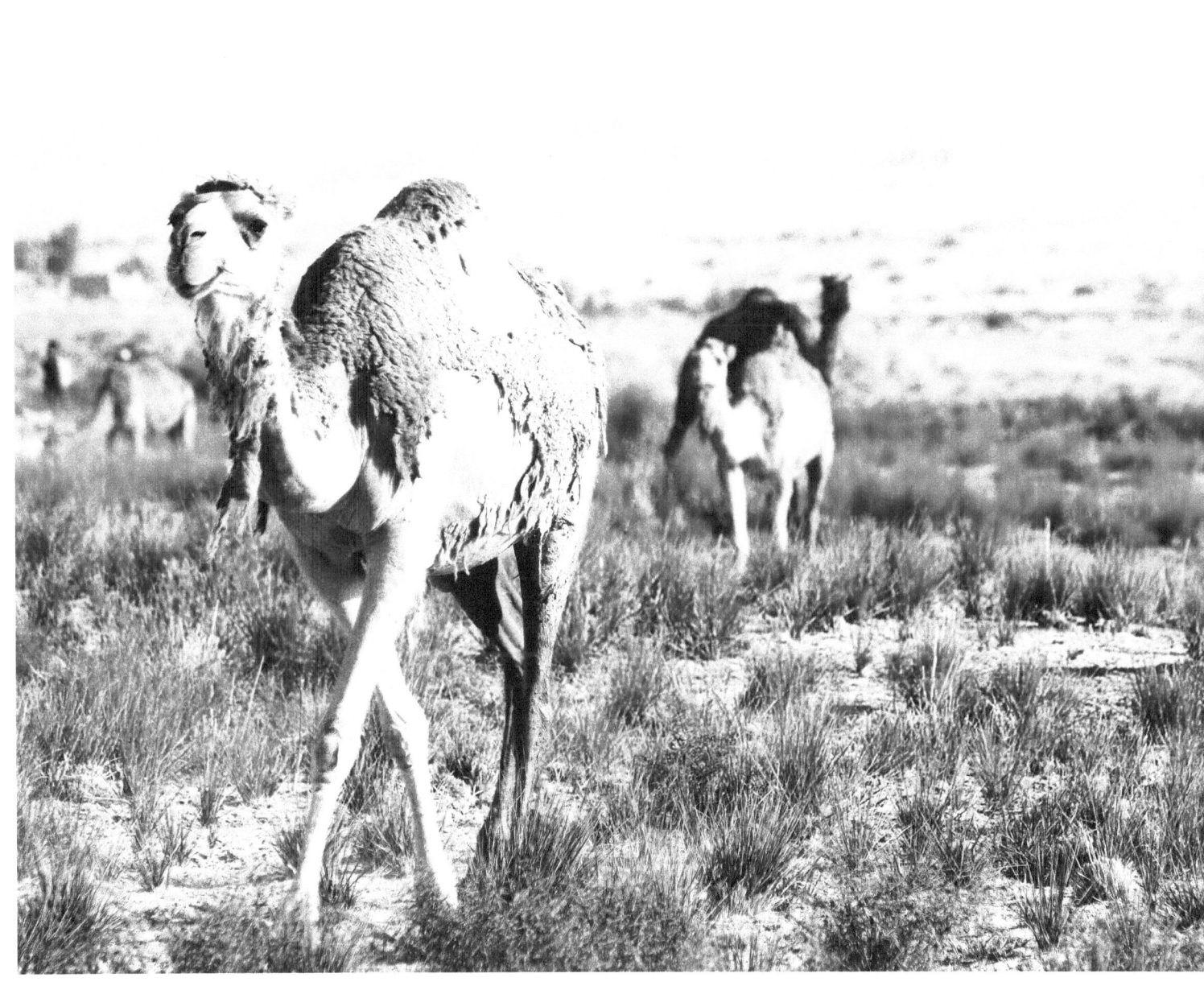

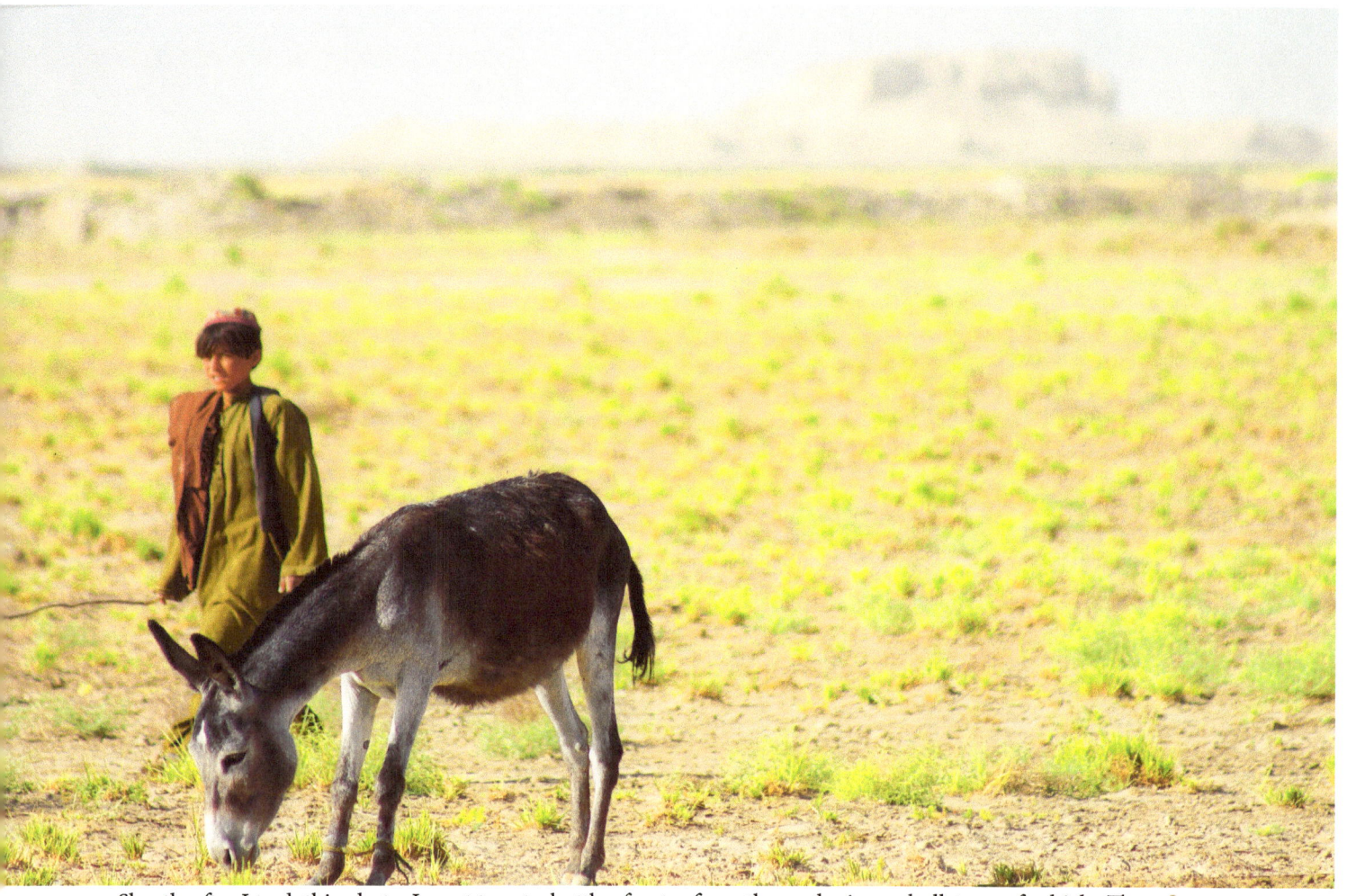

    Shortly after I took this photo, I went to get a bottle of water from the cooler in my bullet-proof vehicle. The water was completely frozen—it was a preserved ice cube! I gave it to the young Afghan, who went back to his family a hundred meters away. I could see people rushing back and forth between the tents. The nomads were passing around the specimen of coolness as if it were a valuable crystal. The little boy then returned to me. Without uttering more than three words, we walked together for about thirty minutes. He was courteous, but he seemed somewhat indifferent to my presence. He was walking near the armored vehicles as if they were nothing. For him, I must have been something like a passing phenomenon, a strange figure that shows up and leaves.

    After some time, the patrol returned from the neighboring village. It was time for me to go back to my vehicle. I was preparing to get going when the donkey started running. To gain his freedom, he would have had to cross an entire desert. With his legs tied together, he went only about fifty meters. He resigned himself to coming back on his own. A few small stones thrown at him had convinced him quickly. Cruelty is the flip side of indifference.

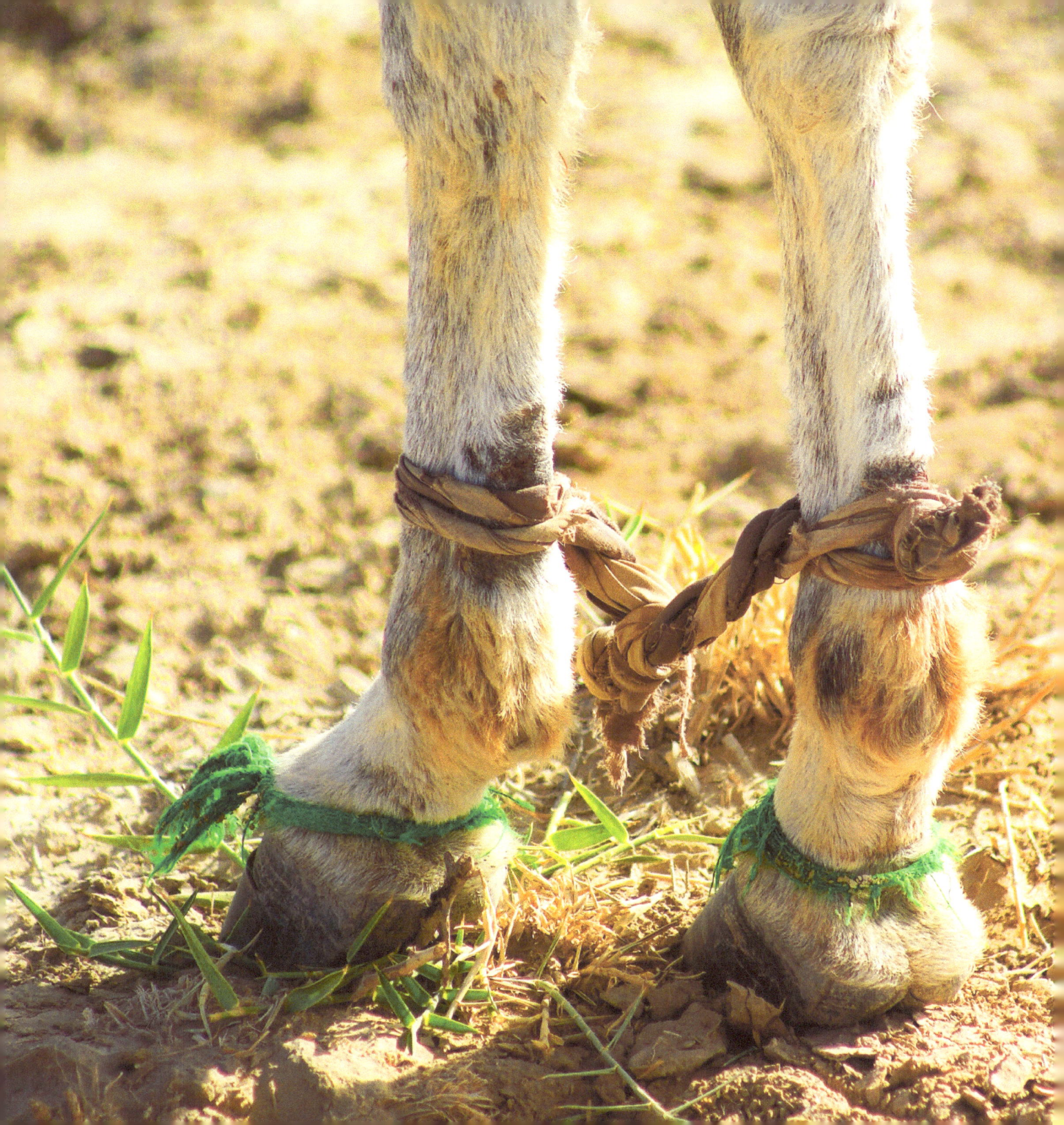

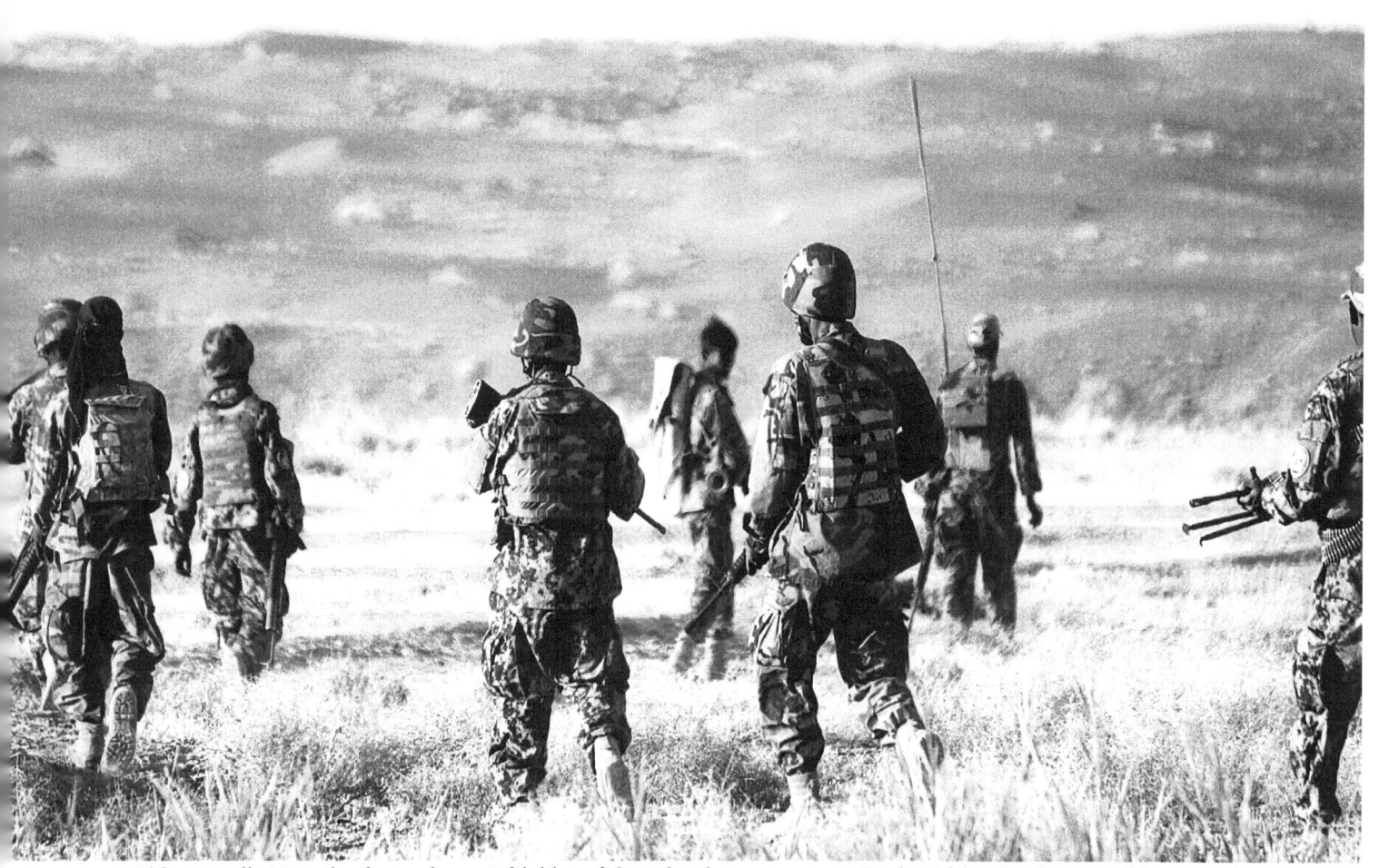

I like to walk. Near the desert dunes, I felt like a fish under the ocean waves. In the Afghan landscape, I felt as comfortable as an actor onstage.

This time, it was Afghan soldiers who were leading the patrol. One soldier carried a type of radio used during the Vietnam War. Unlike Western soldiers, who travel with a lot of equipment, Afghan soldiers carry only the minimum. Both practices have advantages and disadvantages.

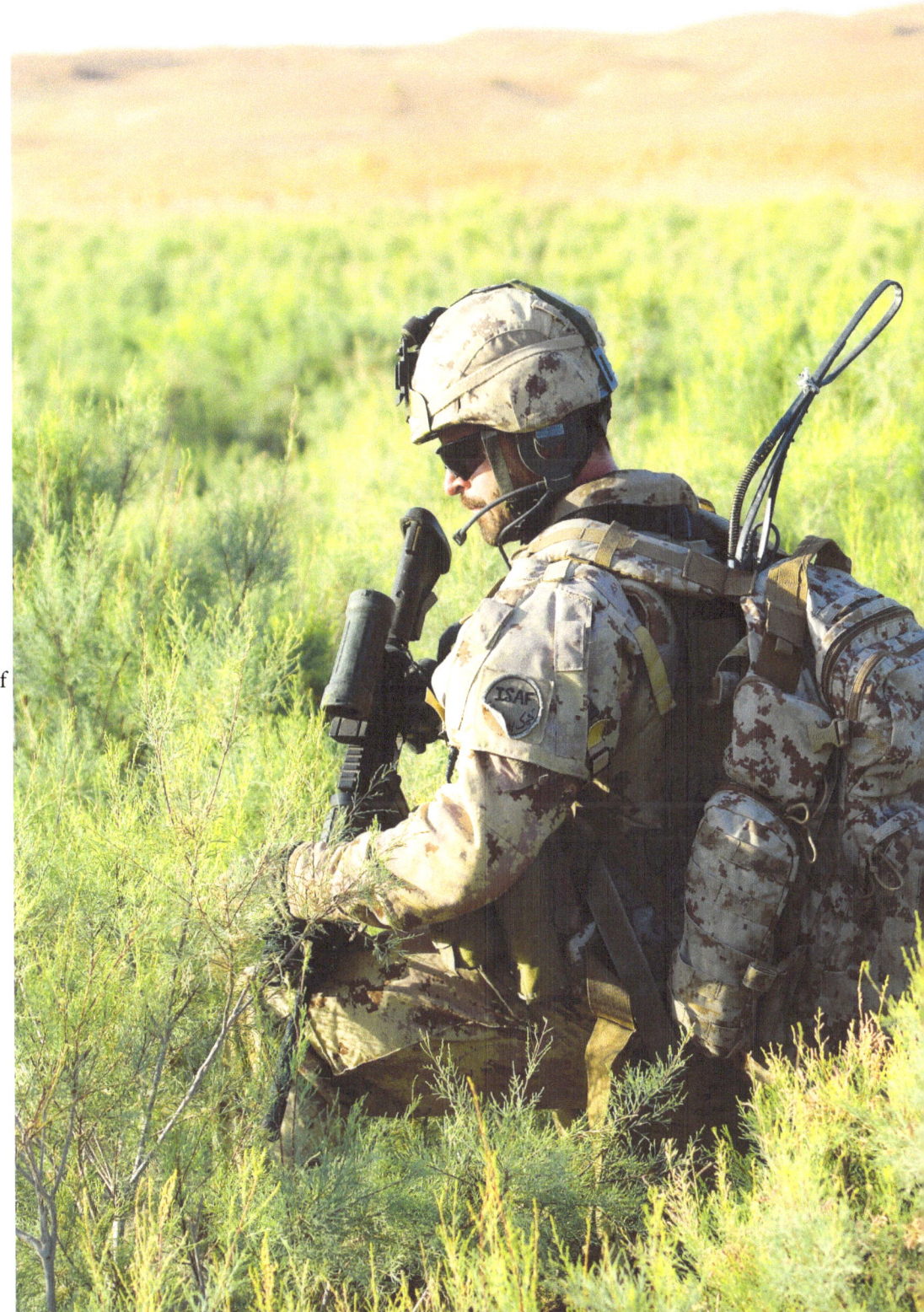

On the bed of a dried-up river, a sergeant was receiving a radio report. The antenna sticking out of his backpack is a true transmitter of life. It enables a call for reinforcements or the fast evacuation of a wounded fellow soldier. For an infantryman, a radio is as important as his weapon.

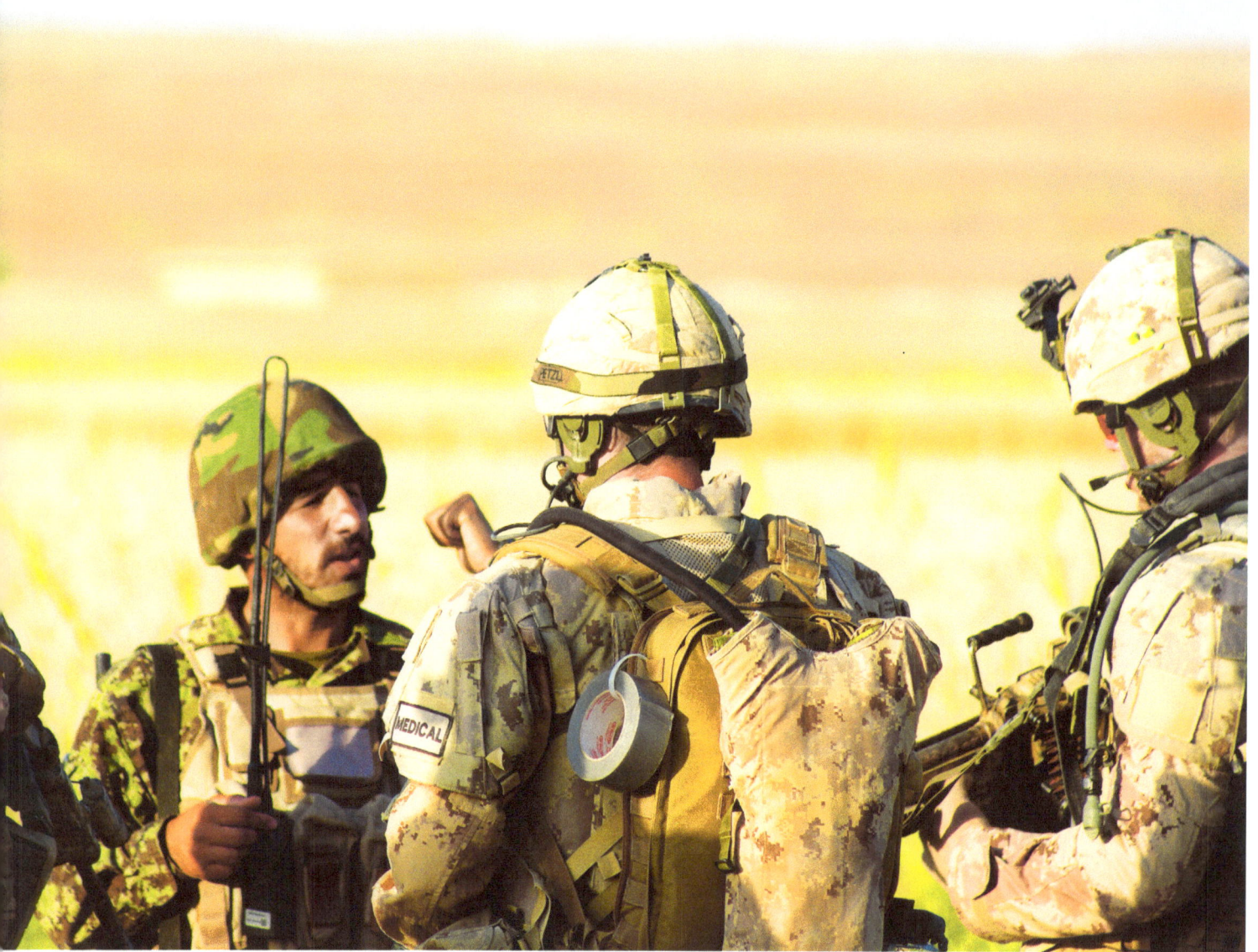

An officer from the Afghan army was explaining the upcoming drills. Over the years, the Afghans took over more and more of the leadership of missions. Our task was to support them. Dare I say that our officers were bored? An army that is bored is an army that has succeeded. Mentoring accomplished!

The "Red Desert" spans several hundred kilometers. Although it is arid, it is not the most dangerous terrain of the region. The villages, streets, and houses are the most dangerous places in Kandahar.

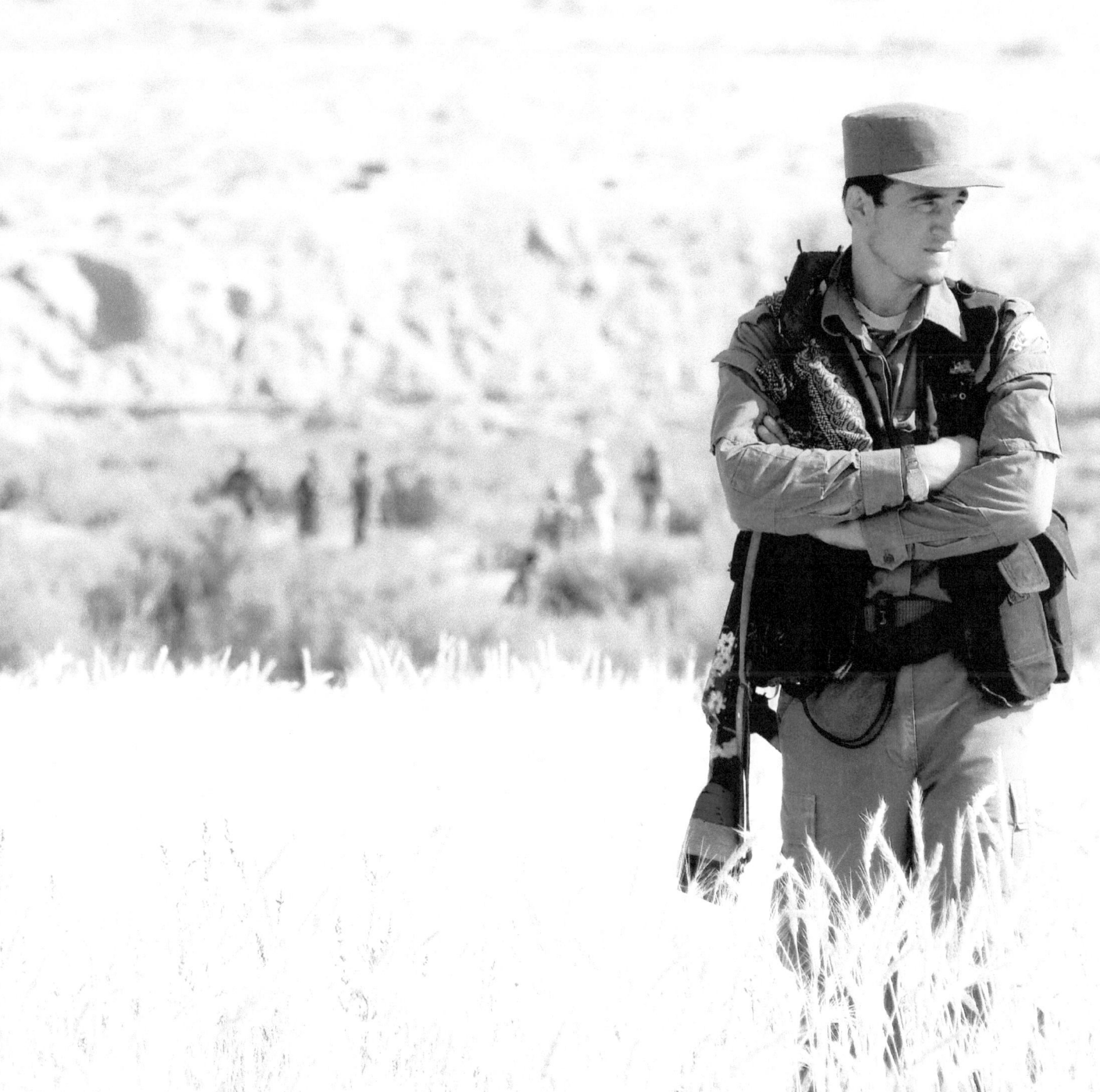

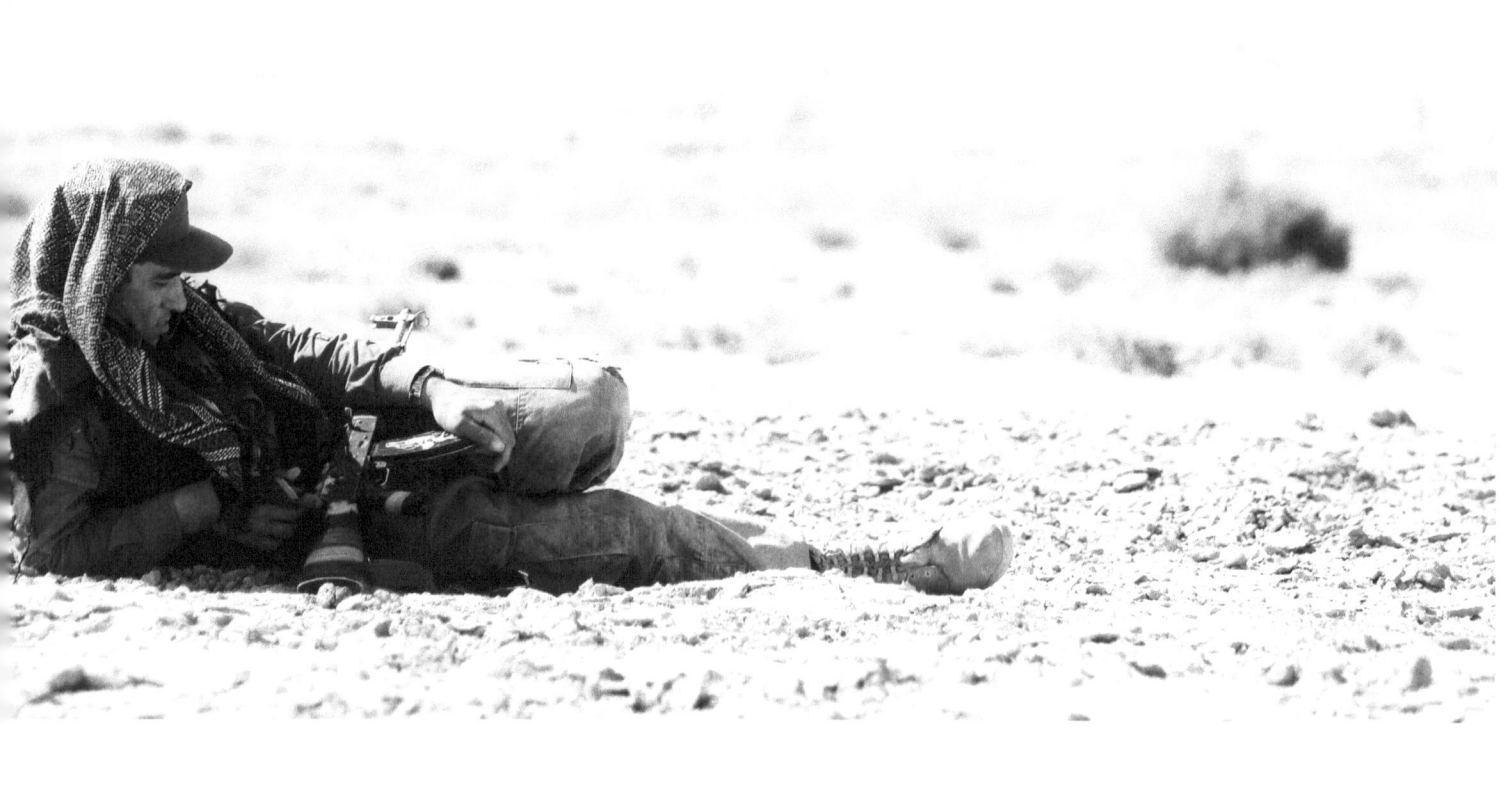

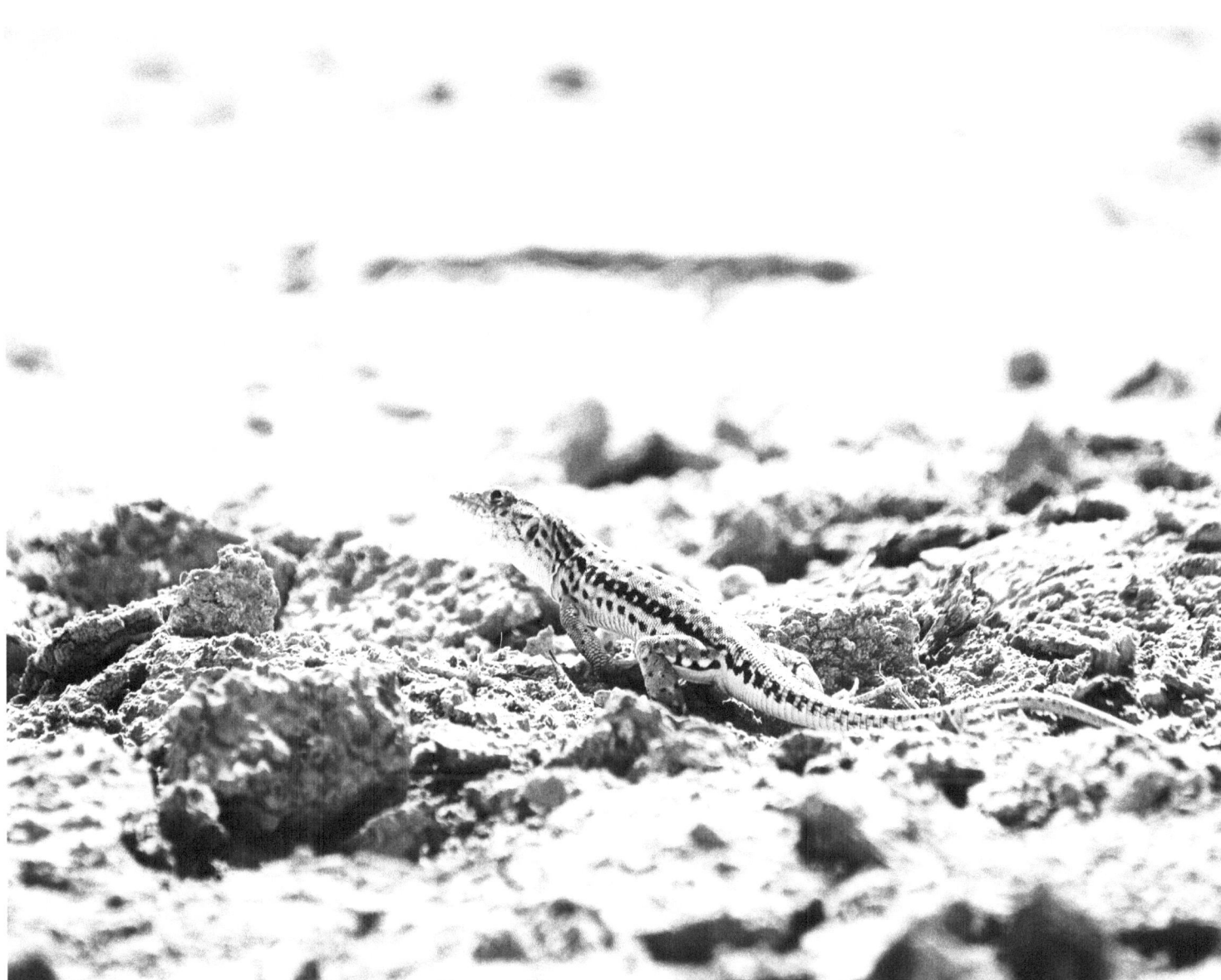

The summer was just starting, but the heat was already unbearable. Seeing that there was no sign of an enemy presence, an Afghan police officer had decided to take a break. Taking advantage of this lull, I sat down with my back against a dried bush. That is when I noticed an interloper walking through our ranks. He was a small soldier with an unusual camouflage. He was patrolling alone, without a weapon. He was not concerned about the war. The war was not concerned about him.

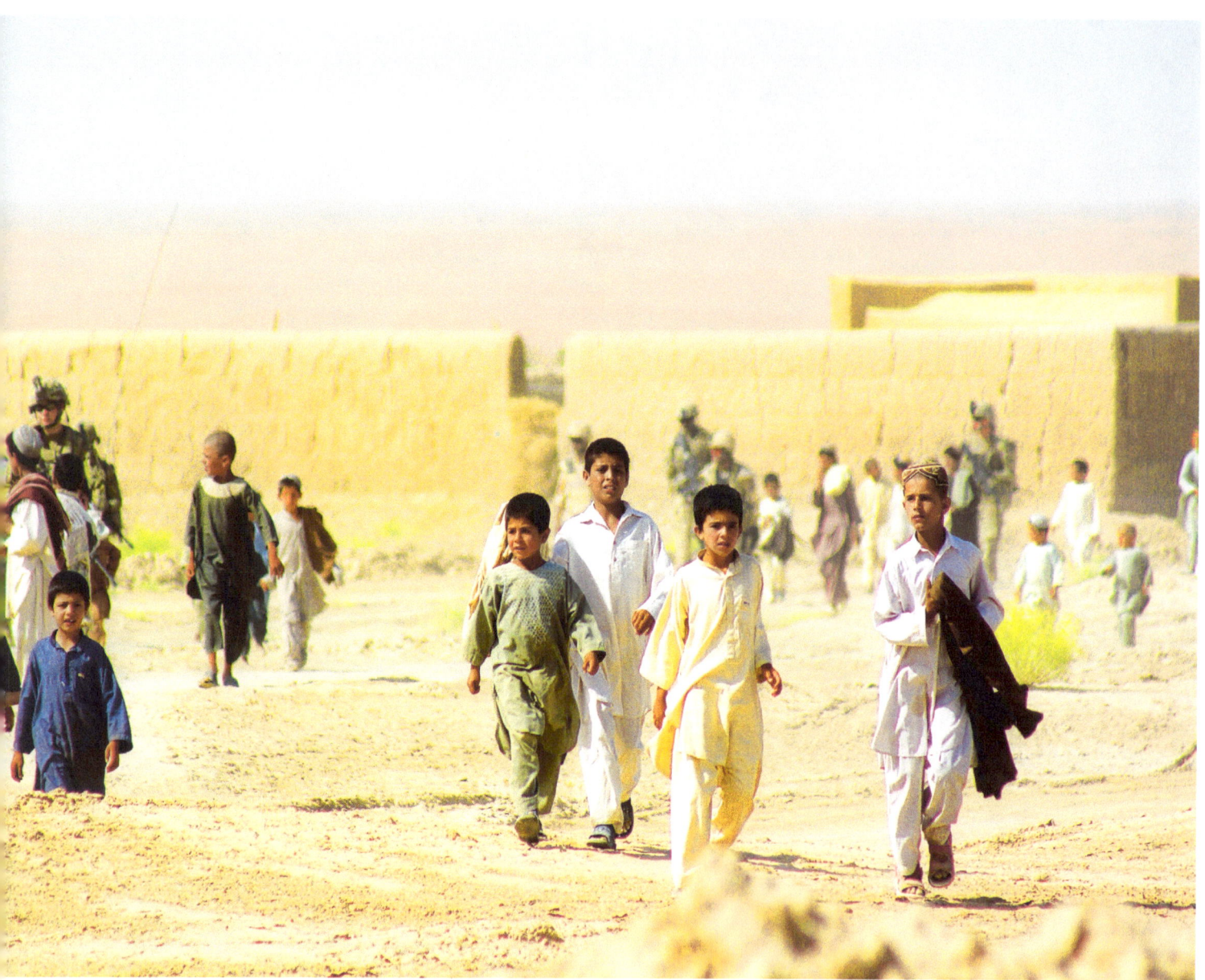

Our bags often contained more candy than ammunition. Children of all ages would come running en masse. The simple act of taking out a treat could work like a magnet on the inhabitants of a village. For this reason, at the end of a patrol, it was preferable to play Santa Claus.

Heading back to the group of vehicles, I photographed the eroded shapes of a former Soviet military base. Situated high up, its military potential had made it an ideal location. The Taliban had probably already mined the place.

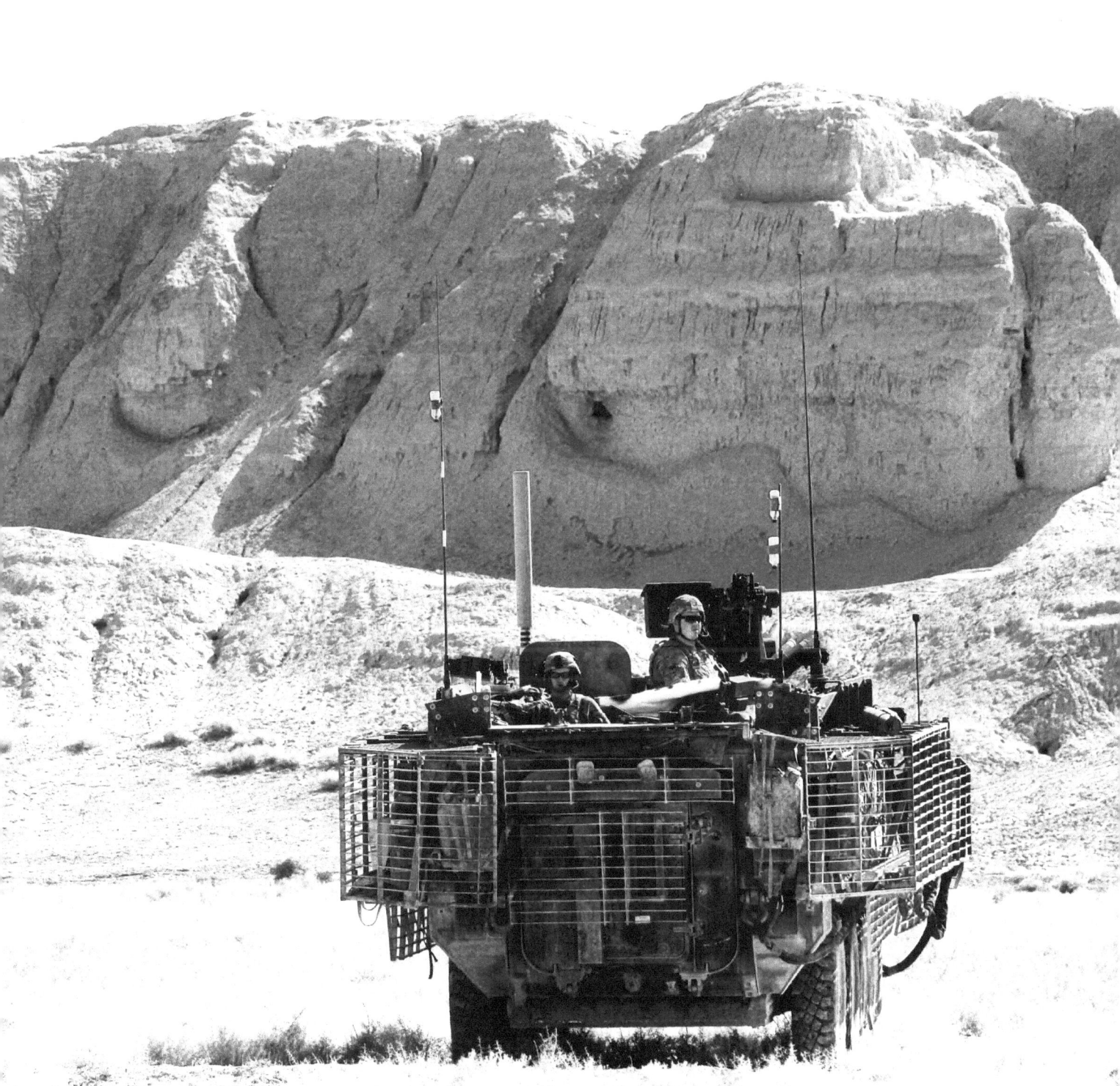

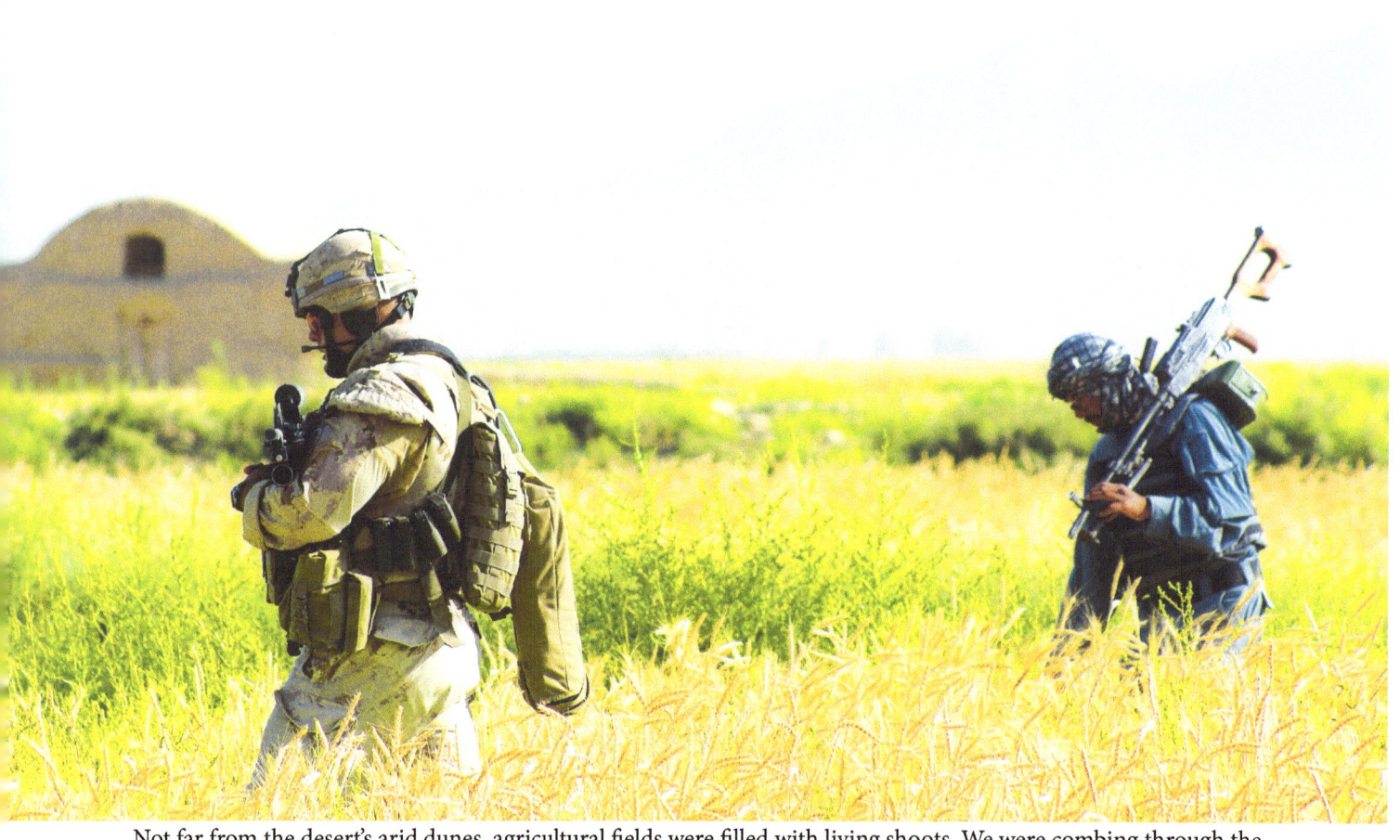
Not far from the desert's arid dunes, agricultural fields were filled with living shoots. We were combing through the fields in search of weapons caches. Surprise! Neither bullets nor bombs—a stunned, worried child motionlessly watched these armed grownups pass by.

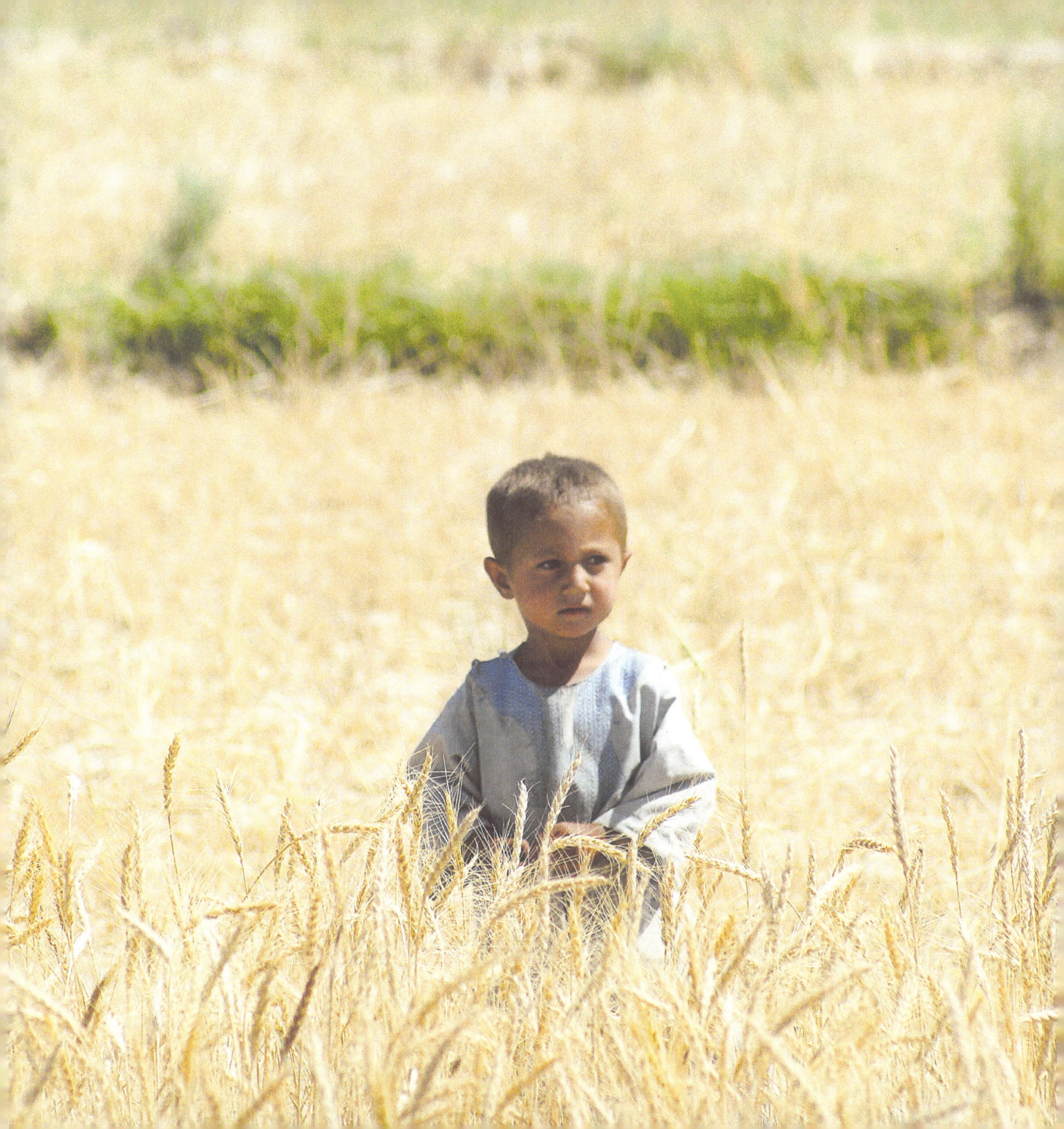

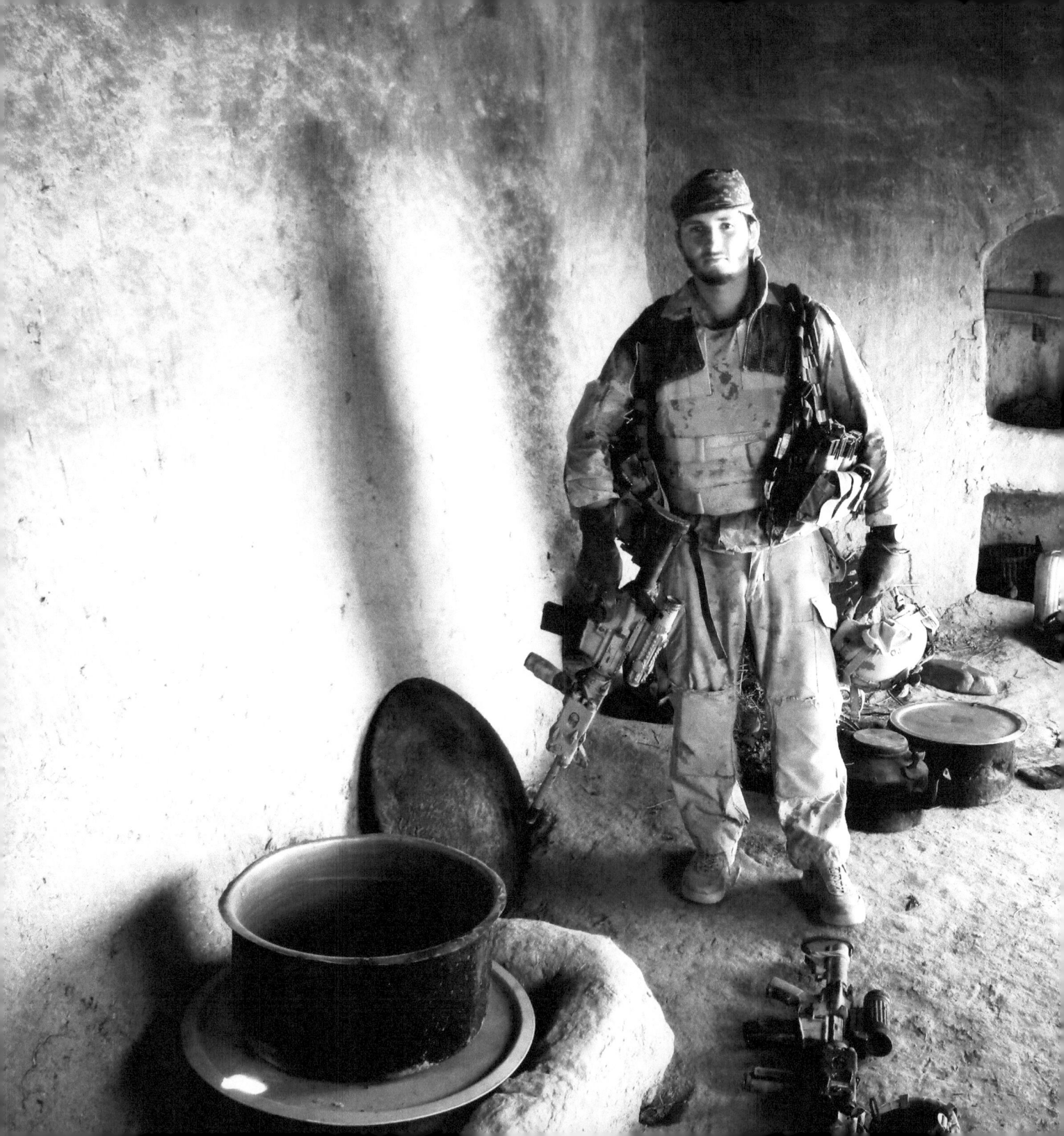

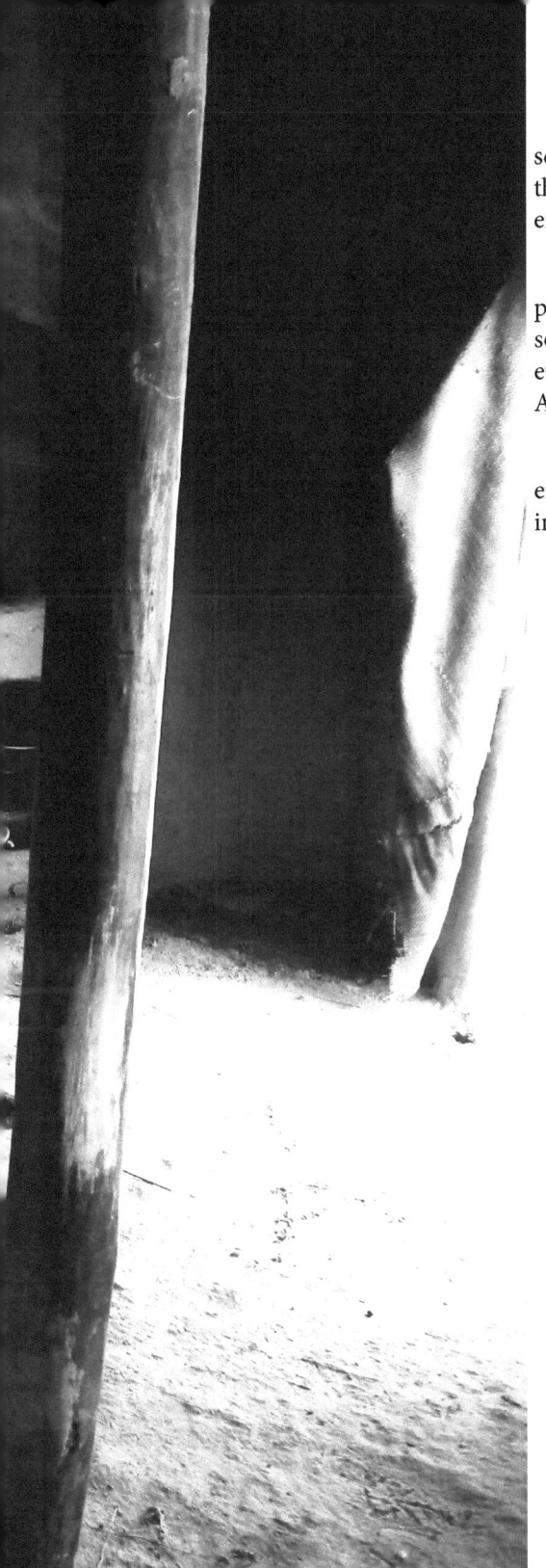

I was continuing my journey through this museum hung with stunning landscapes. This time, the sniper detachment received an order to set up a lookout on the top floor of a building. Several hours later, the four soldiers of my detachment entered an abandoned house.

When there are dangerous operations in progress, residents prefer to vacate the premises. In this kitchen with soot-covered walls, the soup was still hot. I used the soot-blackened wall above the large container as a canvas for a message of peace: I etched the name of my home country and the name of my newly adopted country, Afghanistan. I wrote the two words in Pashto and encircled them with a heart.

This etching might still be there. I like to imagine that a moderate Taliban entered the room a few weeks after I was there, and seeing the inscription's peaceful intention, decided to leave it intact.

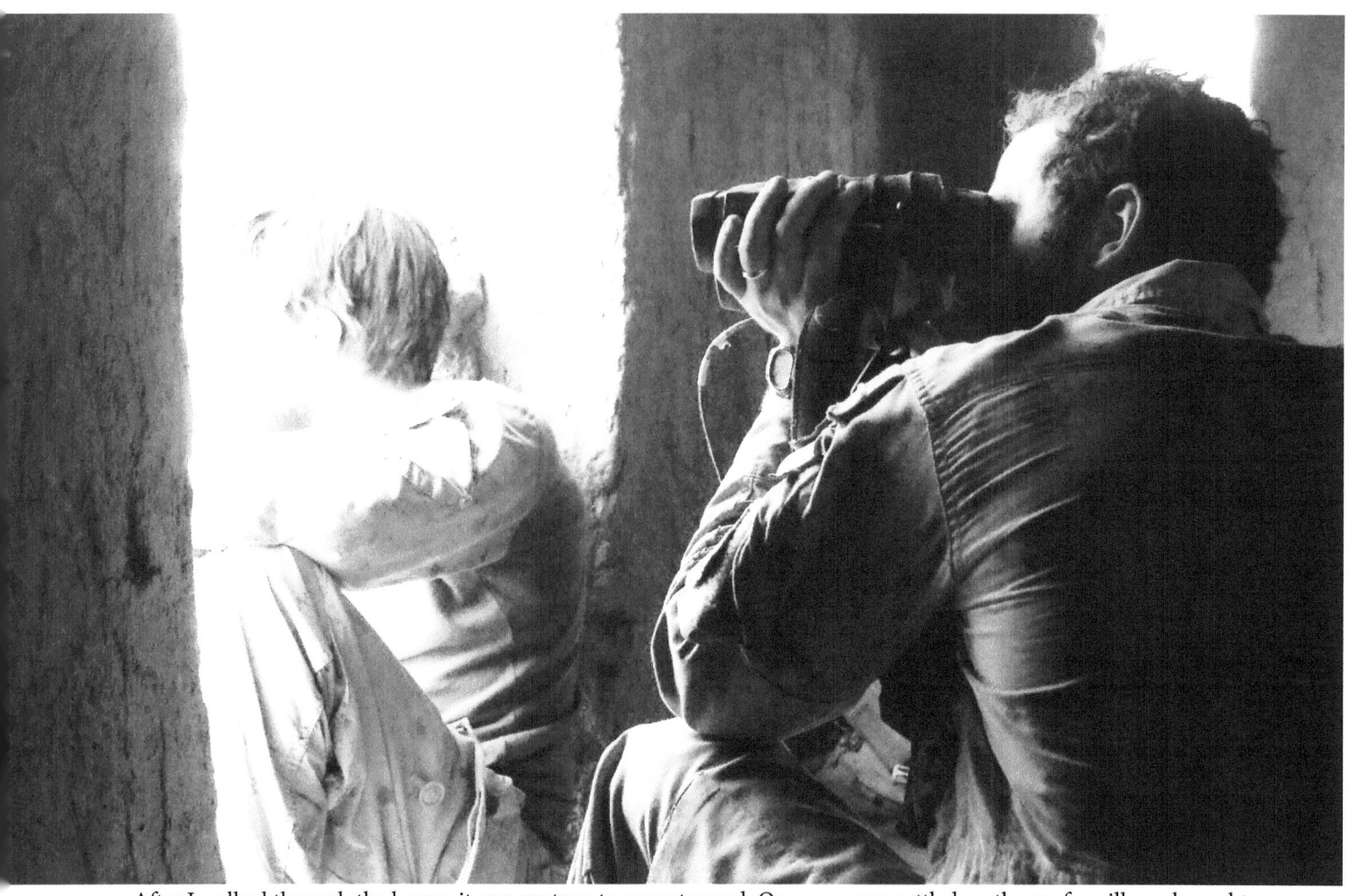
After I walked through the house, it was my turn to mount guard. Once we were settled on the roof, a villager brought us some food. His hands were carrying bowls of fresh grapes, but more important, his face was wearing a friendly smile.

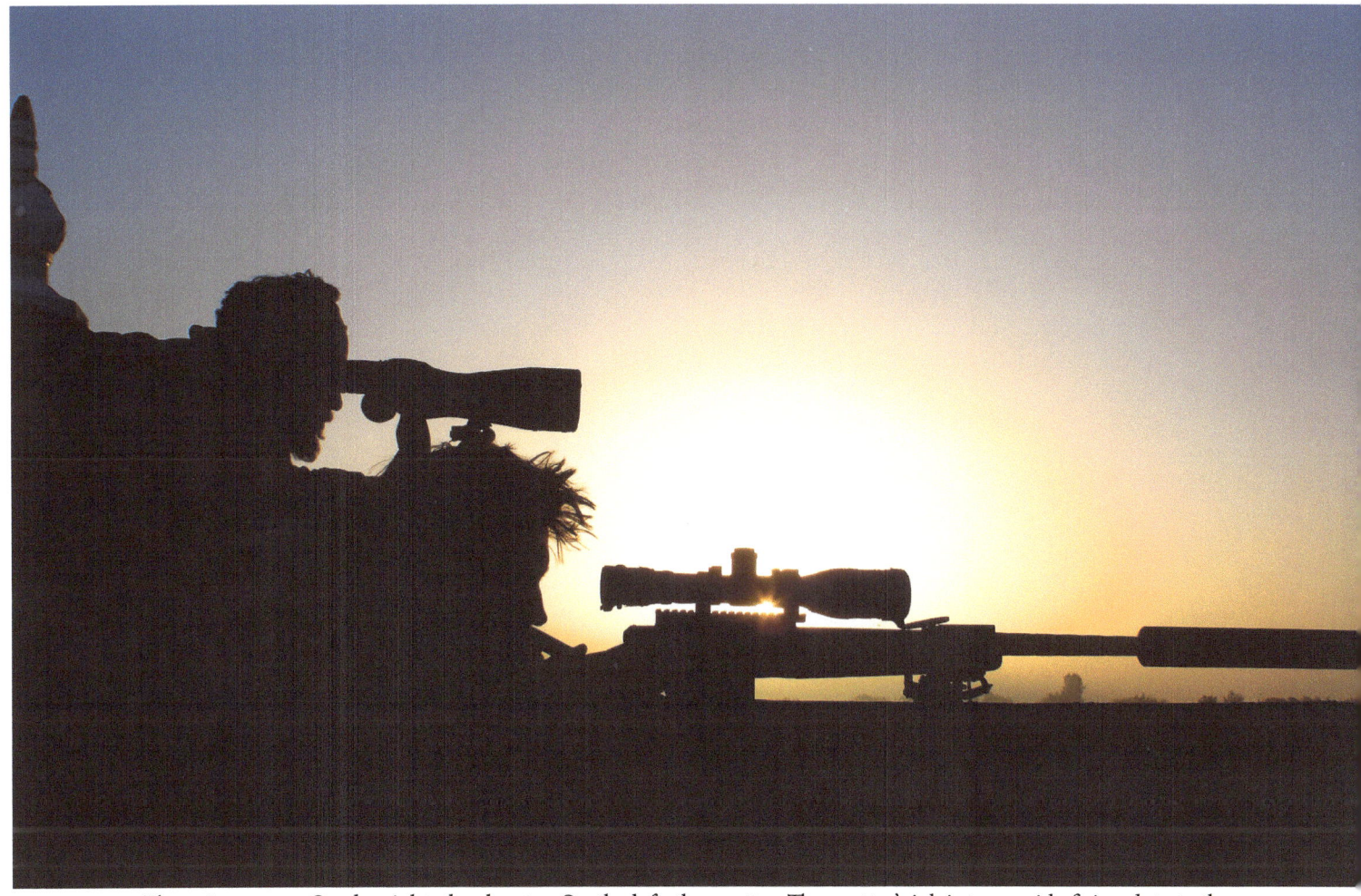

The sniper team. On the right, the shooter. On the left, the spotter. The spotter's job is to provide firing data to the shooter. He must also calculate corrections due to wind, gravity, air temperature, and many other factors. Although his role is less flashy, he is the more important of the two. A good shooter is more common than a good spotter.

I preferred to be the spotter. However, what I saw most often was not armed insurgents, but unarmed Afghans who were trying to live in the heart of a region that had been at war for centuries.

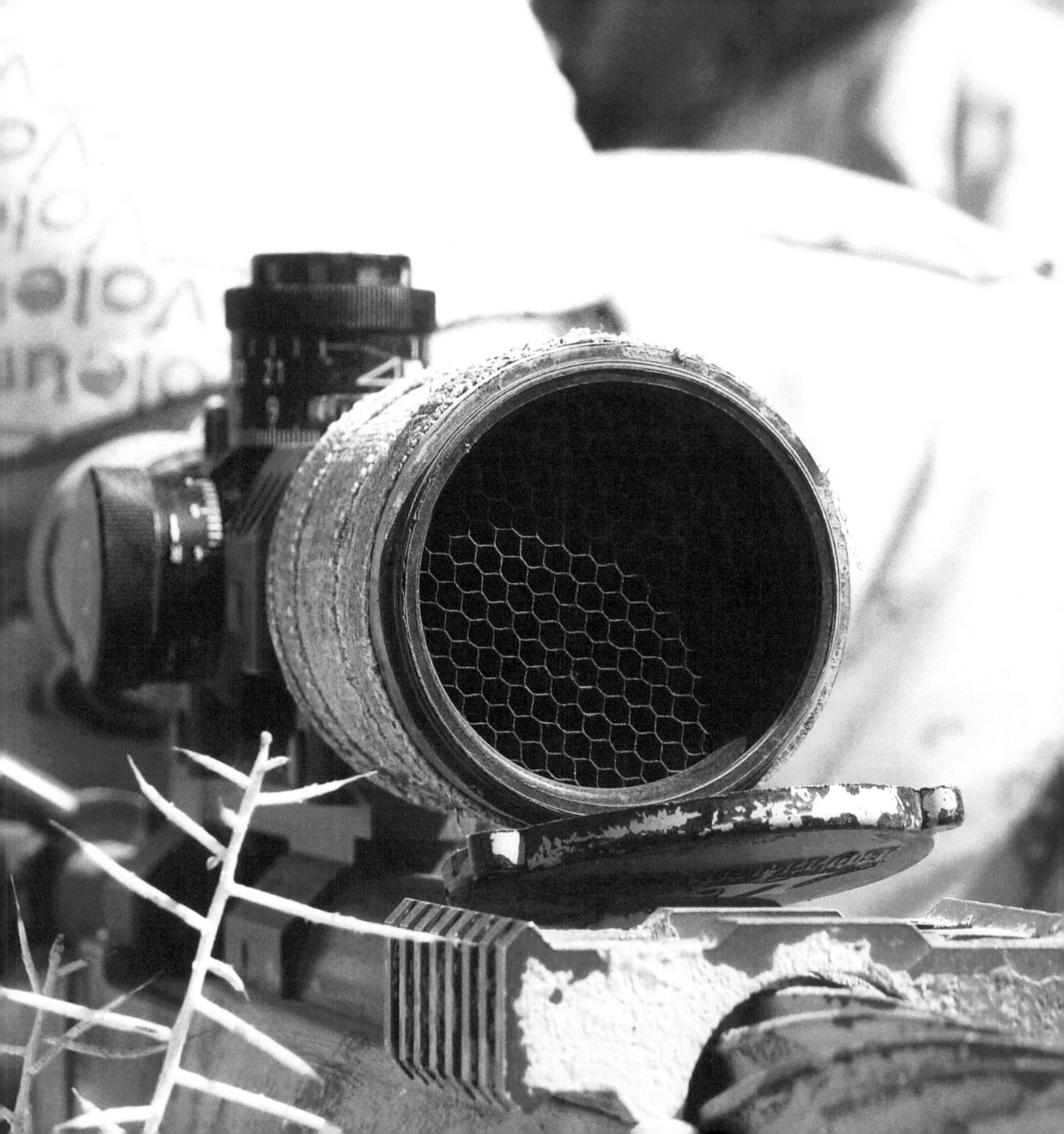

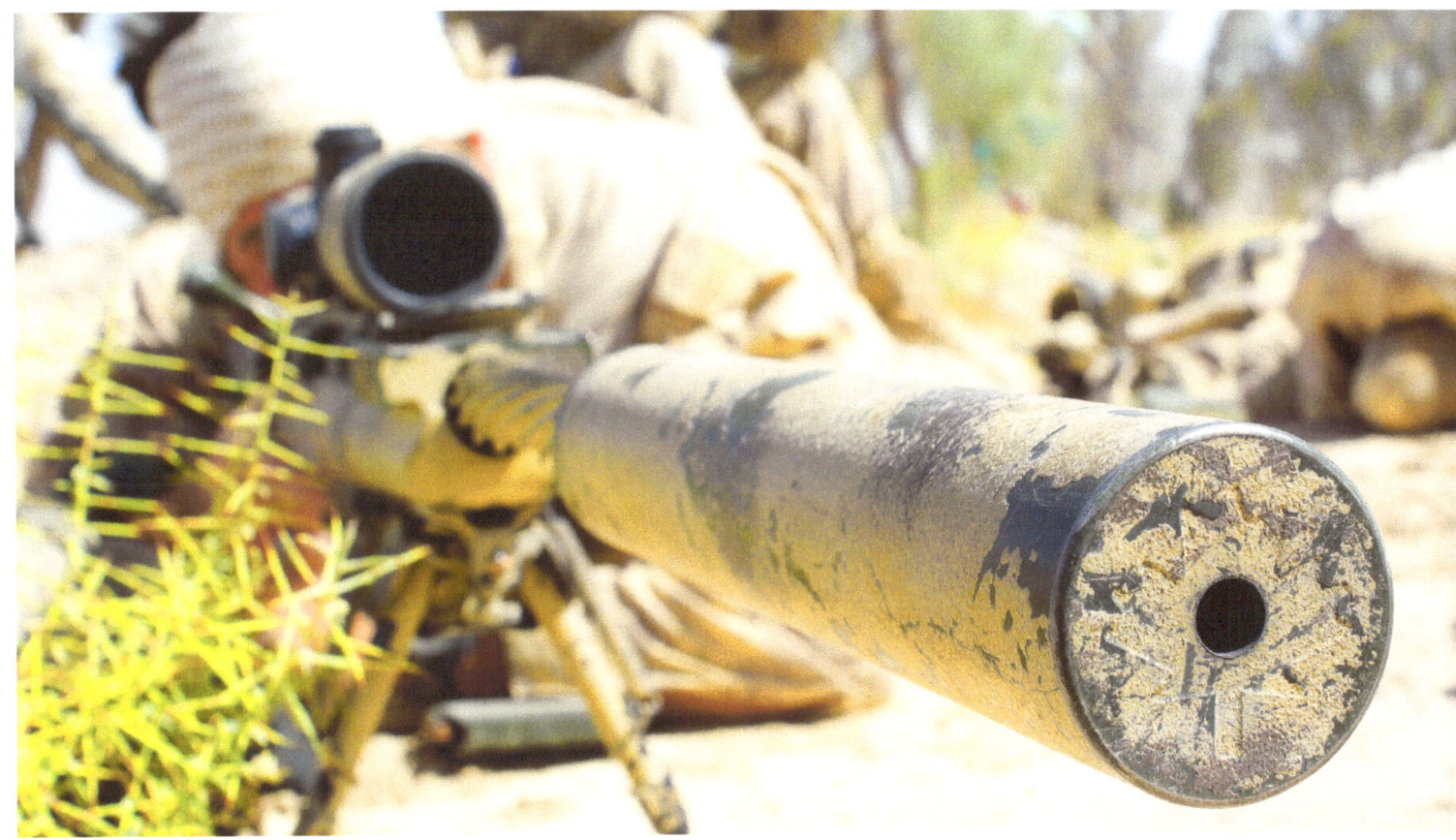

"Honeycomb" patterns prevent light from being reflected off the lens, which otherwise could reveal the sniper's position from far away.

Just after I took these photos of the weapons, I went to take a nap in the shadow of a tree. When I got up, I found myself surrounded... by a group of little boys! I used the opportunity to show them how my camera worked.

A little girl was watching us from on top of her house. I motioned to her to come closer, but she stayed as still as a ghost. She did not show any reaction. I then told the boys to summon the girl, who I took to be their sister. I knew the word in Pashto. She came quickly.

I also knew the word for "gift." Unfortunately, the little girl did not even dare to approach the candy I was holding out to her. She looked like an animal waiting to be punished. So I gave the gift to her brother, who gave it to her. She smiled. She even wanted to have her picture taken with the boys.

Some "graybeards" then came to join us. They put a rug on the ground, telling the children to go get some bread, water, and milk. Meanwhile, the snipers in my detachment were keeping watch over the surroundings. This is how I came to take part in an Afghan picnic in the middle of Taliban territory.

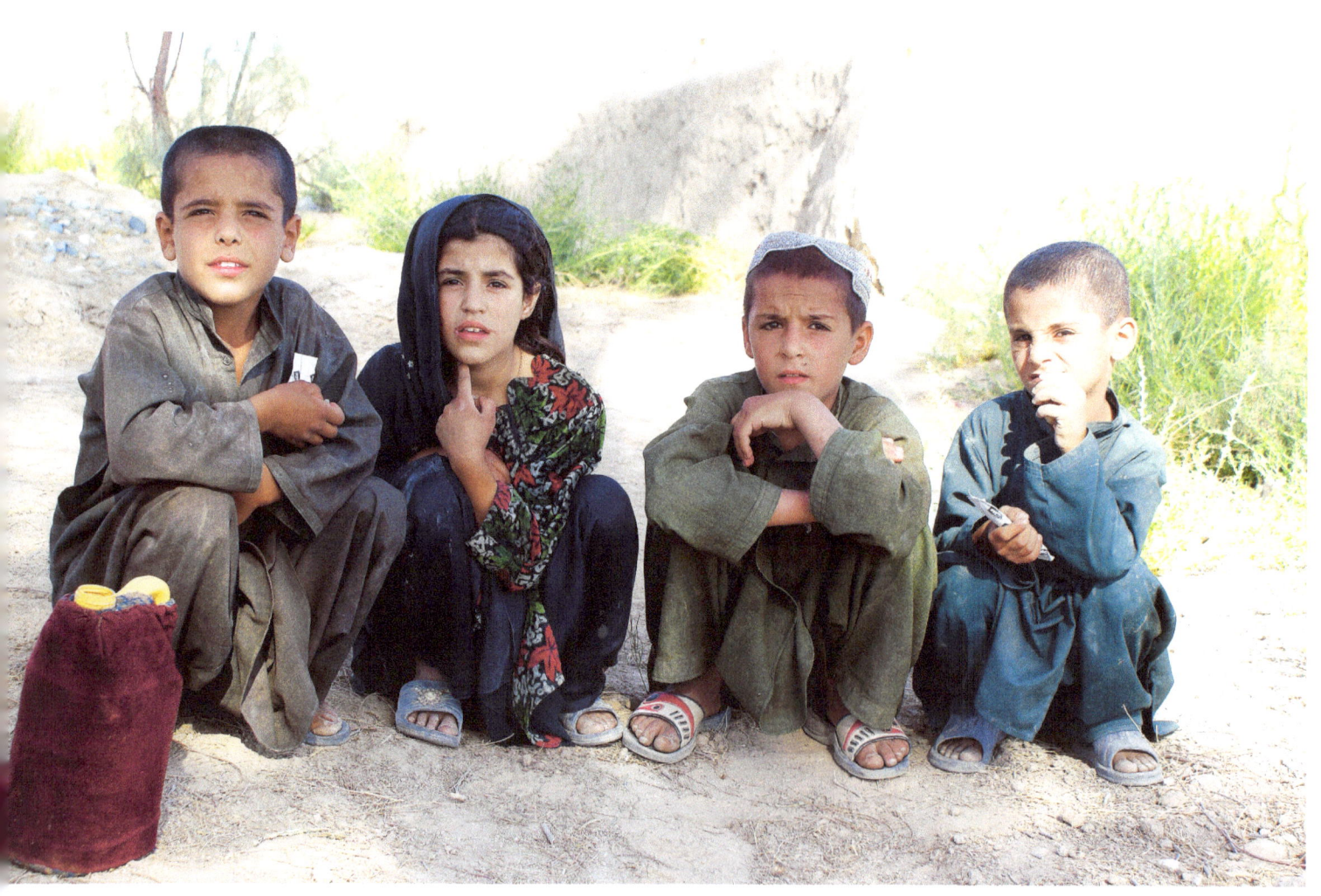

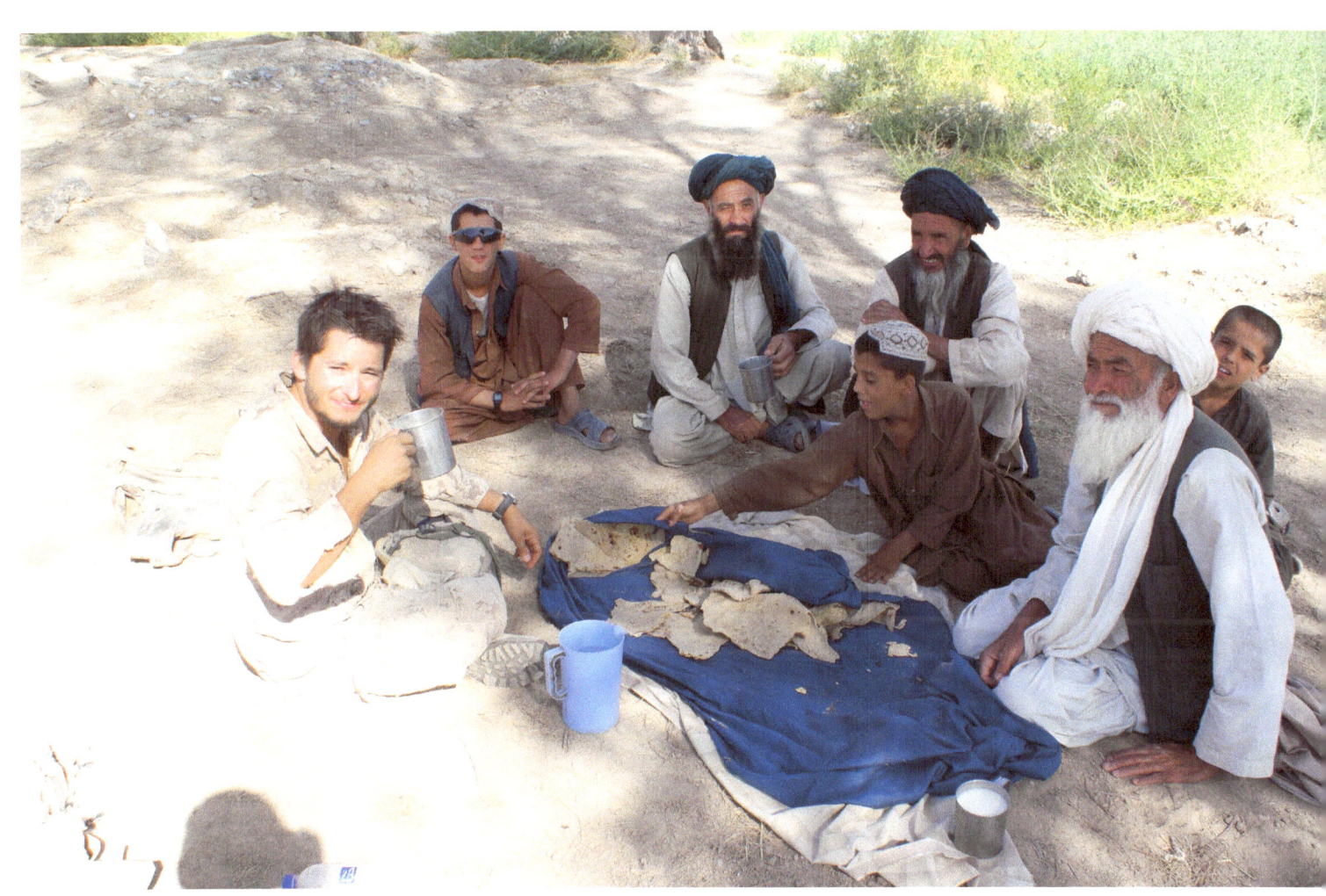

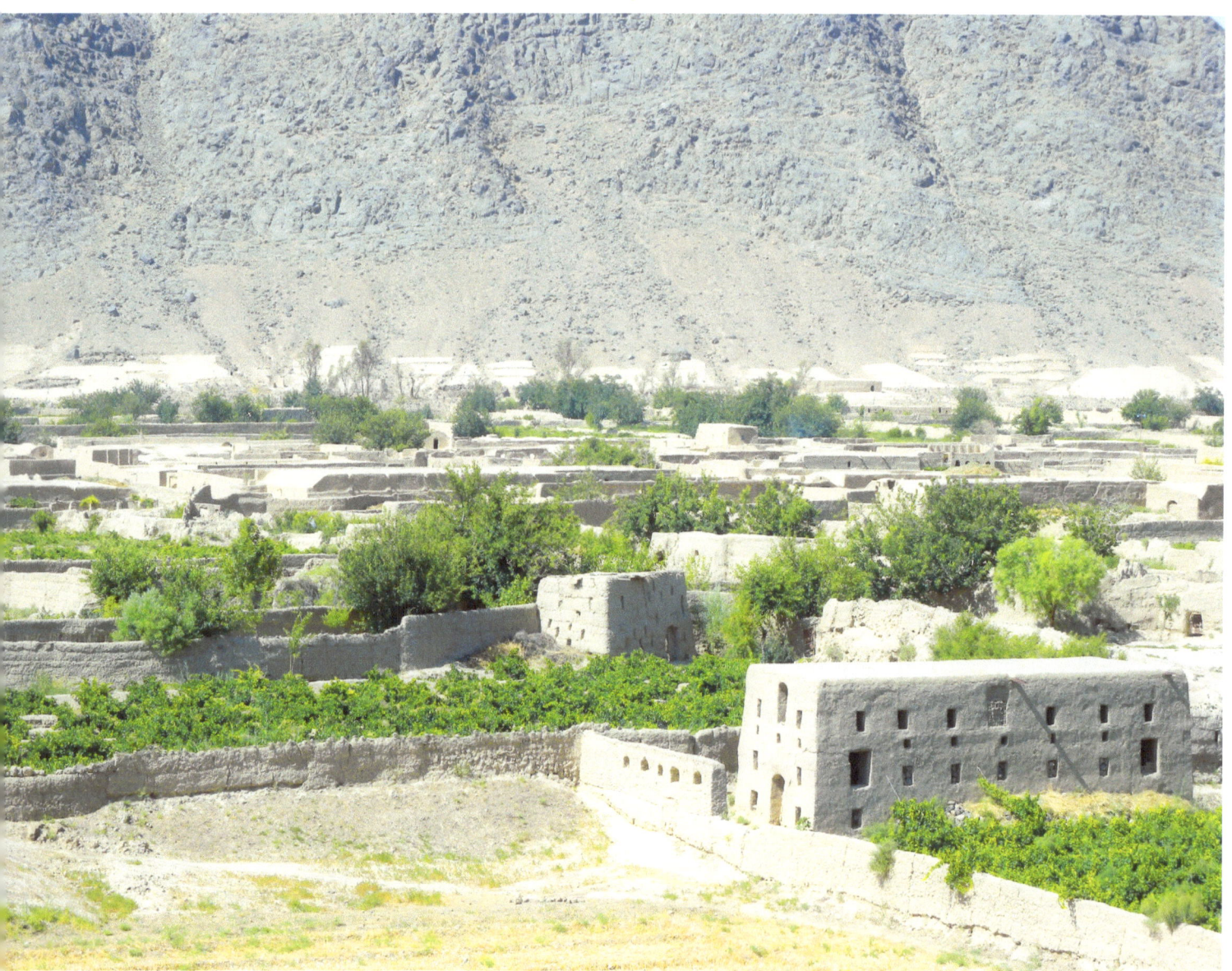

The view from an observation post: a typical village that looks deserted. In the summer, the midday heat is so strong that the residents get off the streets. The small community then looks like a ghost town, yet if one could see past the walls, it would be like watching the inside of an anthill teeming with activity.

At the foot of the sunburnt mountain, unusual white expanses were visible. I looked at them for a long time, wondering what their purpose could be. Several months later, during a conversation with some Afghans, my guesses were confirmed: these white plates at the base of the mountains are used for drying grapes.

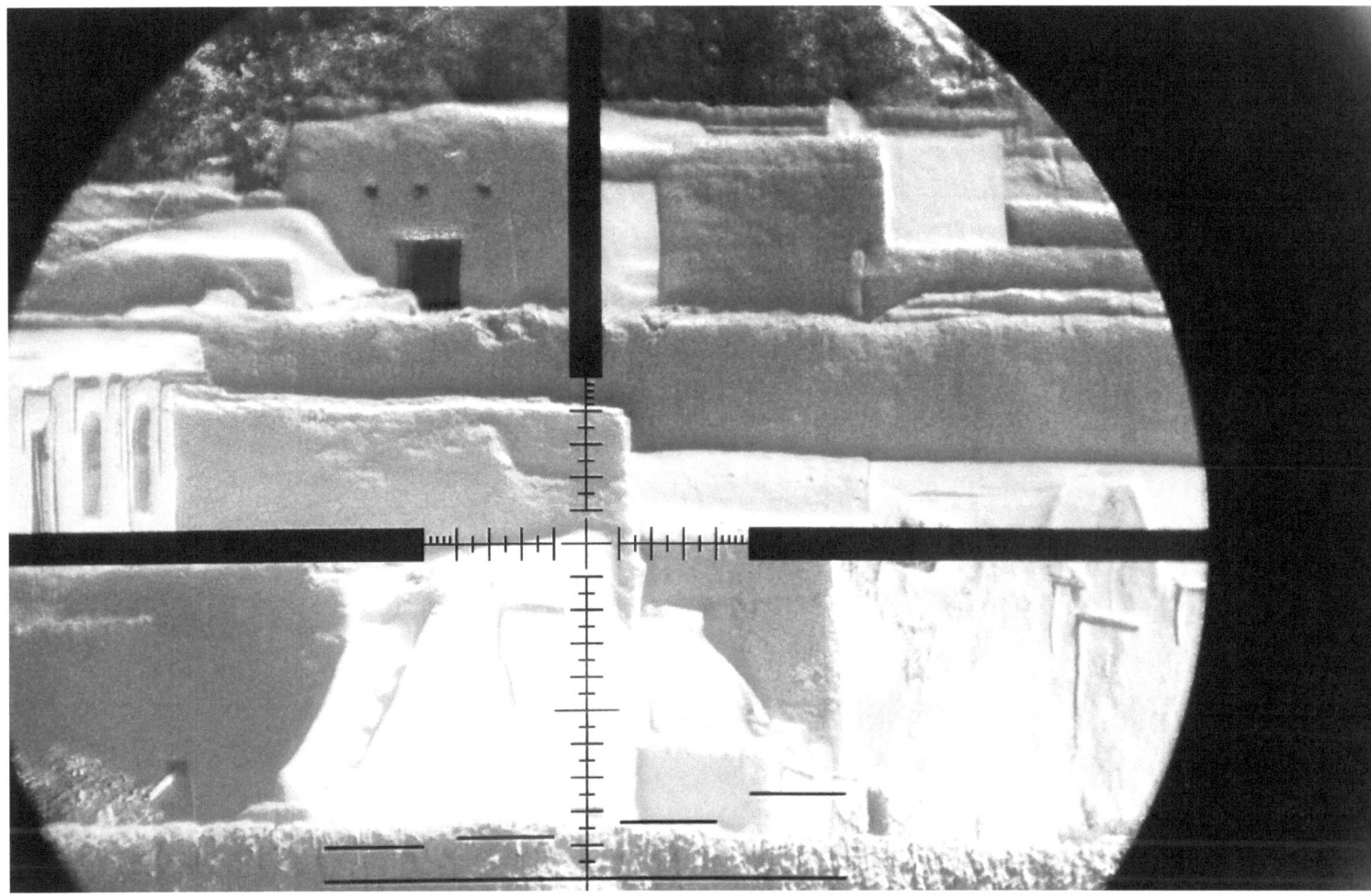

It has been said that "soldiering is 99 percent boredom and 1 percent sheer terror." It is long and monotonous days scanning the surroundings, watching for the enemy to appear even though he generally appears for only a few decisive seconds. Movies give us the impression that a sniper crawls to his target, which shows up standing "on a silver platter." After several hours of sweat and courage, the warrior returns covered in glory and victories. And yet, war is nothing of the sort. Being a sniper is a game of psychological hide-and-seek in which one tries to understand and predict the enemy's behavior. It is like a game of chess in which only half of the opponent's pieces are seen, and in which it takes hours to move every pawn. During a battle in World War II, two enemy snipers searched for each other for days from two opposite rows of trees. The one who lost was the one who decided to relax with a cigarette. His rest ultimately lasted longer than he had planned. In war, especially at night, a cigarette can quickly turn deadly.

In Afghanistan too, hours and even days could follow one another before a single bullet was fired. Despite this, during the long hours of watching, I took pleasure in observing Afghans' daily life. Although my weapons did not shoot often, my camera did.

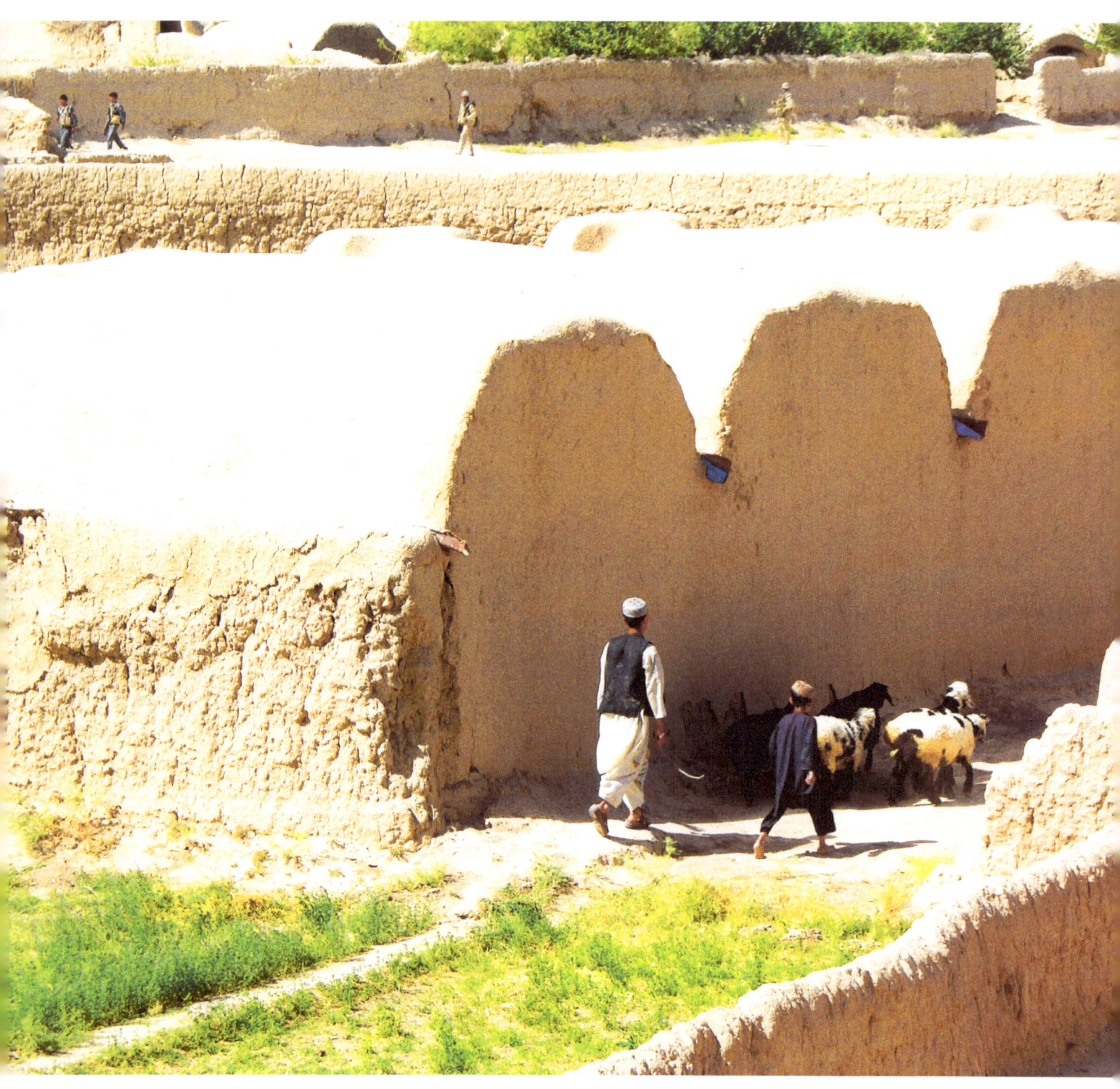

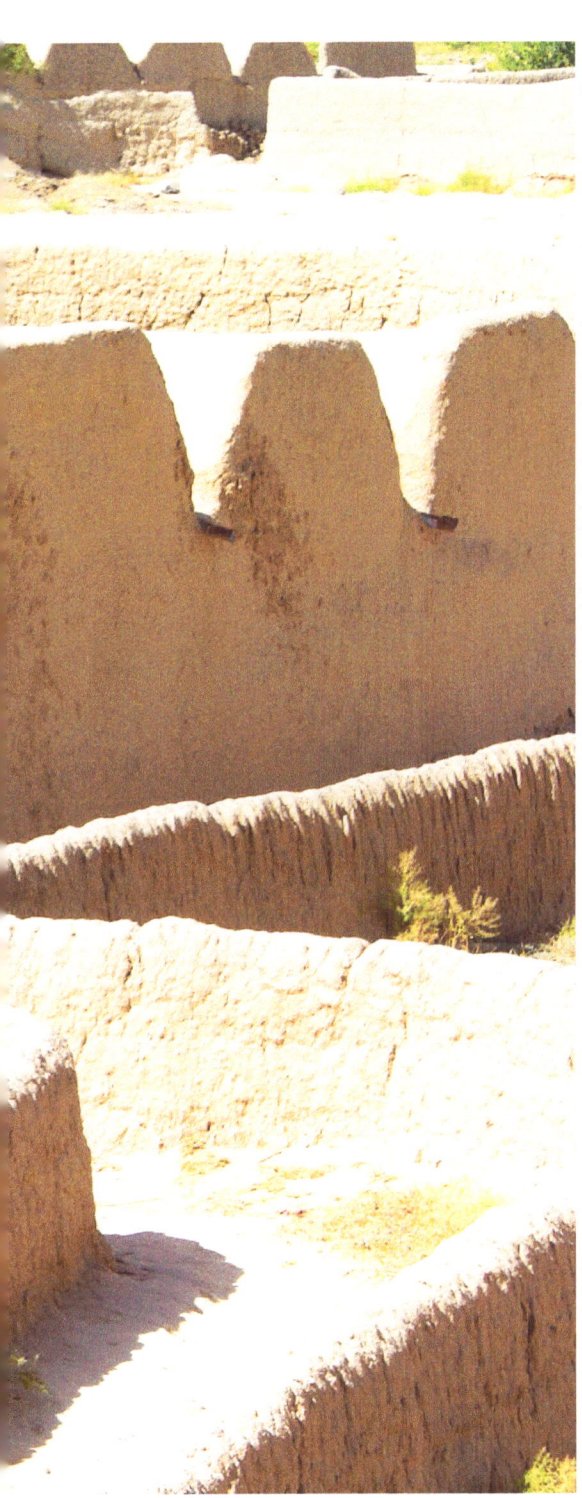

Military operations did not disrupt the routine of this shepherd and his apprentice.

Less than three hundred meters away, in the background, a patrol of Canadians and Afghan police officers could be seen. For days, troops combed the streets of this village. Several bombs were found this way. The tracking dogs were exhausted.

Made from bottles cut in half, drainpipes emerged from the roofs of the buildings. Under each of these undulating roofs, there were members of a family. Perhaps under the first one there was a group of female cousins making tea. Each one was talking about the man she wanted to marry. A bit farther, under another roof, I imagined a boy bringing a jug of water to his friends, who were scribbling the alphabet on scraps of paper. In the room in the back, a woman was taking off her burka and putting on a brightly colored garment. Next door, a young woman was sliding bracelets onto her wrists. She was fantasizing about looking like the Indian model she had seen in a worn photo. She was applying a bit of lipstick. She had the right to do so—there were no Taliban in her family, but they were never very far away. No one could do anything, except these few Canadian soldiers, these strange, bearded beings who were hidden somewhere in the village. This is the description given by the children, who had just come home.

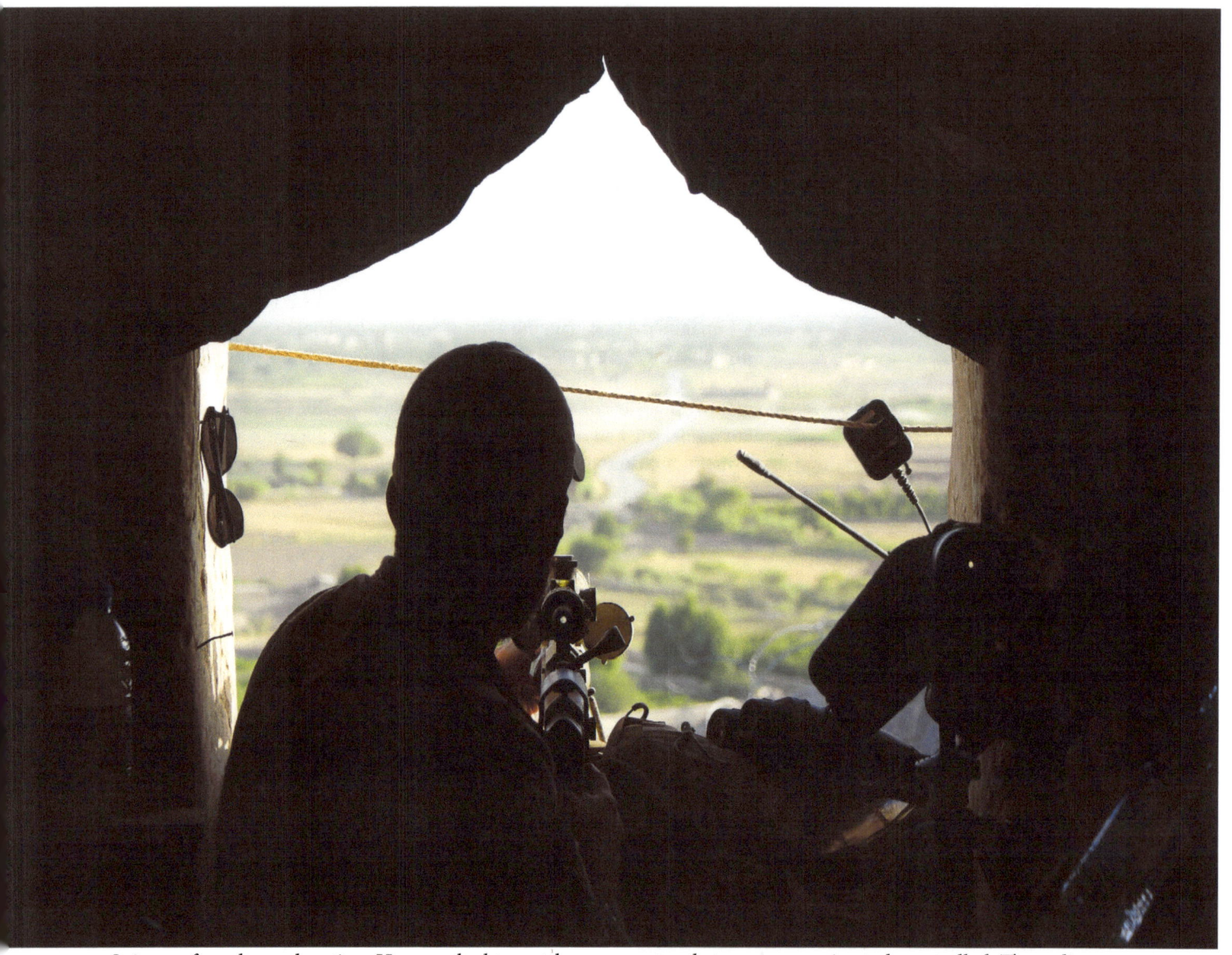

Snipers often change location. Here, we had to watch over a sector that was soon going to be patrolled. The radio antenna can be seen sticking out on the right. In this way, we were able to warn the patrollers of dangers that awaited them. For example, we could indicate the presence of armed men hidden behind blind spots. We could also inform the patrollers about schemes by the village population before their passage. It was sometimes easy to lead the patrollers straight to suspects who thought they were hidden. A sniper needs to be a good psychologist.

Most insurgents are unarmed observers. They wait for the right moment to go get their hidden weapons. They often station themselves on raised areas, such as roofs of houses, and they communicate the position of our troops to their cohorts, who prepare the ambush.

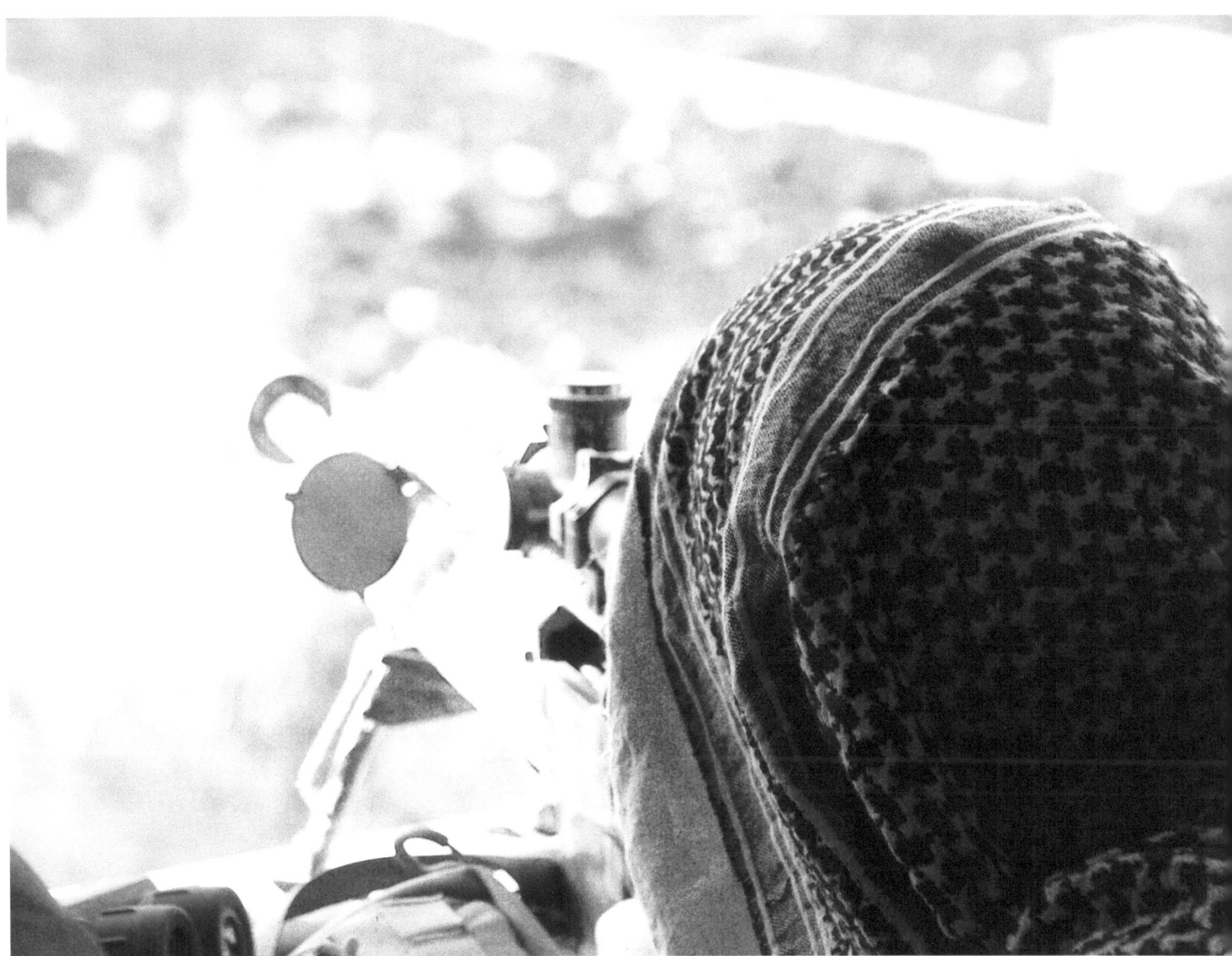

The sniper's weapon must remain hidden inside the building. For the purposes of the photo and memories, we could not resist displaying the weapon through the window frame—it just goes to show that the photographer's artistic side could quickly take precedence over the soldier's instinct! In any case, this patrol was nearly over.

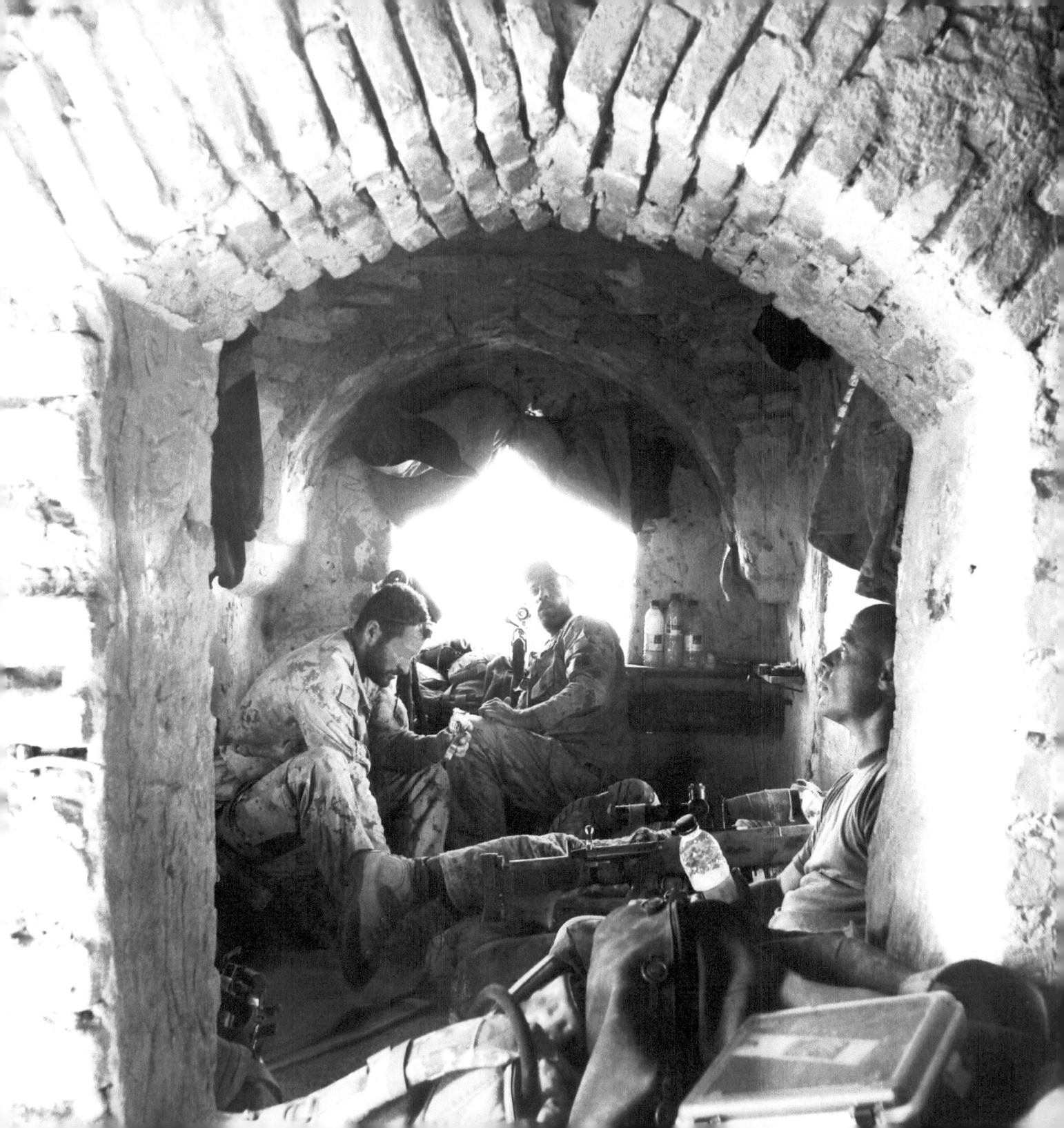

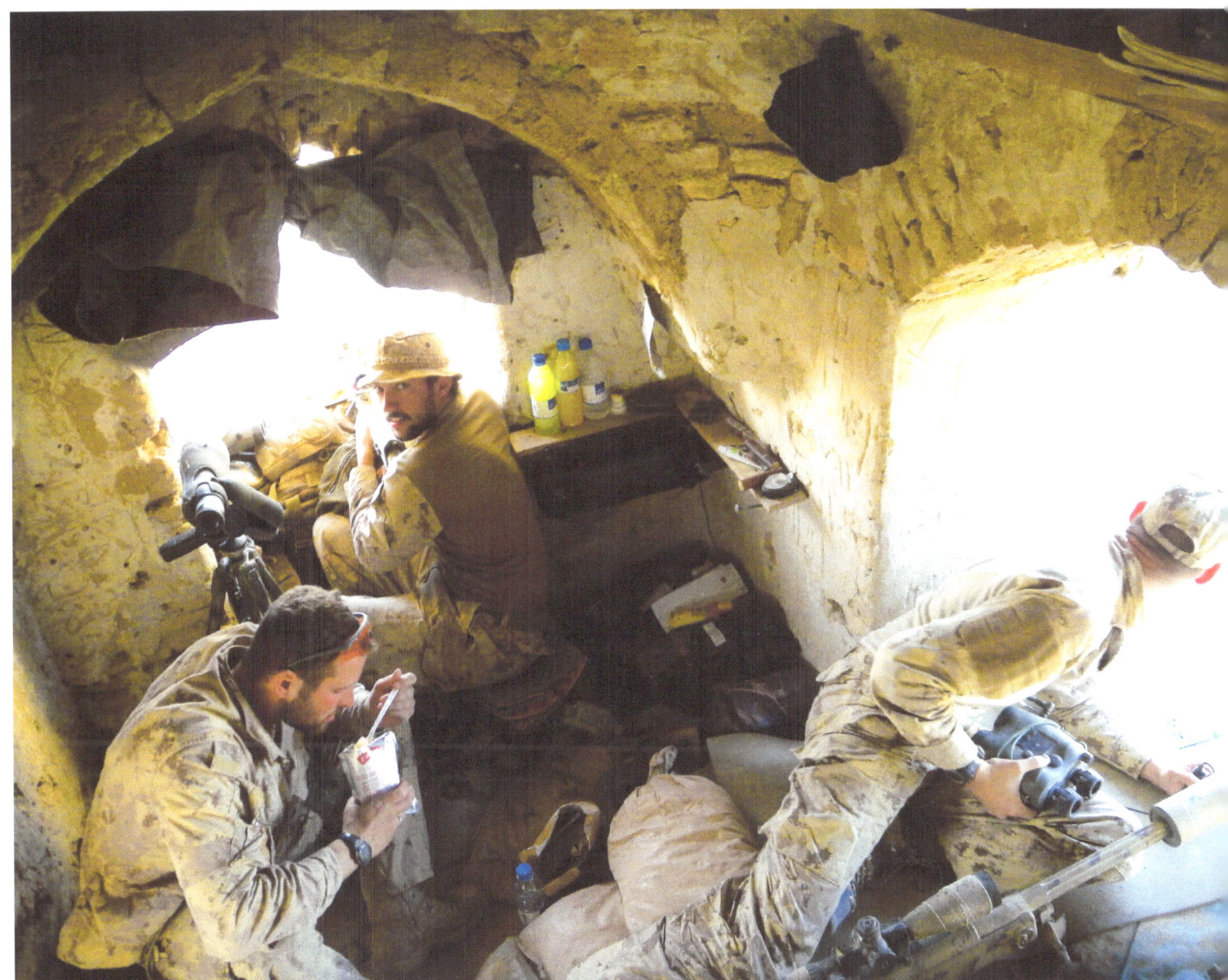

Watch, rest, meal, and in my case . . . photo session! Once a soldier is in position for a long period, a routine is quickly established. During pauses, while the other soldiers watch the Afghans in their daily life, it is the time to dream about our beloved homeland, and moments of peace enjoyed among friends.

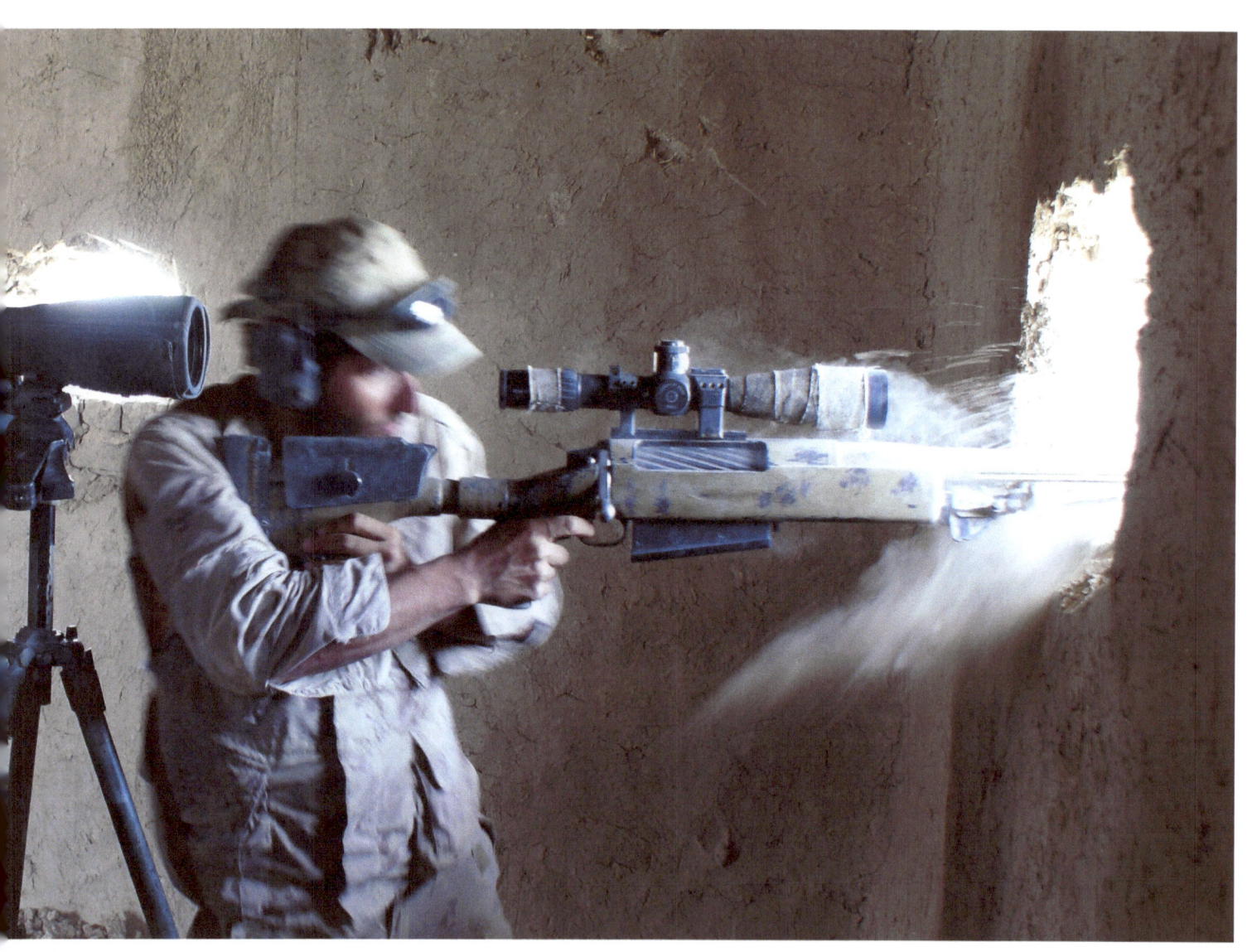

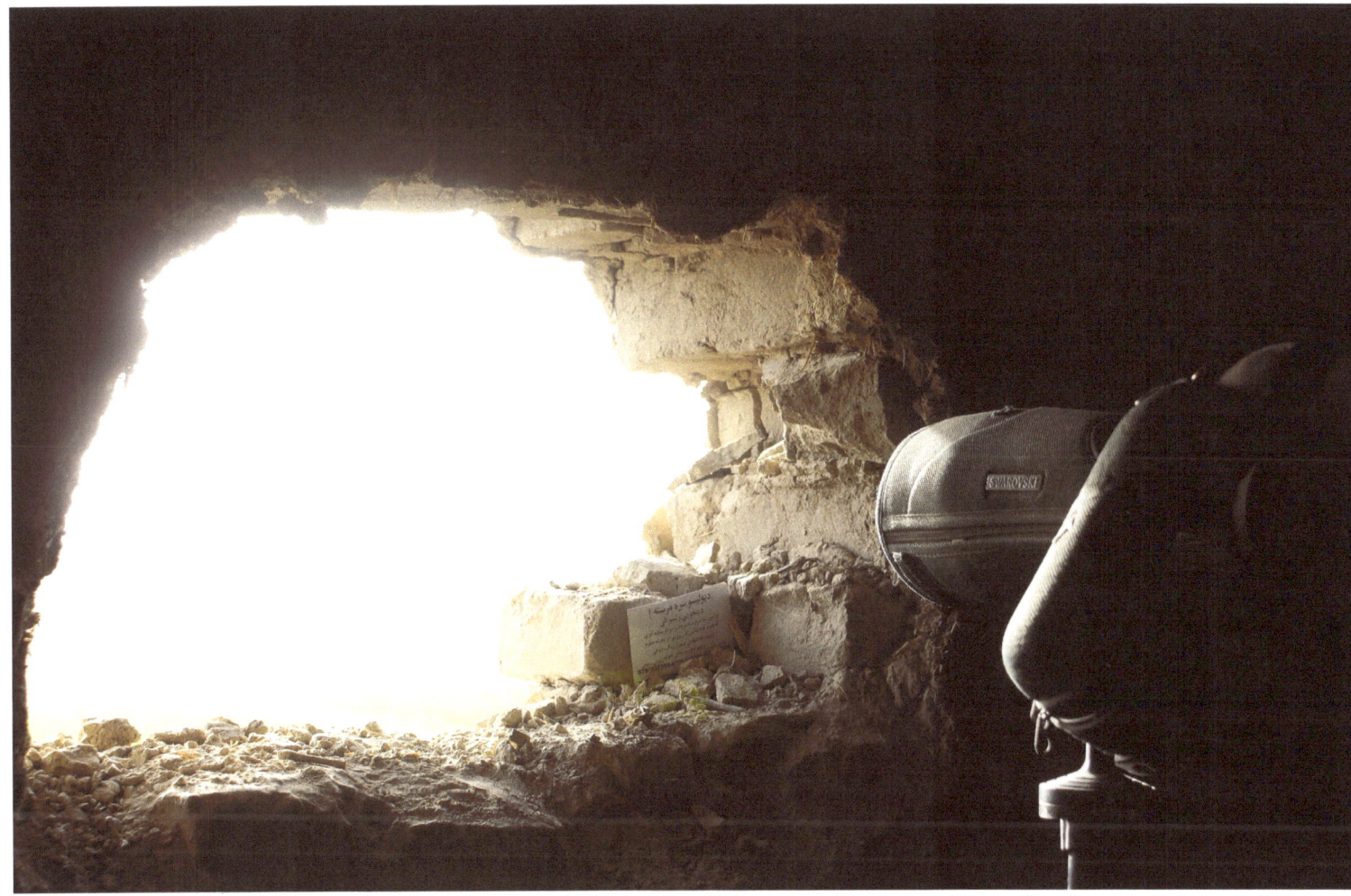

Unfortunately, taking photos was not the only occupation of the sniper detachment. The reality of war too often caught up with the photographer's idealized vision. The weapon's barrel would thus replace the camera's lens. To hit a distant target, we had to shoot just above the head of a Canadian soldier, who was near the weapon's deadly trajectory.

A cow lived near the opening made in the wall. Like us, it had only a few square feet to move in. Surrounded by walls of earth, it led an existence that seemed terribly boring to us, without room to move anything except its neck. In Afghanistan, animals are often seen merely as utilitarian objects that must provide meat, wool, or eggs. As for dogs, they often guard the entrances to dwellings.

Just before departing, we left a small "calling card" from the Quebec City sniper detachment. The little piece of cardboard was addressed to the owner of the property, and it indicated whom to call to be compensated for the holes we had made.

The soldier was setting out on his next mission. The photographer was inventing another one for himself. After a night of walking, we had set up an observation post in the mountains, among burning rocks that were blackened like coal.

The horizon I was photographing contained the last moments of many soldiers who had fallen in the line of duty. Some were young Canadians. Others would soon die. A book could be written on everything that had happened in this simple viewing angle of my lens. The Afghan horizon is a graveyard of civilizations.

The intelligence services had told us that a group of insurgents was moving toward our sector. After we had been watching for several hours, a man on a motorcycle stopped between the mountains, leaning carefully near the road. He looked around attentively, assuring himself that he was alone. I was lying down. The shooting distance was not challenging. The cross of the reticle divided into four the shape of the man, who continued to look as far as he could see. Turning his head, he rested his gaze on us. However, we were hidden in the mountains. He could not see us. After a few seconds, his head continued turning.

Finally, the man took something out of his long, dirty pants. I smiled. I removed the cartridge from the weapon and my eye from behind the lens. I left the man alone in the privacy of his act.

Many things happened during those few days in the mountains. Without even shooting a single bullet, we had followed the trace of several bomb layers. We had in this way photographed their houses, their friends, and their faces, all making them waste bombs that they had laid with so much difficulty.

Eventually, having run out of water, we had to walk to the closest military camp. Back at the camp, I took the opportunity to look at the photos. On my camera's memory card, images of innocent children were juxtaposed with images of dangerous landscapes. Several files later, there were photos of friends drinking coffee in a little restaurant on a large base in Kandahar. The children looked as happy as the soldiers eating in the air conditioned room.

For the whole evening, snipers gathered on couches in an improvised living room near the infirmary of the military camp. Clustered under a red-tinted light bulb, we watched movies on a computer. Some soldiers had tubes and intravenous needles attached to their arms—in order to rehydrate us, the medical team injected water directly into our veins.

Long live these small vacations! But they did not last long. The next day, another mission was planned. The orders were given, the weapons cleaned, the ammunition distributed. The vehicles were ready to leave.

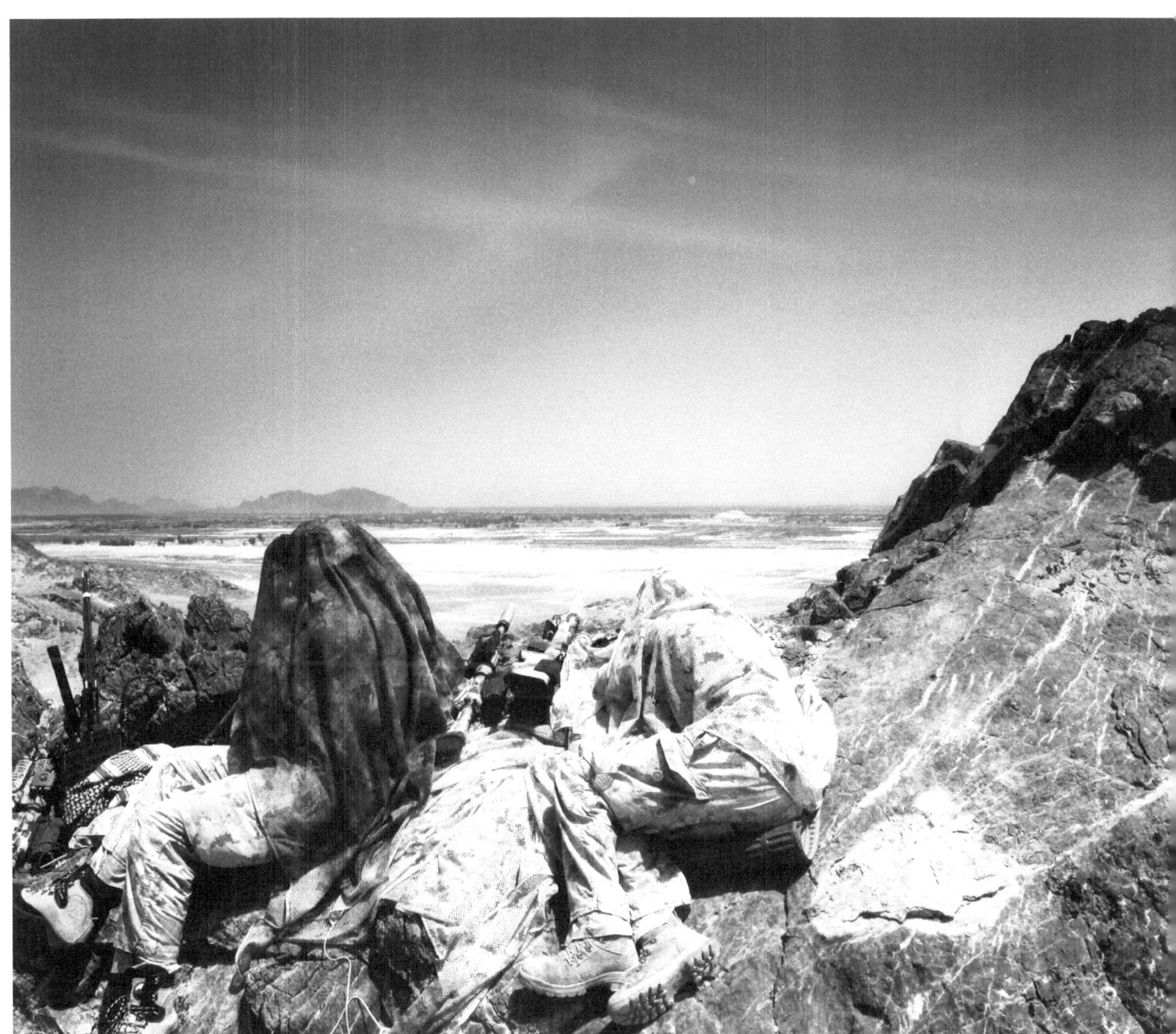

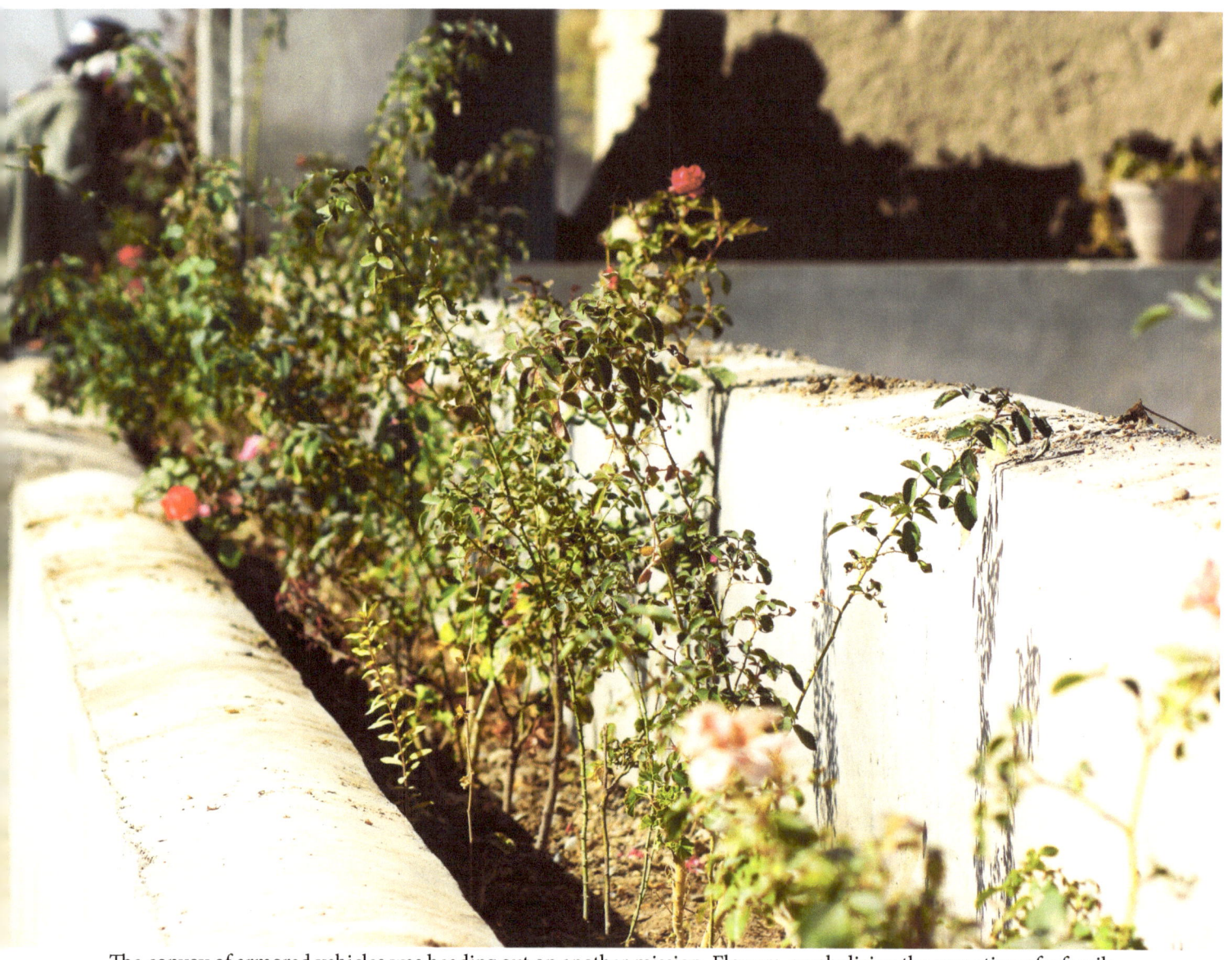

The convoy of armored vehicles was heading out on another mission. Flowers, symbolizing the sprouting of a fragile peace, were emerging hesitantly between the fortifications of the entrance of the military base. Numerous bombs had exploded here in recent years. Their breath had destroyed these delicate ambassadors from paradise. Yet the flowers kept returning!

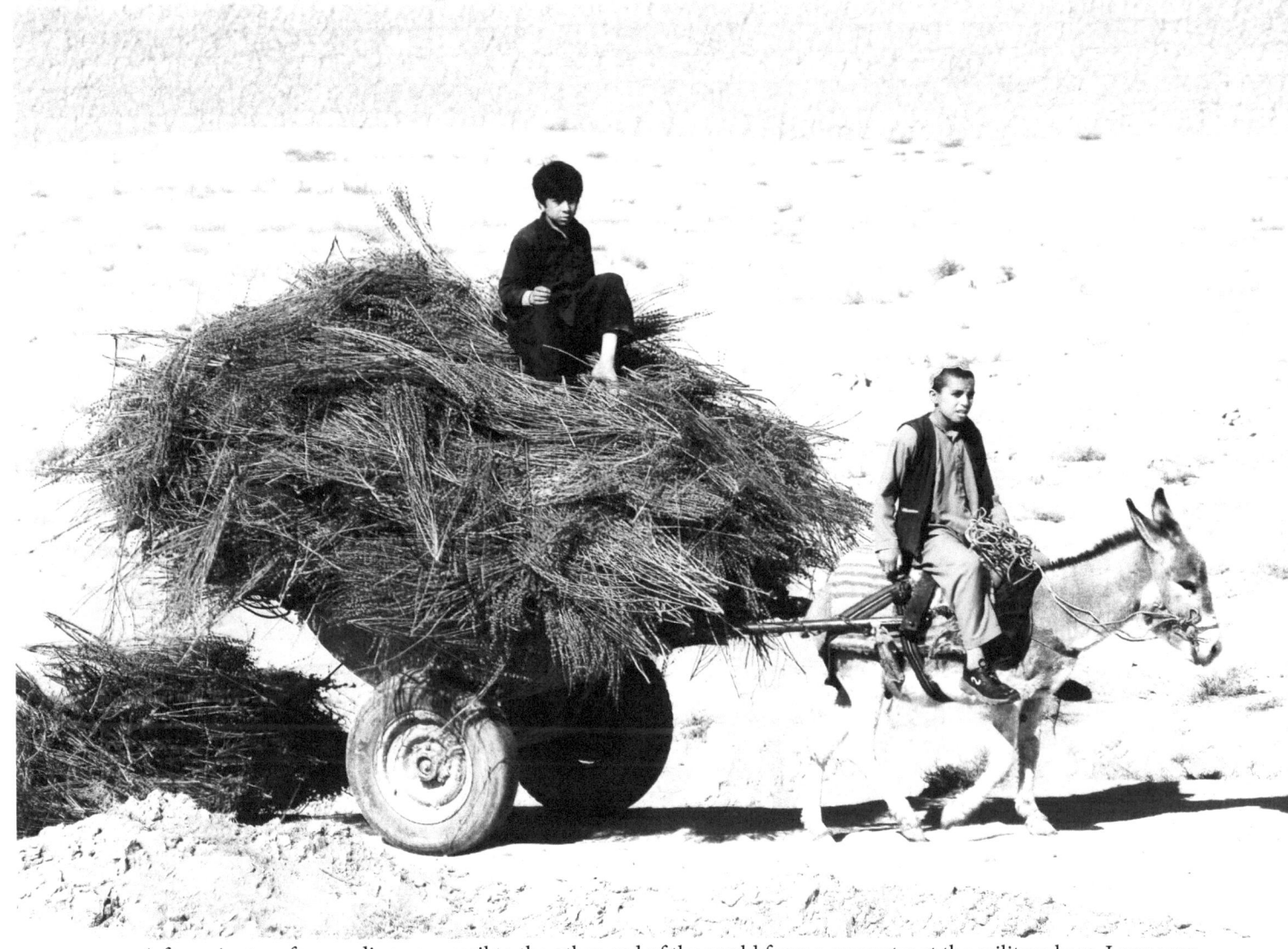

A few minutes after sending an e-mail to the other end of the world from a computer at the military base, I was passing near a cart that called to mind the Middle Ages.

In Afghanistan, even the children work. Arms that can move are arms that must help. Whoever can work must work. This is how the Afghans think.

In the background, the various layers that make up the walls can be seen. Days of work go into building these surrounding walls that cost nothing more than time and earth. I am convinced that if modern civilization came to an end, Afghanistan would feel virtually no effect.

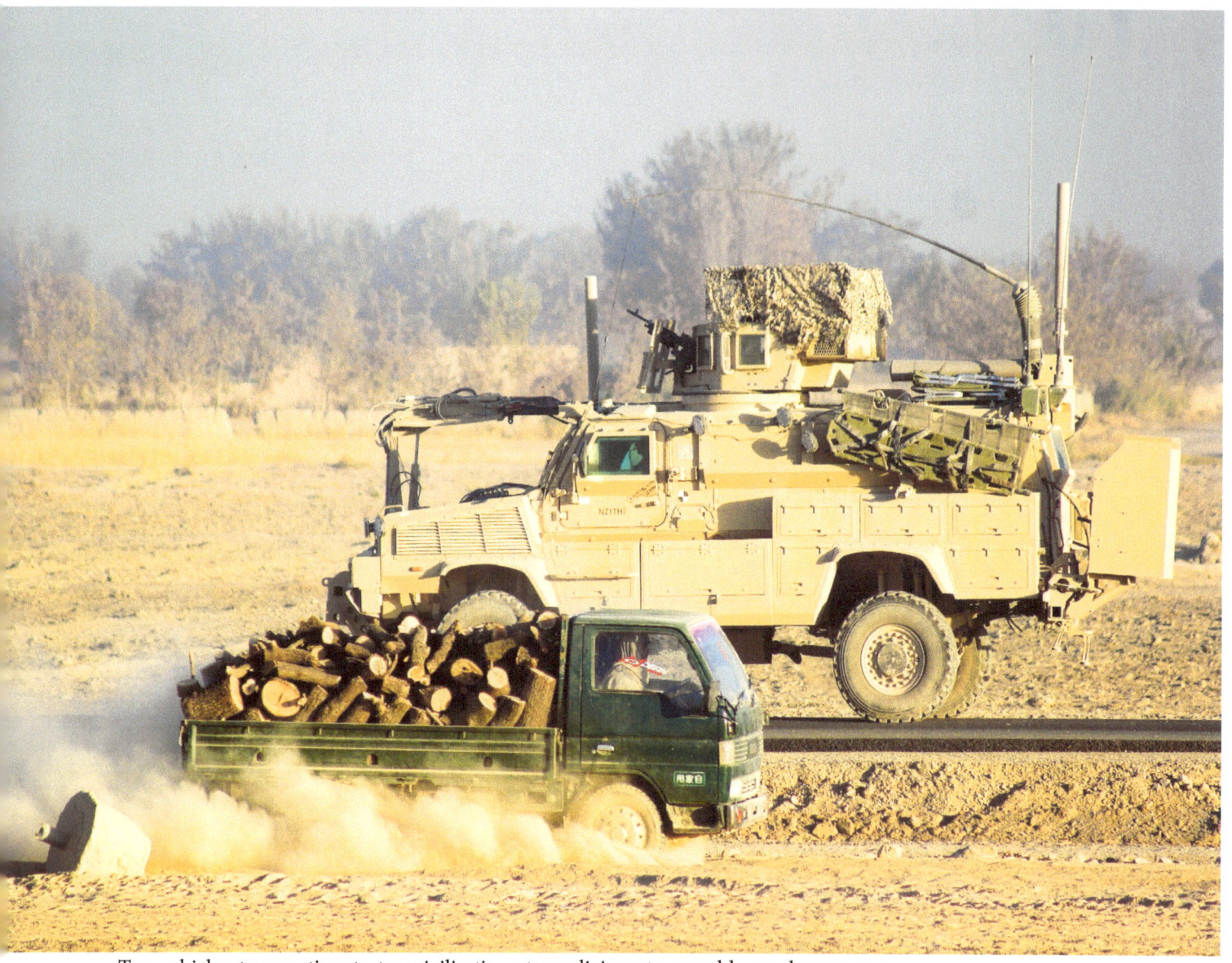

Two vehicles, two continents, two civilizations, two religions, two worlds: one human race.

Military vehicles always had the right of way. The Afghans knew this.

A bit farther on, my vehicle was passing near a cemetery that was covered in scrub. A man was engaged in private prayer before an old, worn grave. Was it his grandfather, or a respected chief religious elder? Or perhaps he was pretending to pray in order to watch us and alert the insurgents? I would never know.

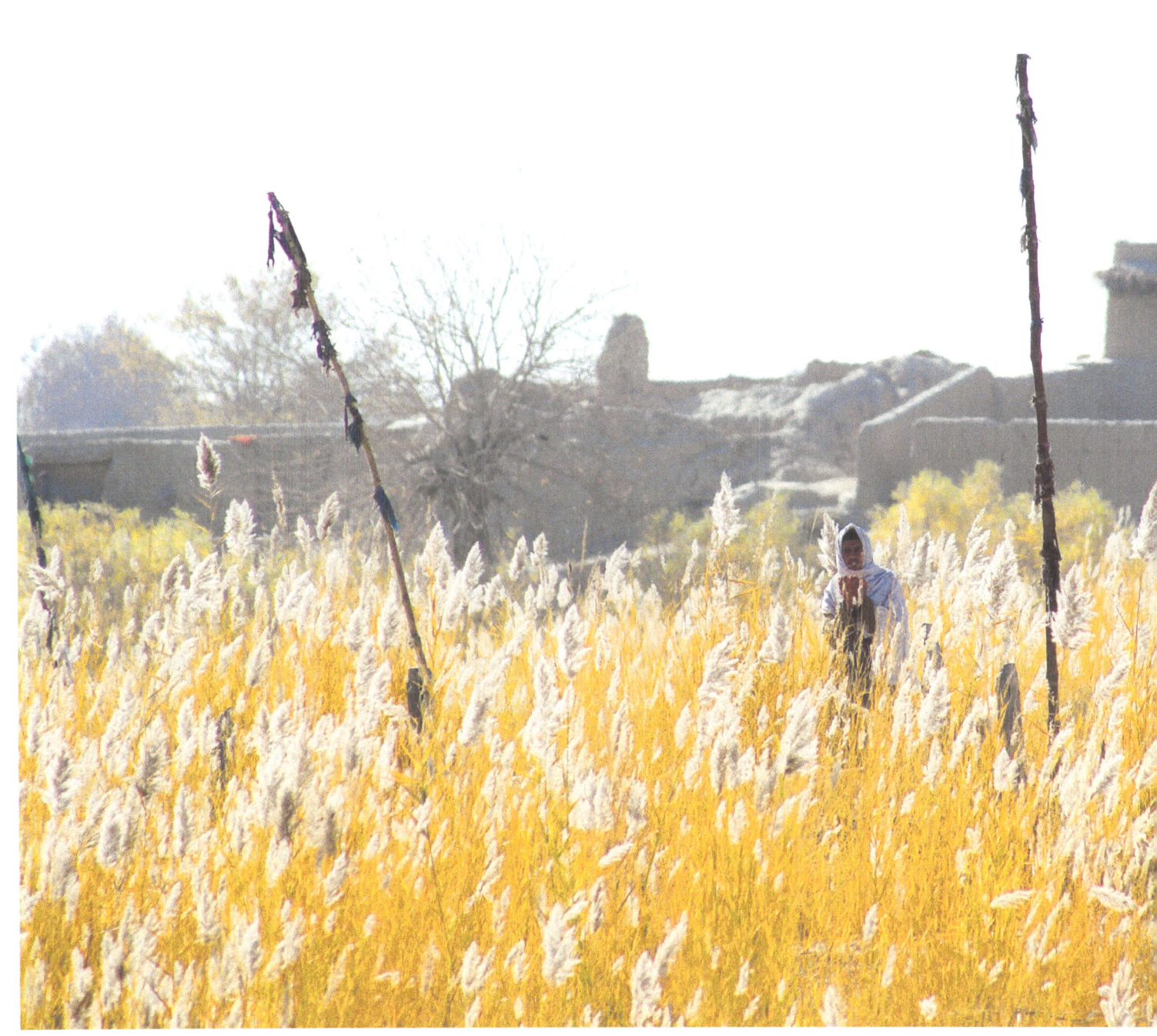

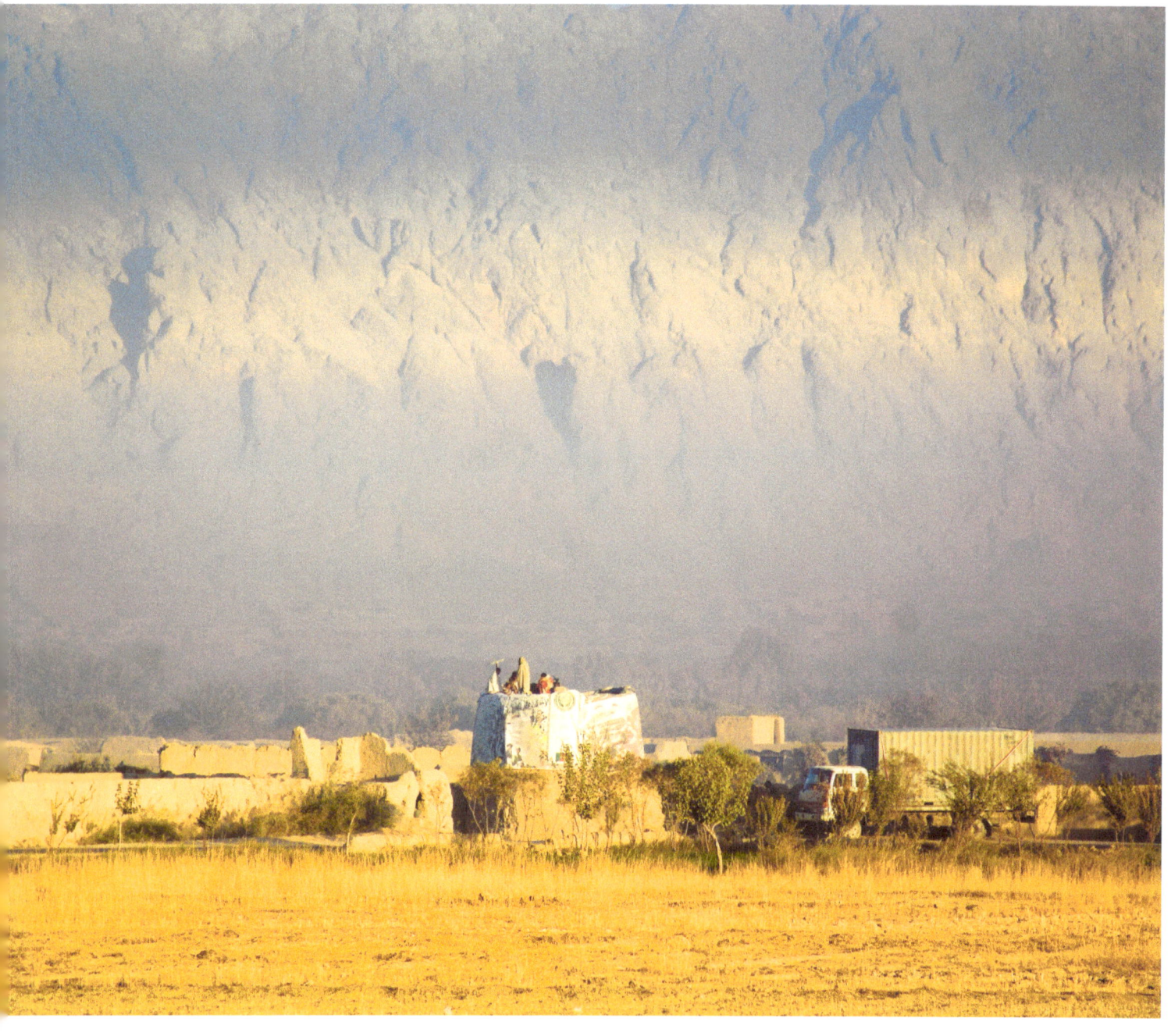

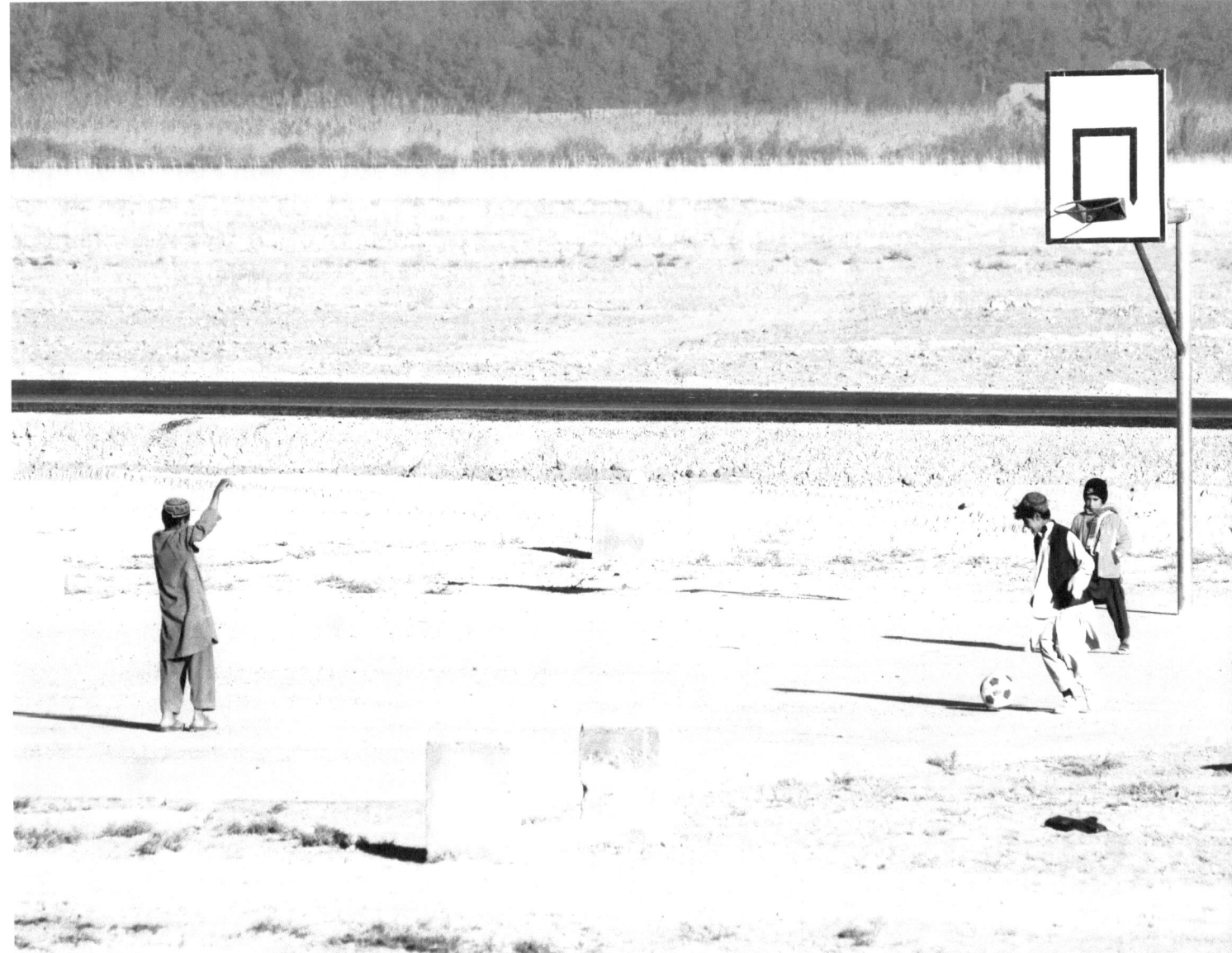

The humidity and morning mist were mixing with the smoke from coal fires. These fires kill as much as, if not more than, the fire from bombs and weapons.

A bit farther along our route, some children were entertaining themselves in a small park. A moment of peace. No armed man on the horizon. No Taliban to puncture the ball or threaten the families of children devoting themselves to "foreign sports." The Afghans were having fun in complete freedom. And while photographing them, I was enjoying myself almost as much as they were!

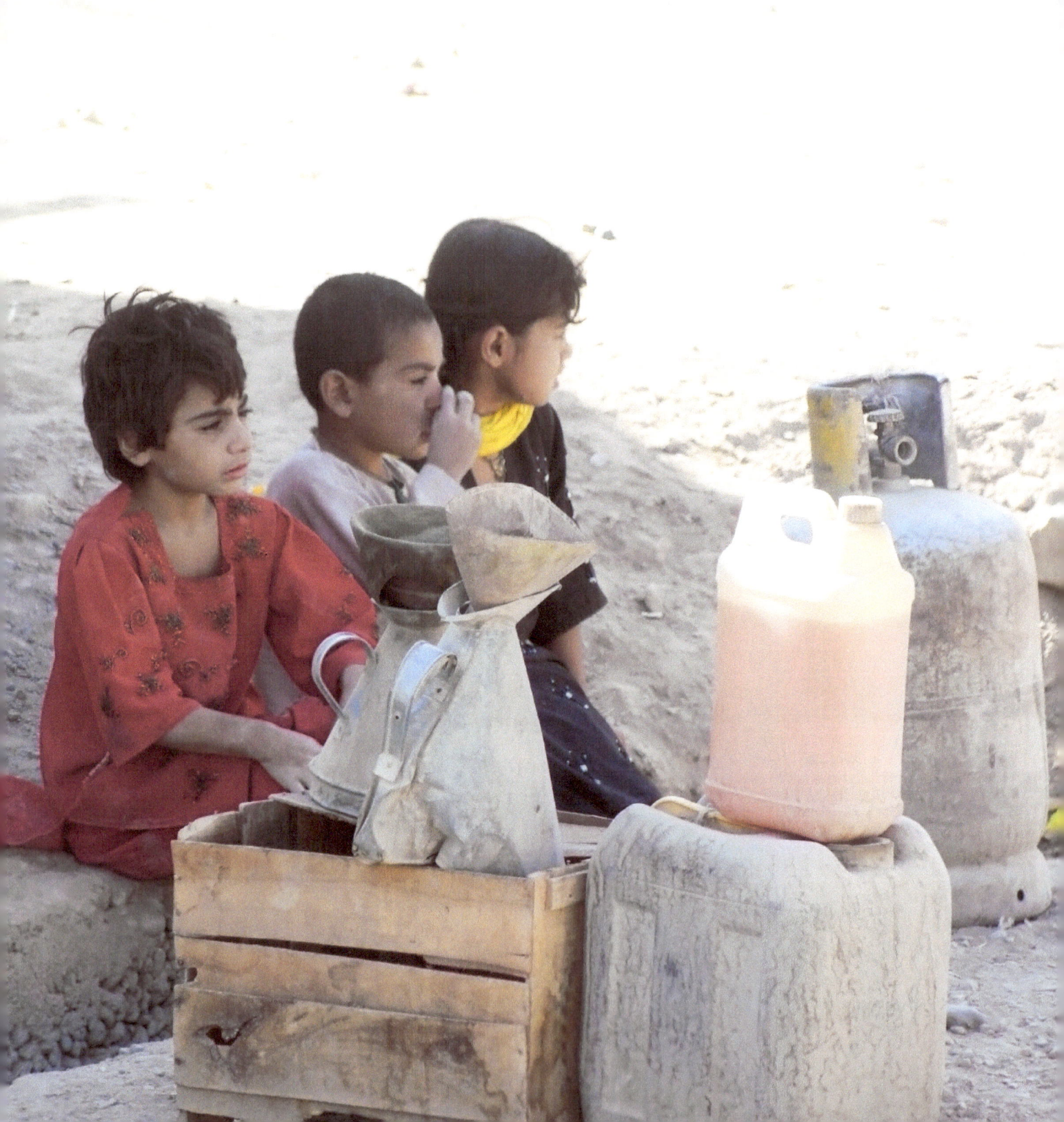

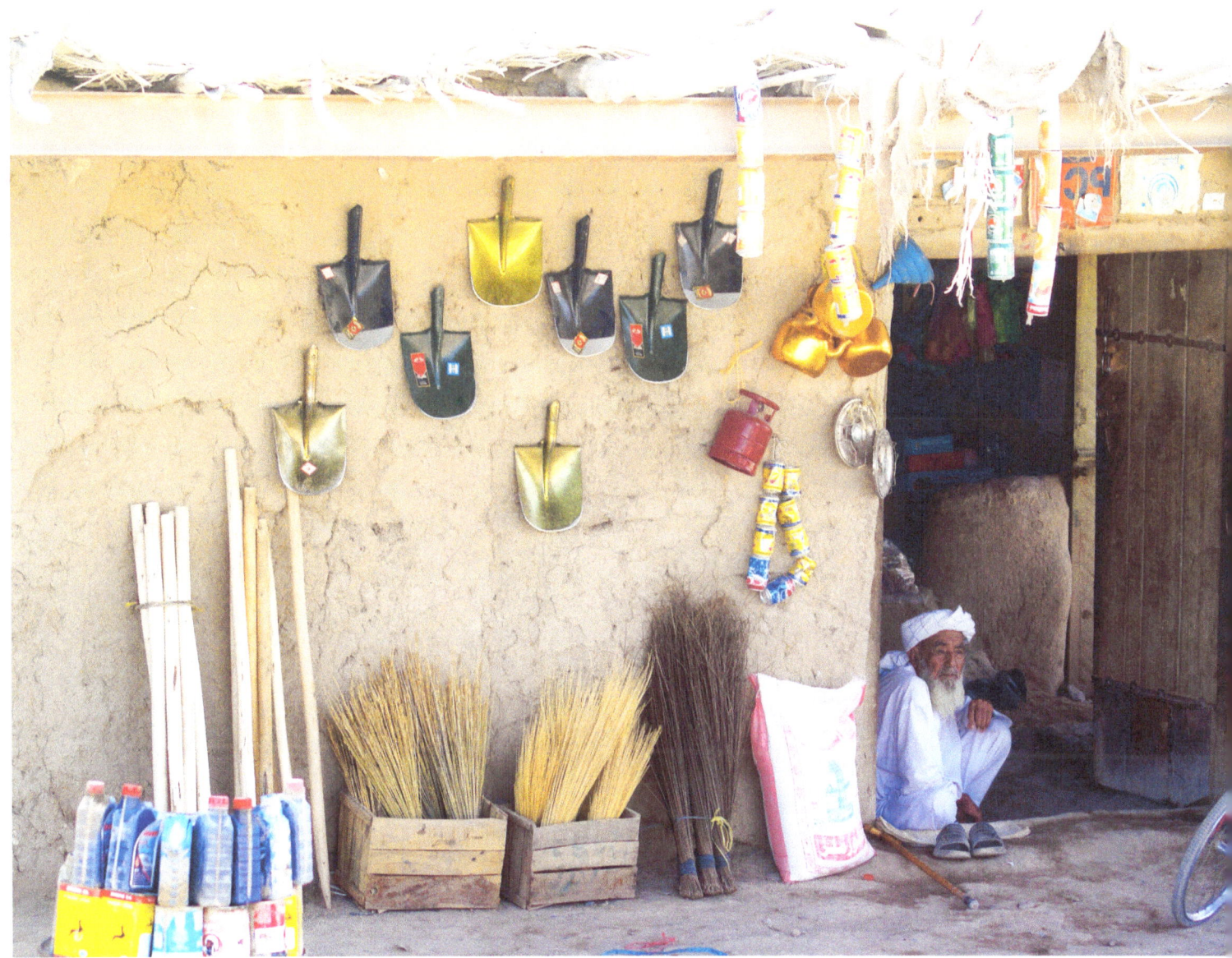

The convoy was passing in front of the corner store of a small village on the outskirts of Kandahar. There were brooms, shovels, broomsticks, kettles, energy drinks, and even a small red gas cylinder that Afghans use to heat tea. This old man had undoubtedly been watching foreign troops parade by for decades. Perhaps he himself was a former warrior? Perhaps he had stopped a troop of Soviet assault tanks with his last friends of the time? Perhaps he had lost half his children?

After years of conflict, some great warriors are content to return to a simple, tranquil existence, like the great leader of the Roman Empire, who after having saved his country refused honors and rewards, and went home to push his plow in the fields.

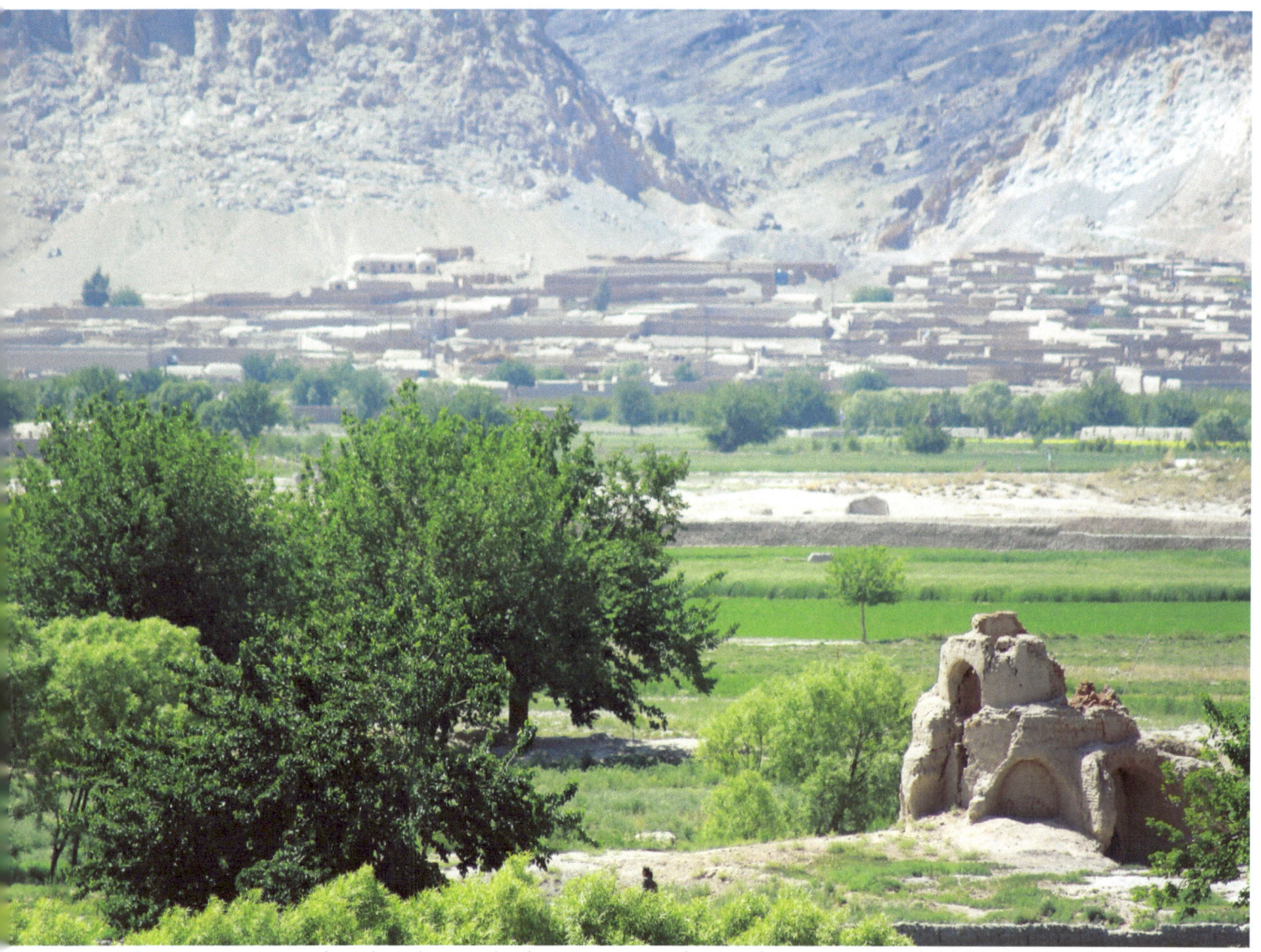

When summer approaches, the colors are dazzling. It is a magnificent sight! It reminds us that life will always be stronger than death, that winter will always give birth to summer, and that even a desert can give rise to a forest that is green like Eden.

Right: a friend of mine once said about this photo: "When you shoot a subject, it's better to leave space in the direction of its movement and not behind it. It's a principle of photography." I answered, "I would have liked to, but I was in a vehicle and there was a good chance that there was a bomb on the road. Also, I had barely arrived at the destination when there was an explosion one kilometer from our convoy. Another Canadian had just died."

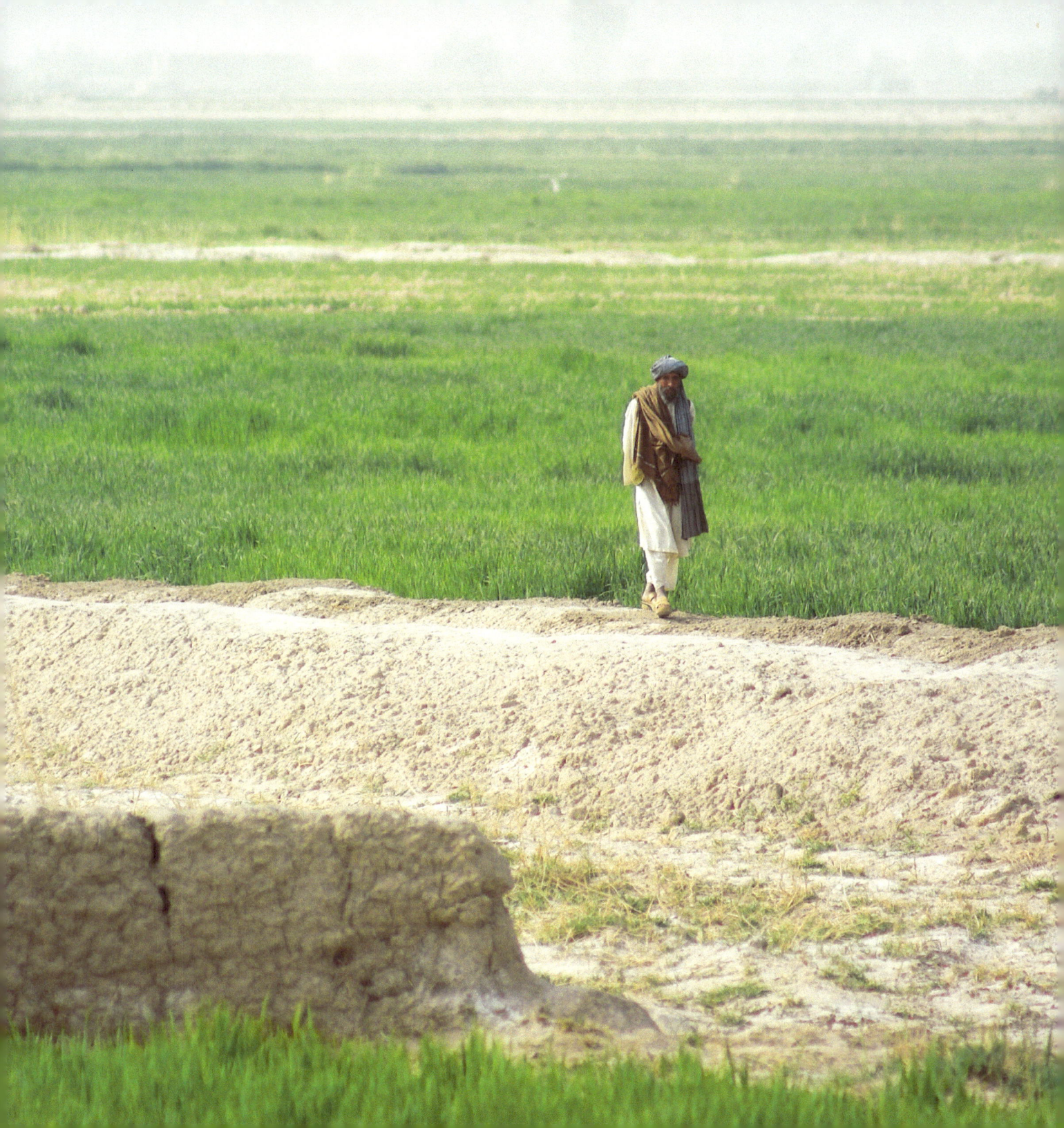

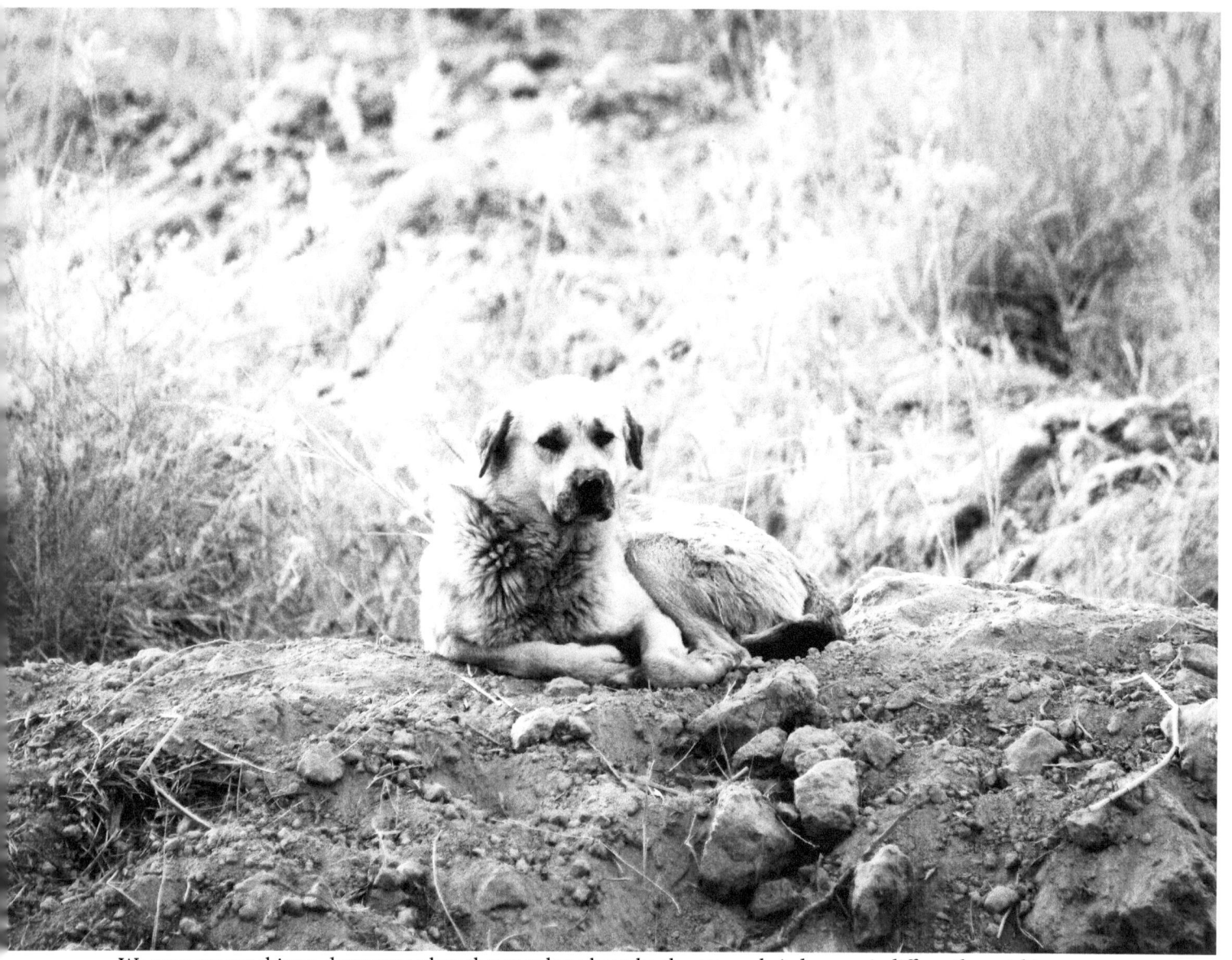
We were approaching a dangerous place that may have been booby-trapped. A dog was indifferently watching us pass. He did not seem to have a master. Far from humans, he was free of dangers.

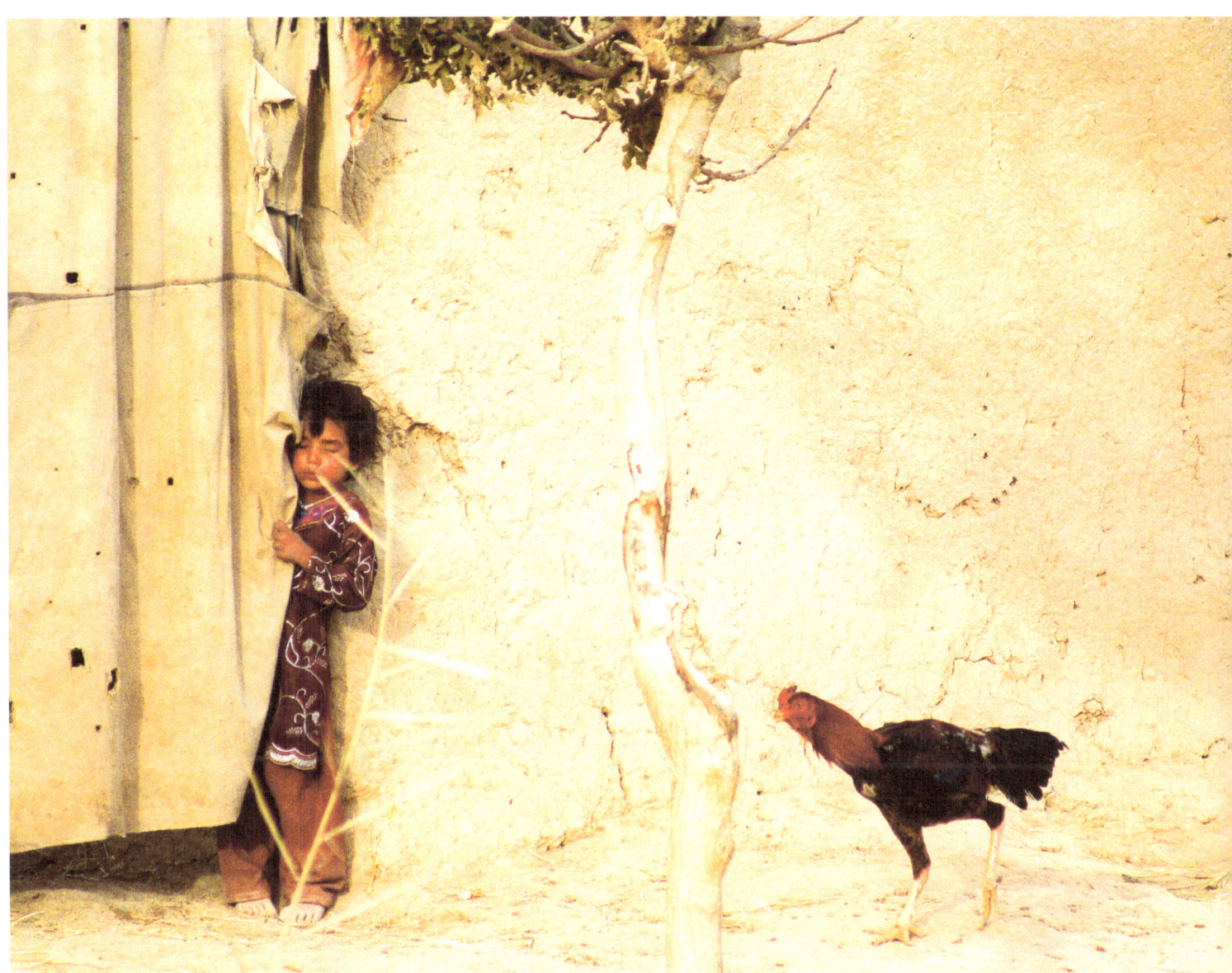

 I turned my camera toward the other side of the street. While a proud rooster was hiding as the convoy approached, a little girl dared to come out and watch us from the entrance of her house. She was still young. She was still half free—half uncovered, half covered. She was allowed to show herself, unlike adolescent girls, who are required to cover themselves with a burka and stay inside the family enclosure.

 In a few years, the rooster will continue to pass between his dwellings and the outside. Little boys will go outside to play. They will go back inside and give orders to their sister, who will slip on a burka and go shopping.

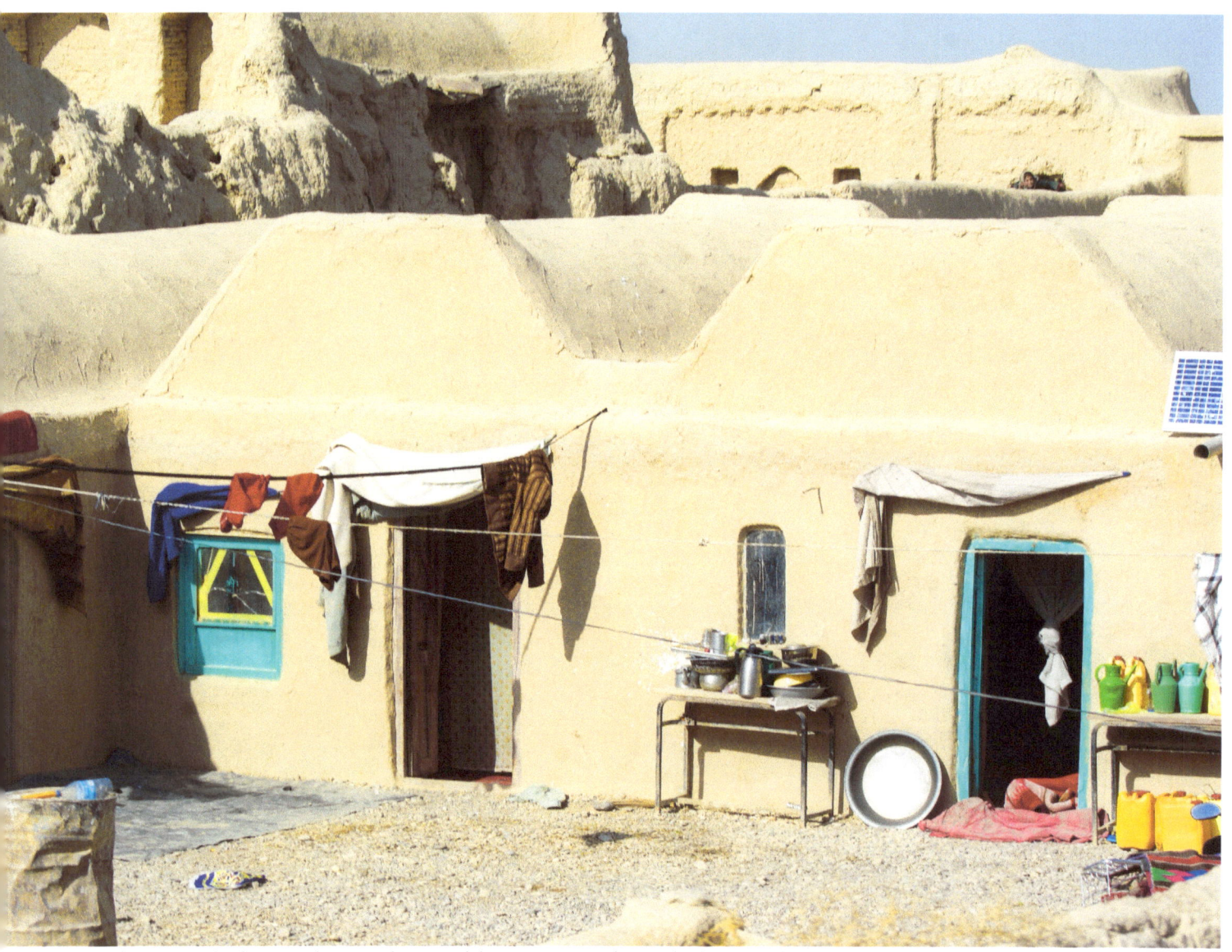

    The convoy had stopped. From the top of the gun-turret of my vehicle, I could see over the walls. A woman with a beautiful smile had just greeted me. In order to help orient ourselves, we liked giving names to the places we often saw. Some mountains were given the names of animals they resembled (dragon back, big fish). In homage to the young woman, I named the house "Fatima," and then communicated the information to my cohorts by radio.

    A number of roofs functioned as trenches against bullets. Some insurgents used them. This time, a solar panel was visible. As is often the case, it may have been stolen from a street light. Here, it is every man for himself—generosity is a luxury that is too costly.

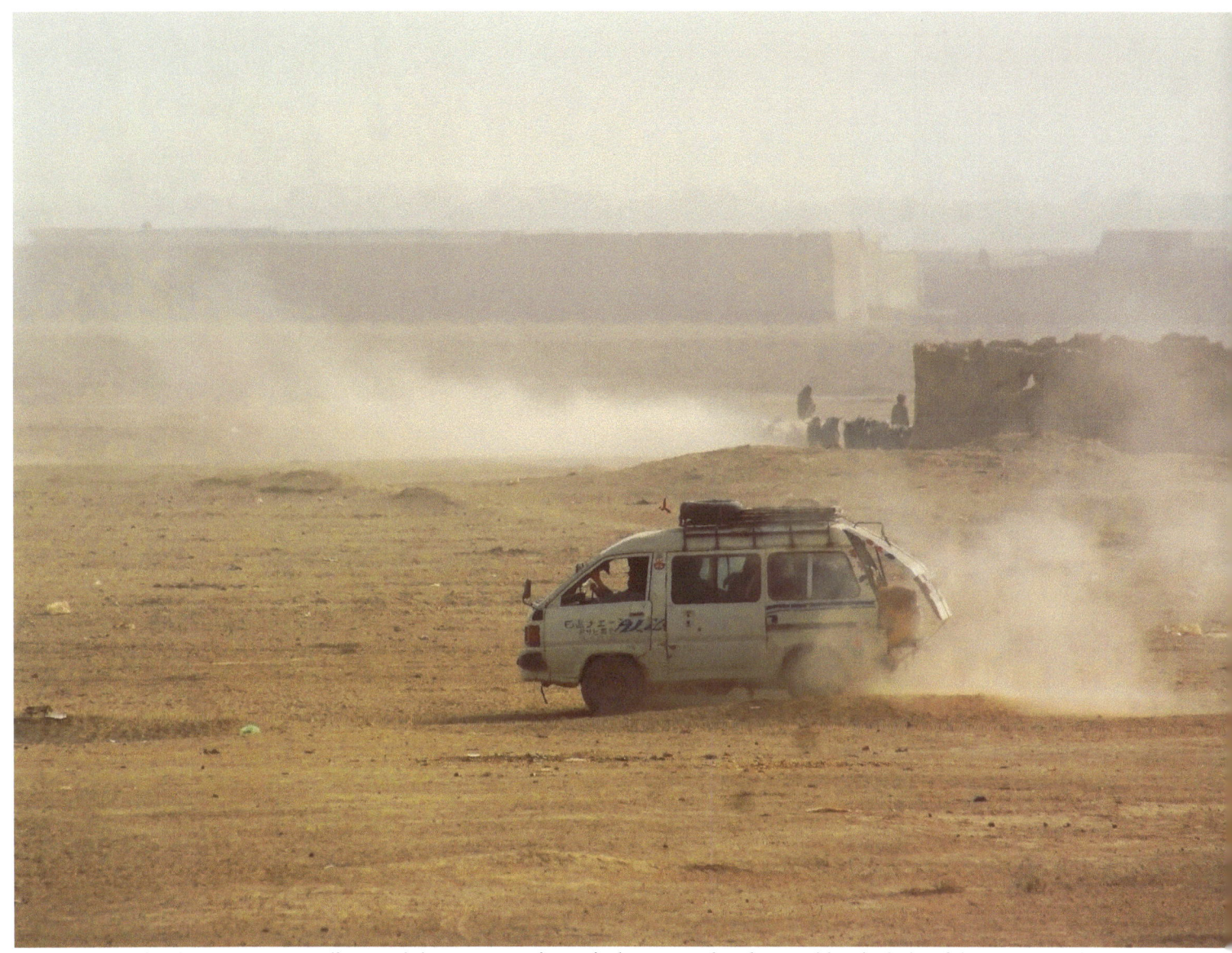
The sky was turning yellow, and then orange. The sun's shape was already invisible. The light of the sky was softening, and the sky was emanating a uniform light. A sandstorm was approaching. My eyelashes had already been turned white by what looked like a fine ash. In Afghanistan, wherever there is air, there is dust.

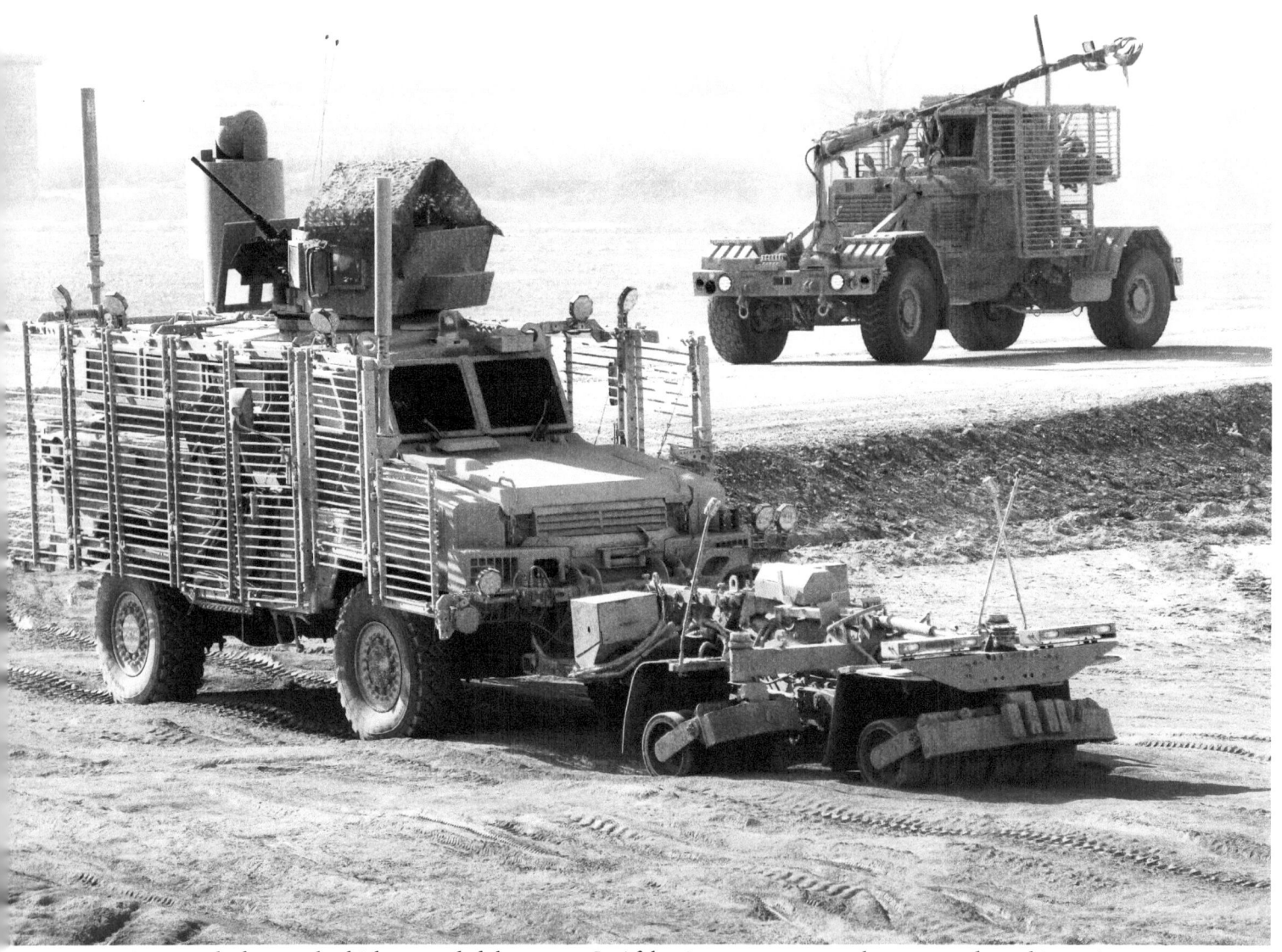

An arsenal of unusual vehicles preceded the convoy. In Afghanistan, weapons are the most modern objects. As a result, vehicles that looked like space probes were juxtaposed with huts made out of branches. The insurgents probably felt invaded by extraterrestrials. During the first year of the Kandahar hostilities, the Taliban did not know about the destructive force of a modern army. They charged by the dozens armored vehicles that were equipped with shells and ballistic computers. Seeing that their friends were being decimated by the hundreds, they then hid in trenches. With the help of a remote-controlled missile, an operator drinking his coffee in an air conditioned control post then transformed these defensive holes into graves filled with earth and corpses.

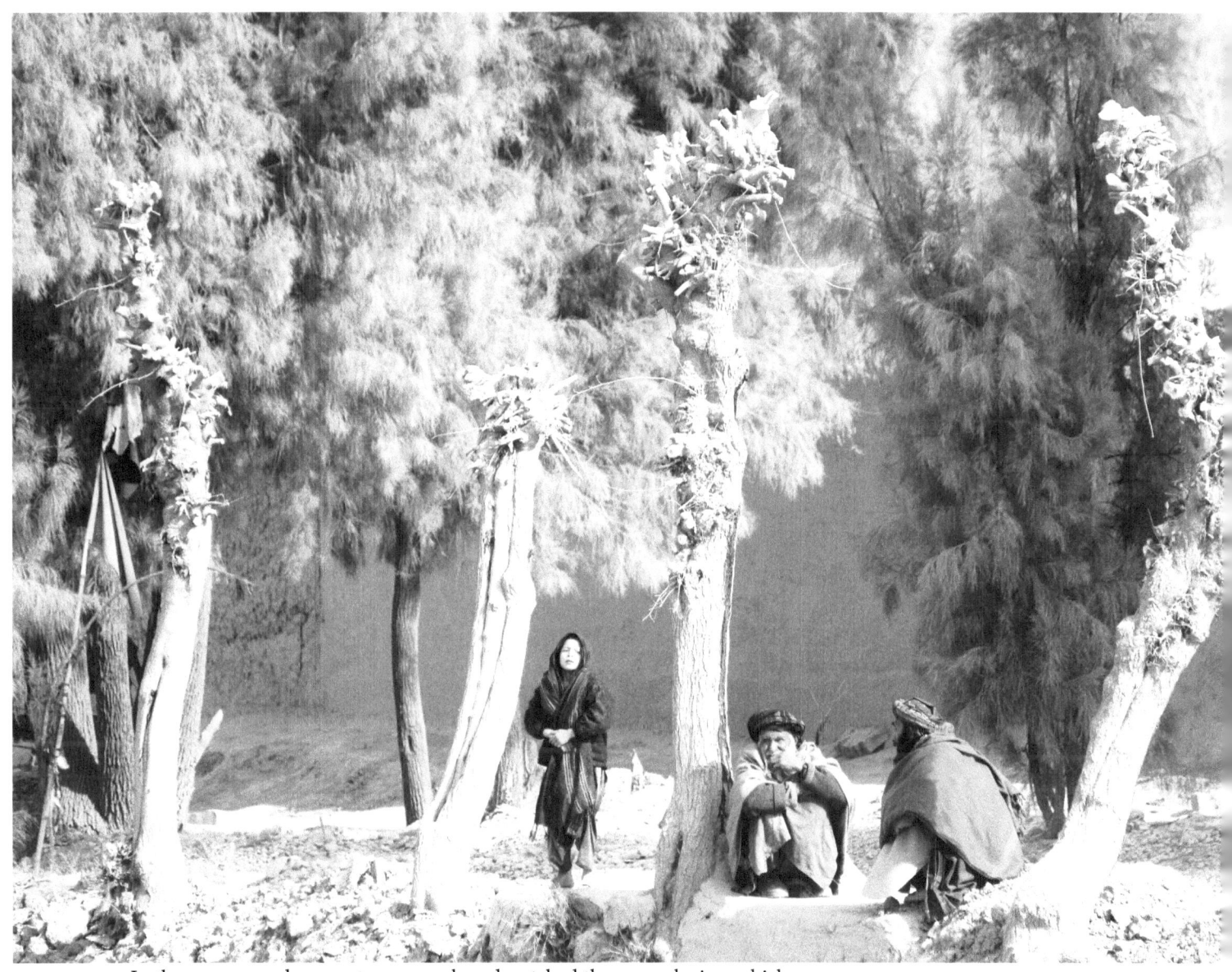
In the area around a cemetery, a graybeard watched these perplexing vehicles pass.

Despite the murderous effectiveness of the weaponry, in Afghanistan, the key to victory lay not in all these gadgets that were worthy of science fiction films, but in our friendly behavior toward the population. The majority of Afghans are innocent and wish merely to live in peace. The greatest victory is to succeed at being loved by one's enemy. If this is not possible, one must then be loved by the friends of one's enemies. All Afghans have at least one friend, cousin, or brother who is close to the Taliban.

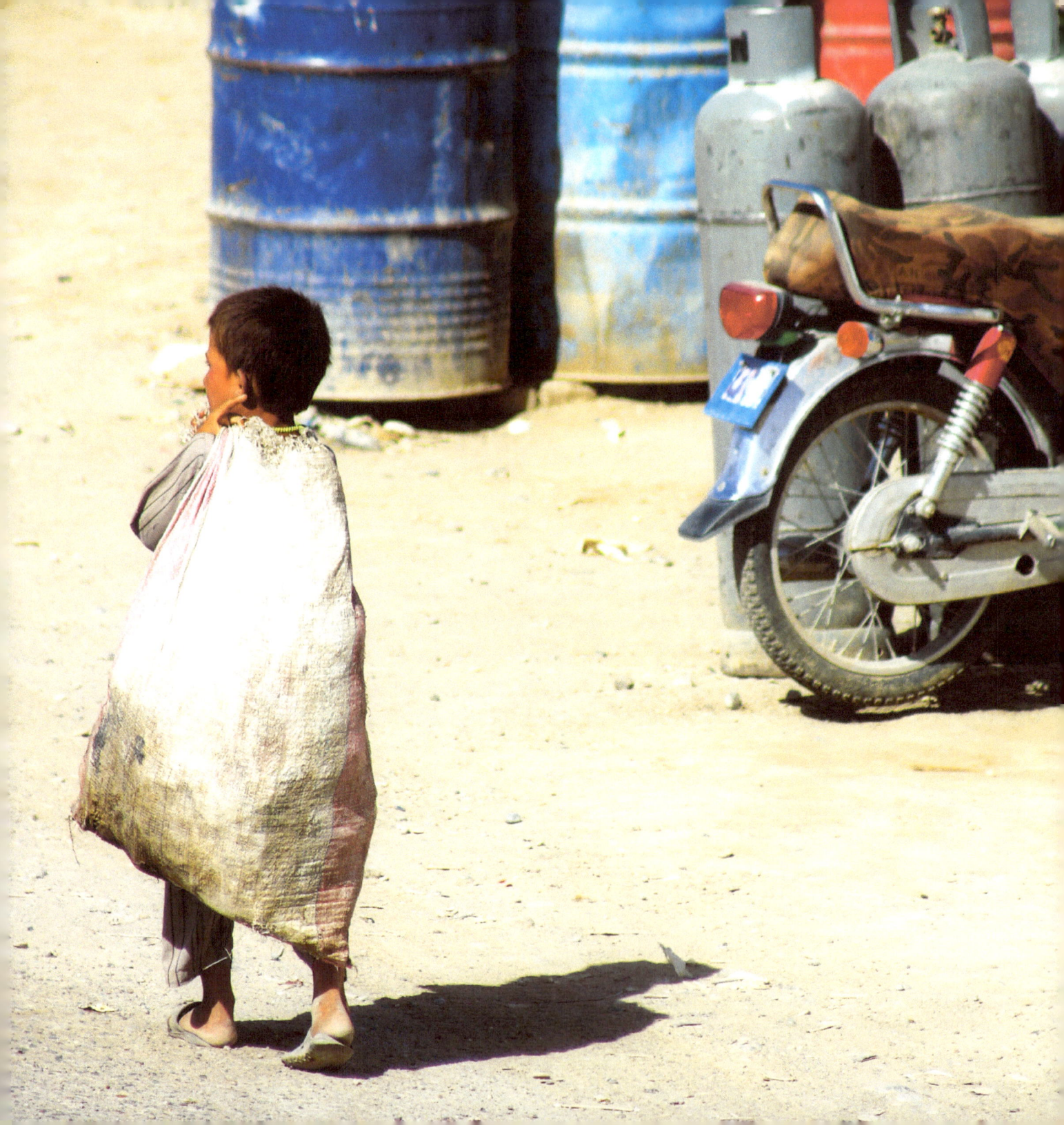

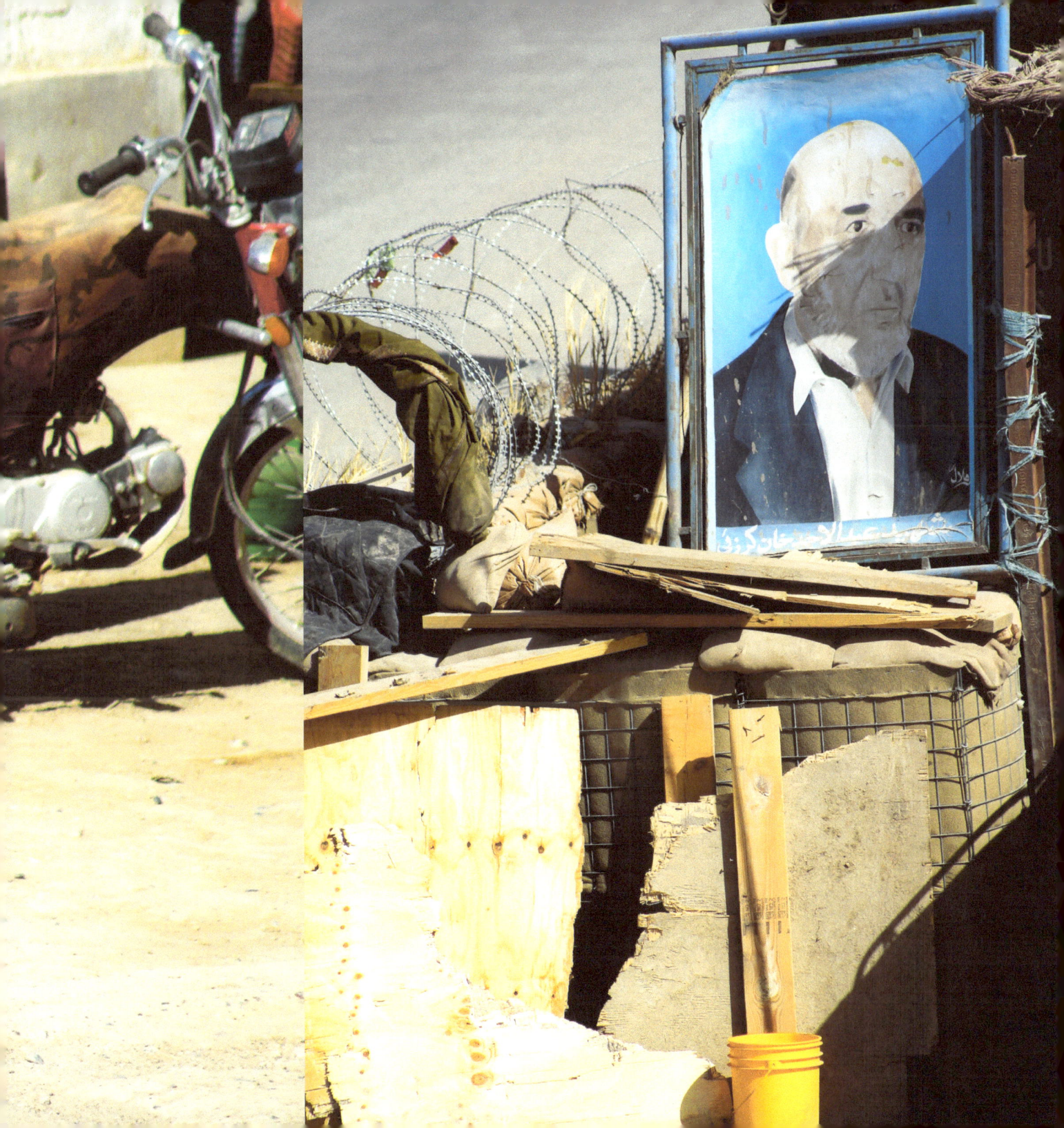

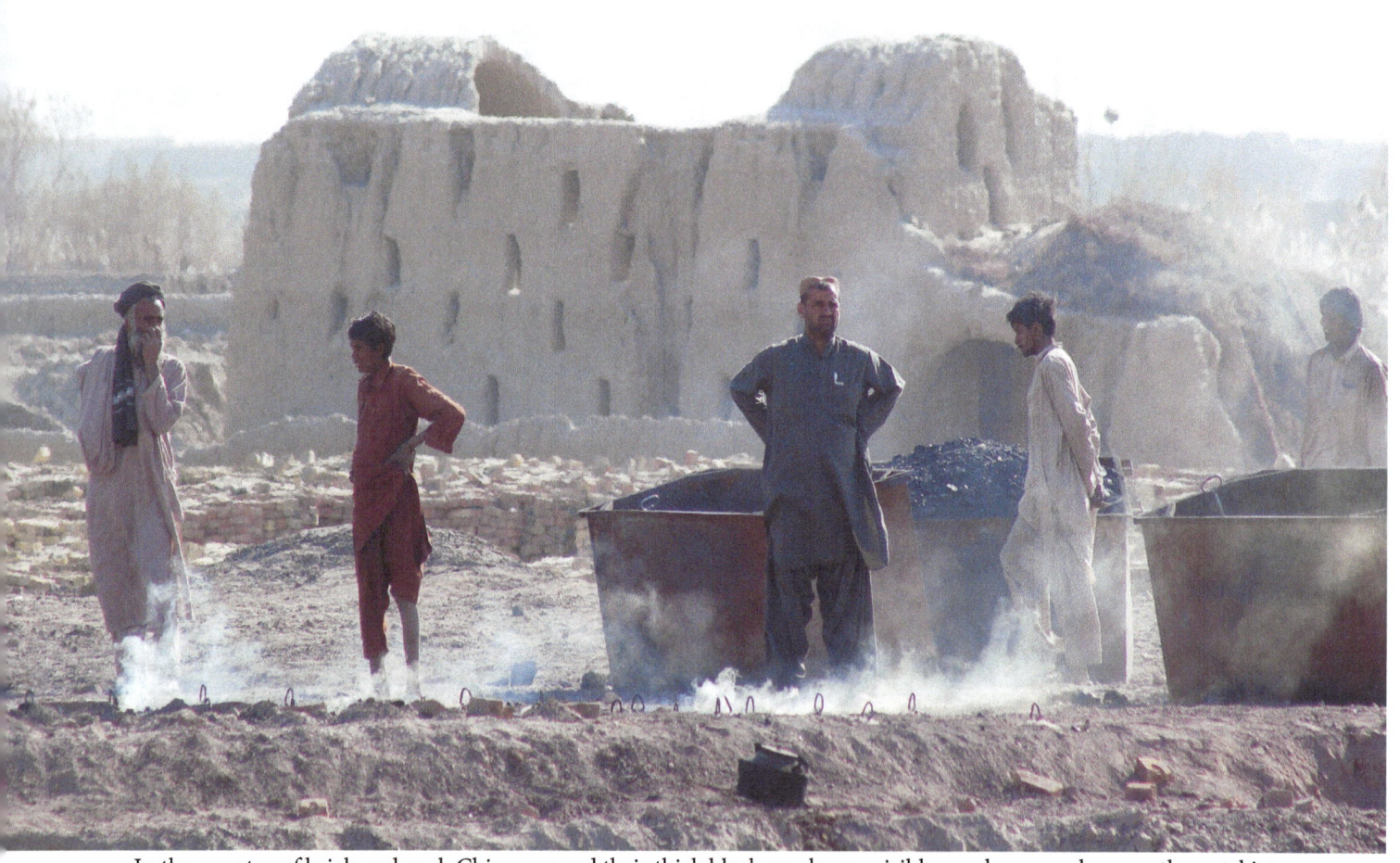

In the country of brick and coal. Chimneys and their thick black smoke are visible nearly everywhere on the outskirts of Kandahar.

On this cold winter's day, laborers were warming up over gigantic ovens. Behind the laborers was what looked like a castle with fortifications pierced by multiple arrow slits. It was a grape dryer with a roof disemboweled by war and abandoned to the erosion of time. This type of building is always oriented from east to west, and this helped us situate ourselves during patrols.

Preceding page, right: the neglected entrance of an Afghan police station. As in the West, during a political campaign, Afghans exhibit their allegiances by displaying portraits of their "candidates."

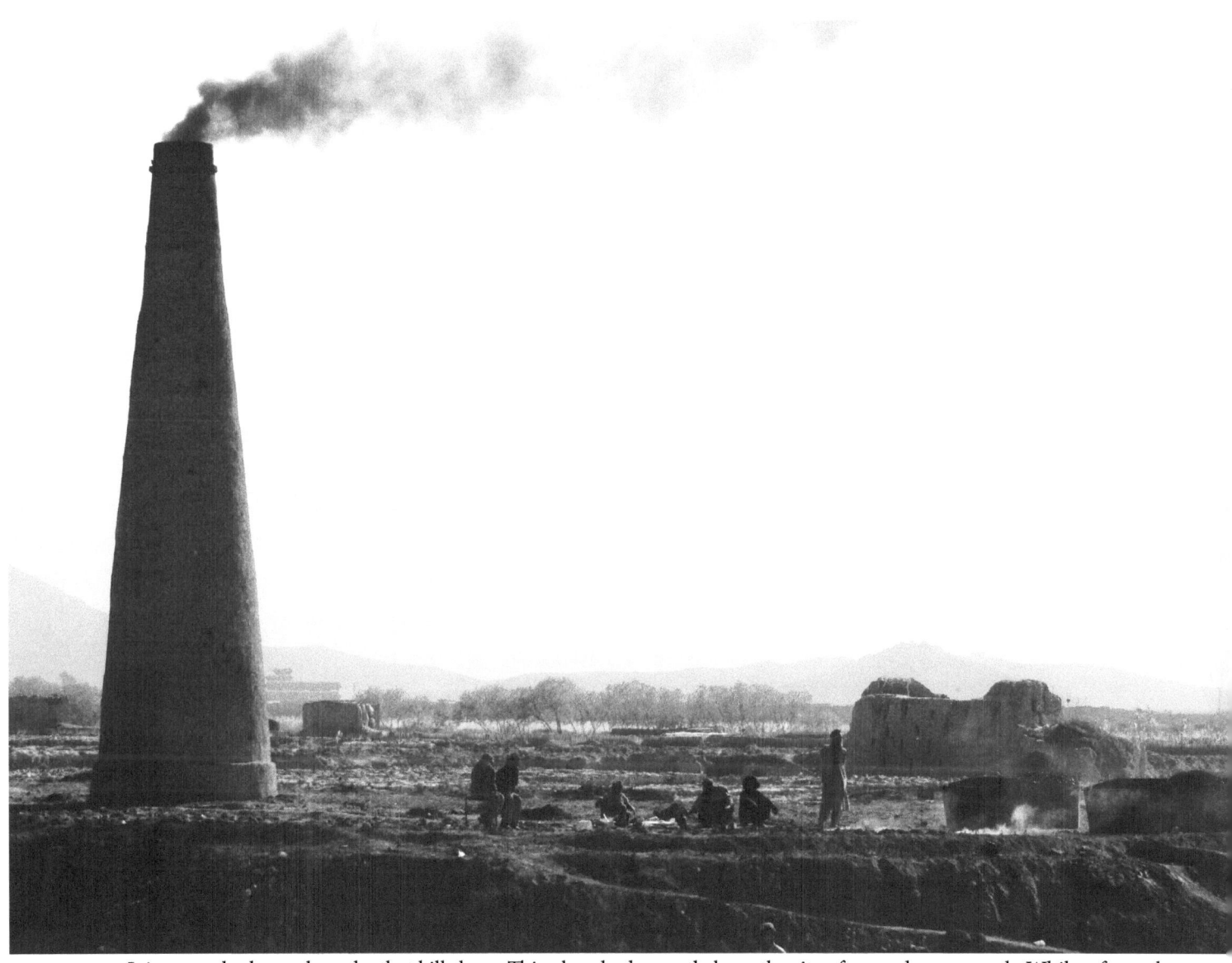

It is not only the coal smoke that kills here. This place had recently been the site of a murderous attack. While a funeral was being held near the factory, a man showed up. He calmly dismounted his motorcycle and joined the family and friends who had gathered for the funeral. In view of everyone, he took out a weapon and killed a person who had refused to obey the insurgents. Then he got back on his motorcycle and left dispassionately.

The funeral could continue. Another could begin.

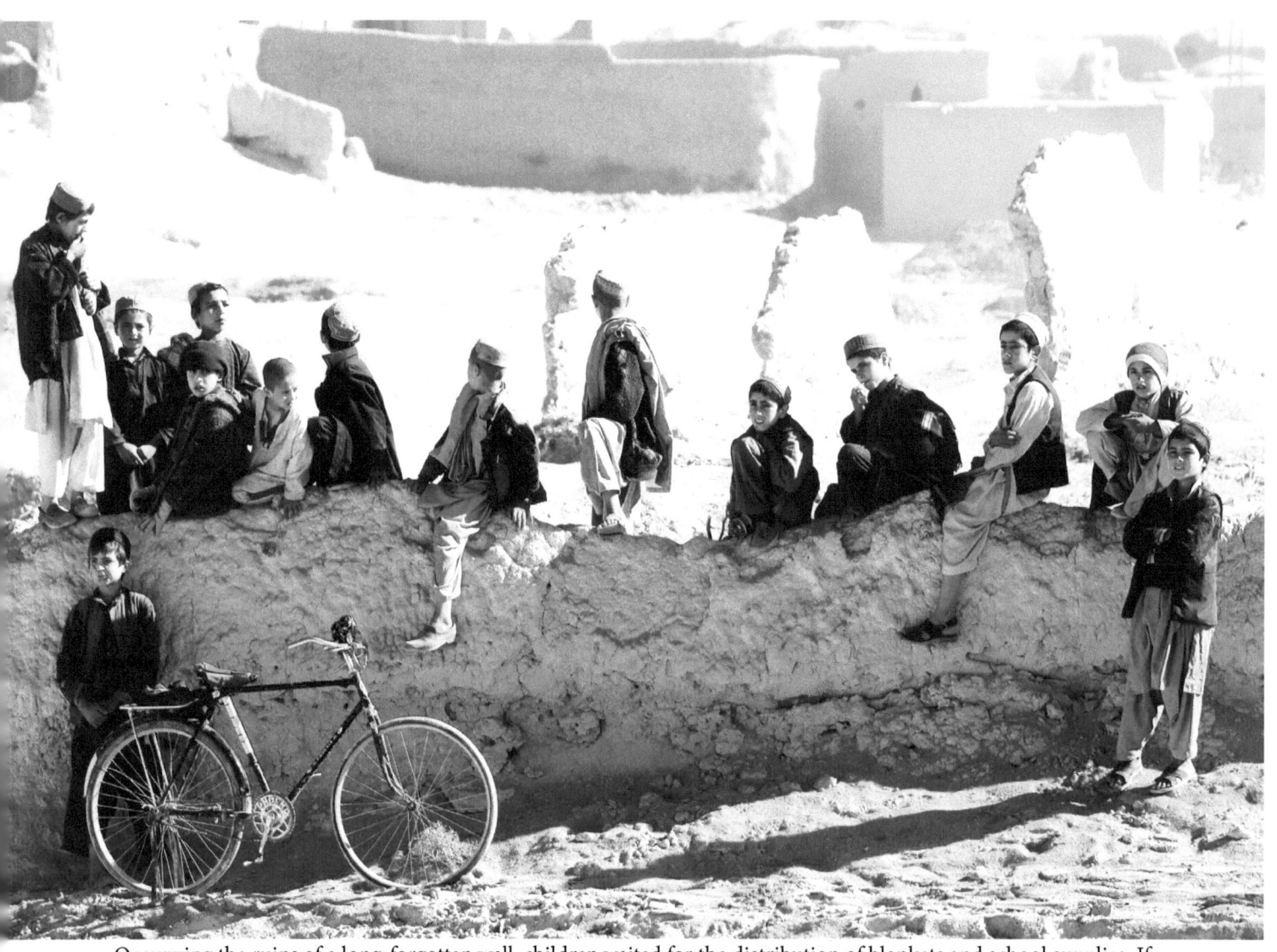

Occupying the ruins of a long-forgotten wall, children waited for the distribution of blankets and school supplies. If the statistics are truthful, some of these children would be dead by now. Yet they were already survivors.

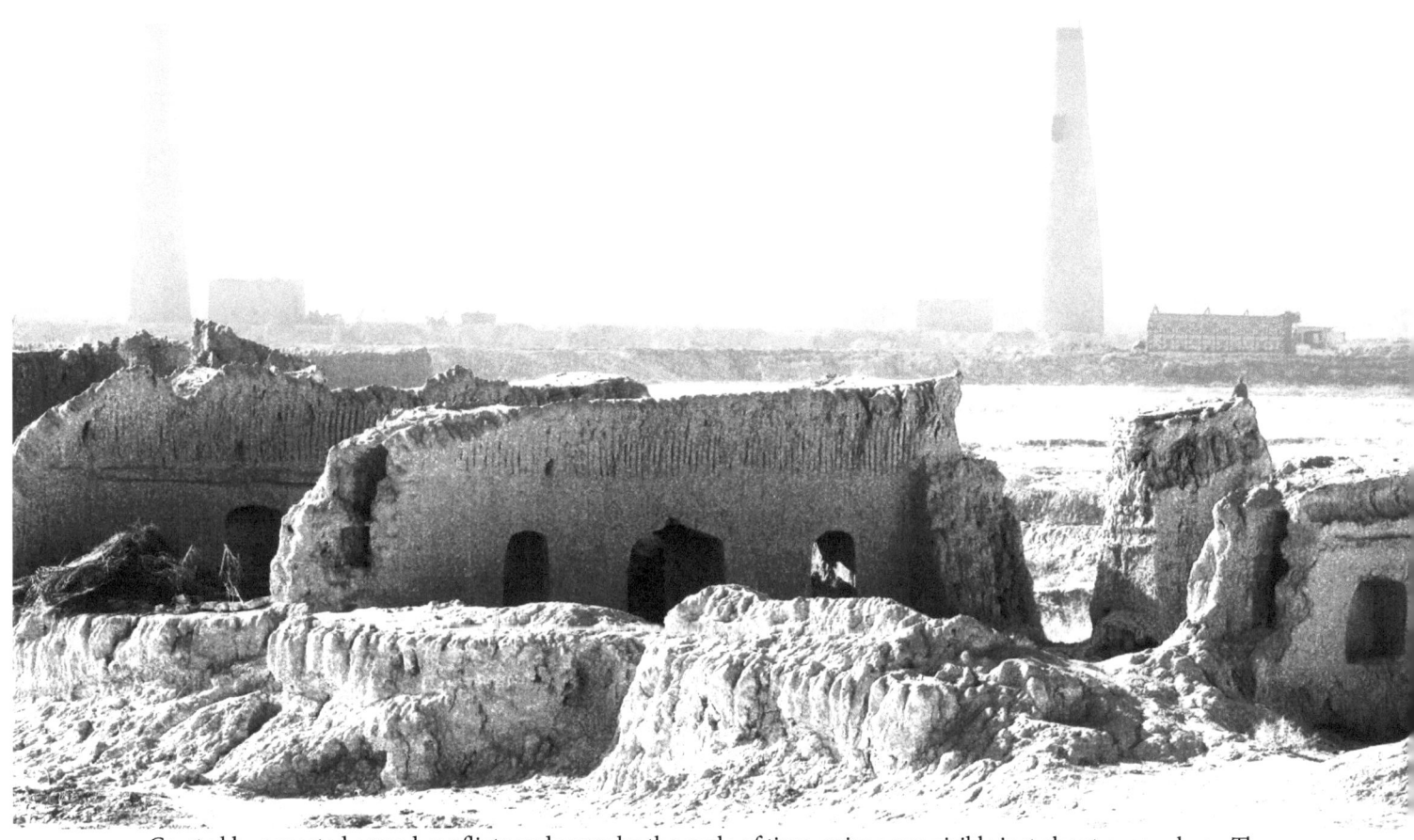

    Created by repeated armed conflicts and worn by the cycle of time, ruins were visible just about everywhere. They sometimes spread over the area of an entire village. They were often caches or booby-trapped places. As they were hardly coveted sites, poor nomads would go there and hang their canvases. Syringes could always be found there, and sometimes traces of blood, the last witnesses of massacres that will never be resolved.

    Millions of Afghans fled the war against the Soviets. In recent years, many have returned to Afghanistan. Others will never be able to—they are buried on foreign soil. Some think those people are the luckiest. In Afghanistan, only the dead see the end of war.

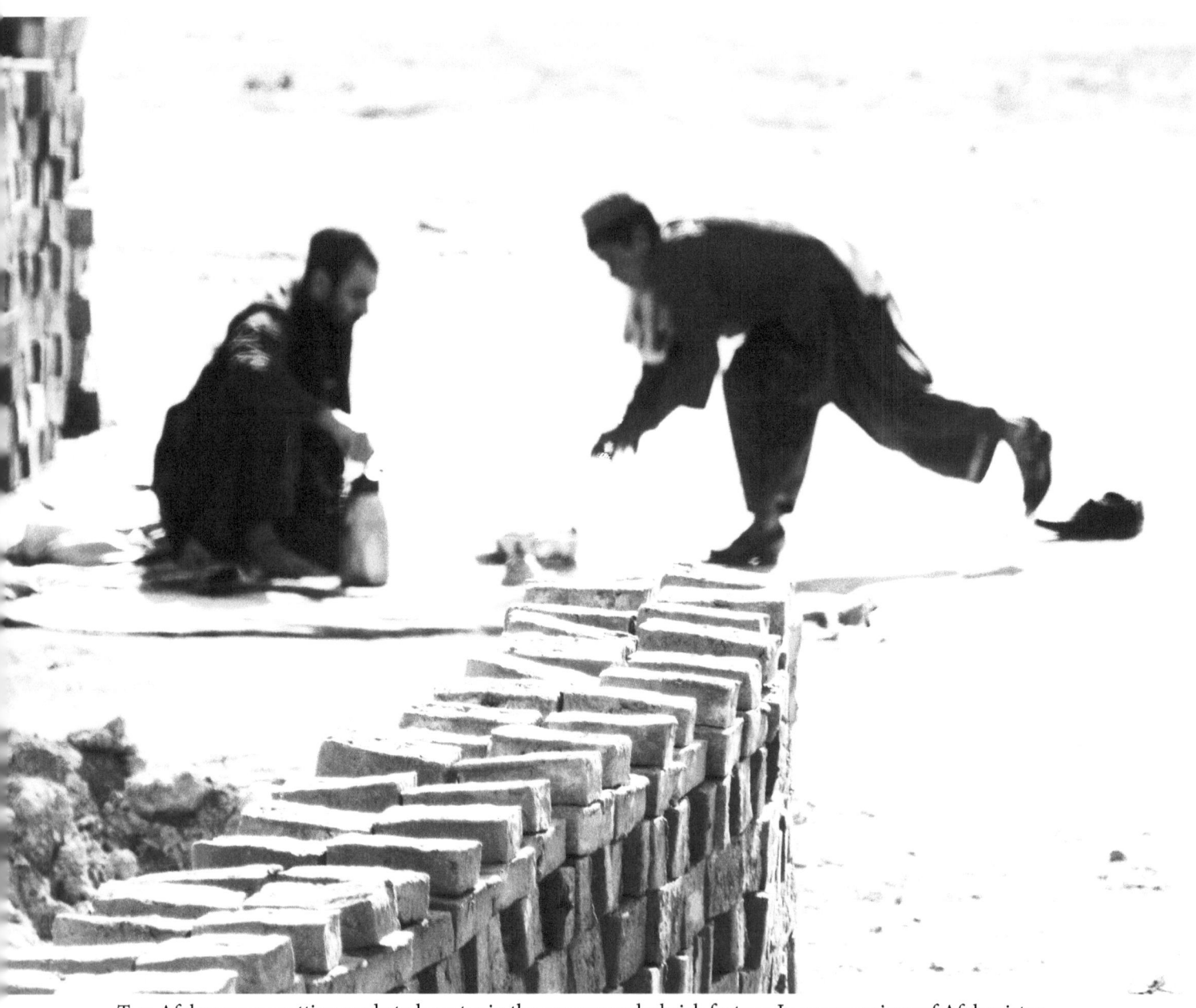

Two Afghans were getting ready to have tea in the area around a brick factory. In many regions of Afghanistan, there is no television, cinema, or video games. As in the olden days, people entertain themselves by getting together and talking. They talk about these oddly dressed soldiers who are patrolling in the villages. They talk about this soldier who looks mean and that one who looks nice.

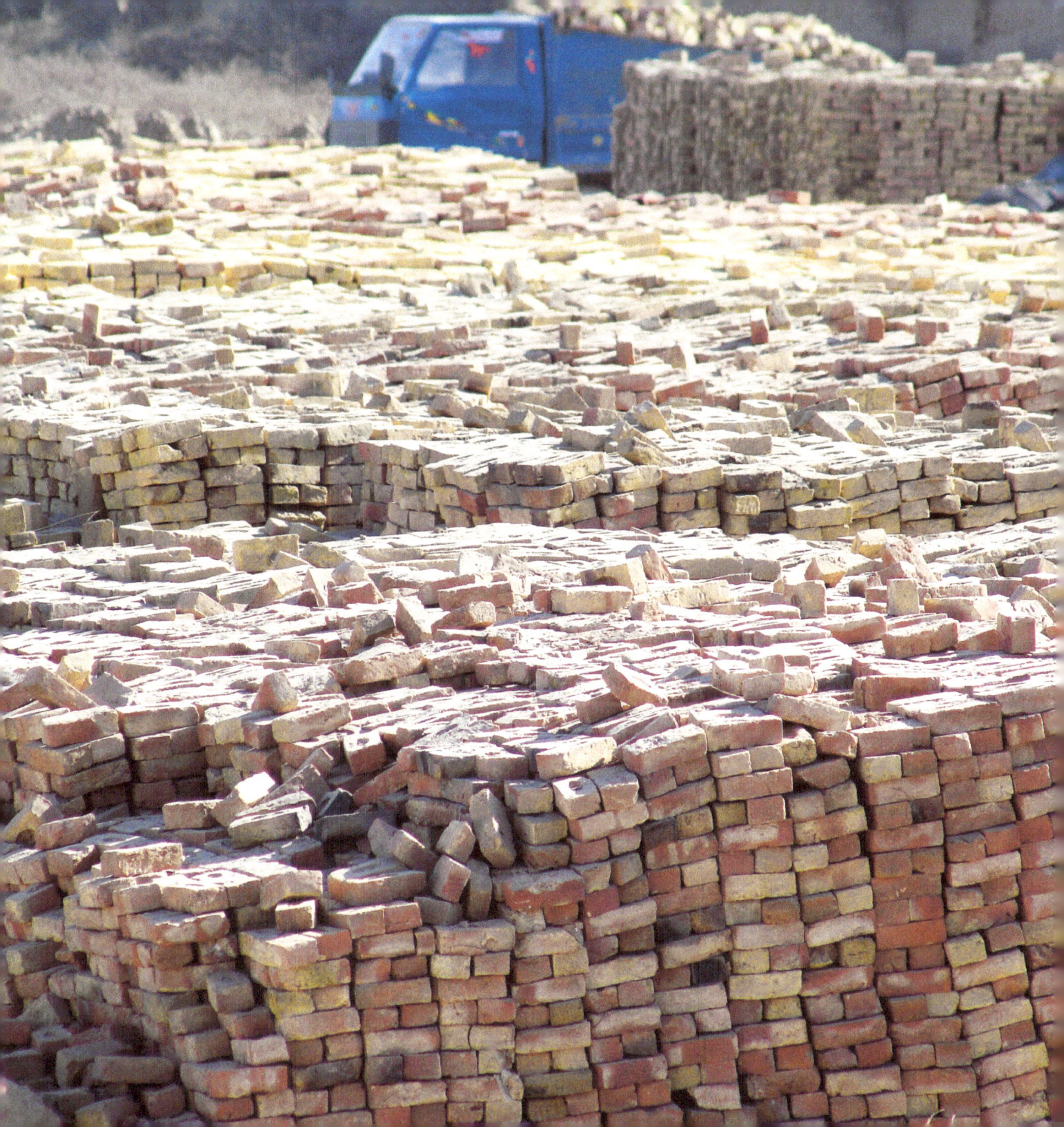

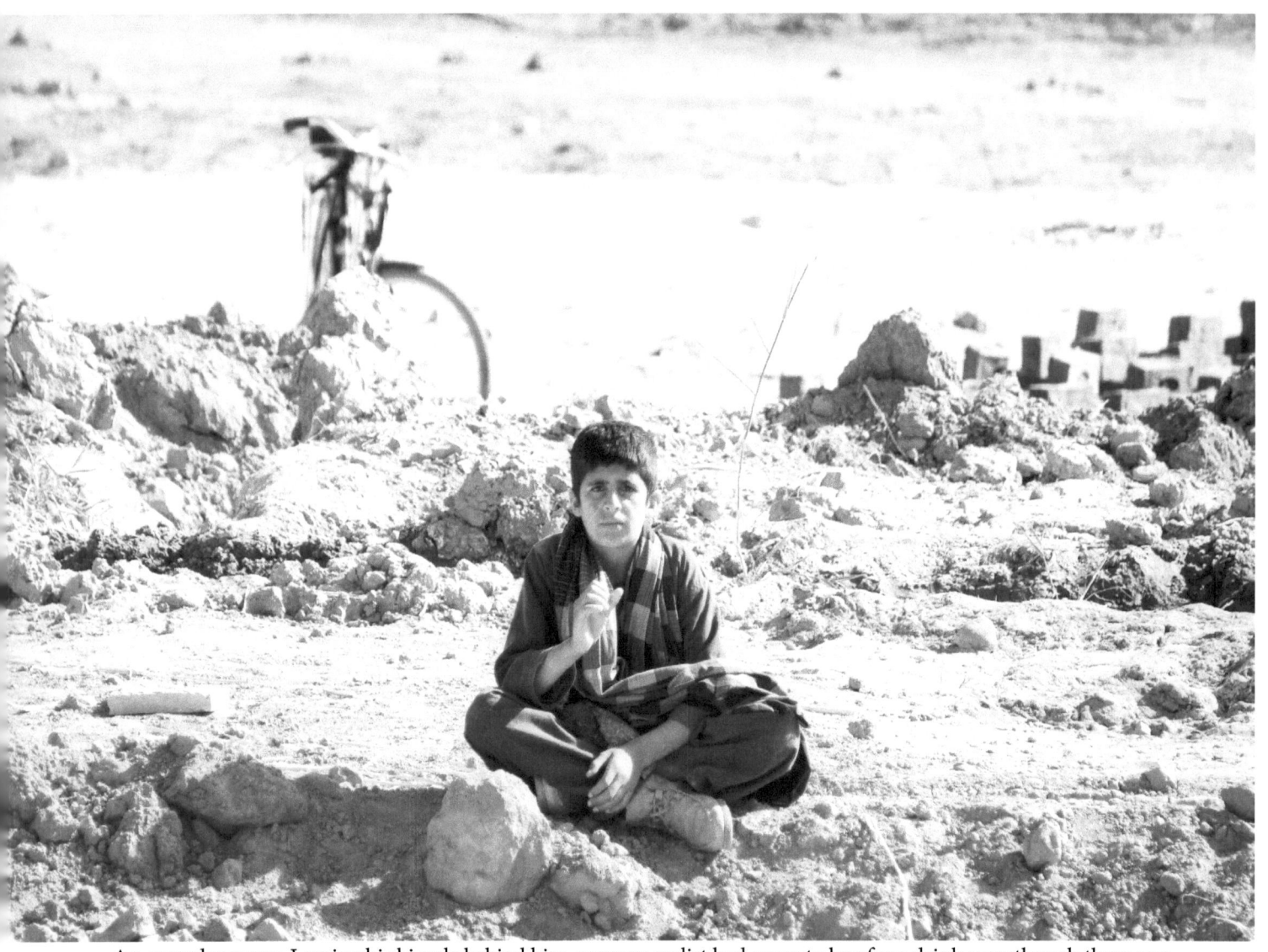

An everyday scene. Leaving his bicycle behind him, a young cyclist had come to beg for a drink even though there was a well of potable water close by.

A bit farther on, this cricket game reminded us of the colonial influence of British India. Under the Taliban regime, this sport, like many others, was banned.

A few moments after we watched this small athletic event, radio communications were announcing the imminence of airstrikes in our sector. We knew that some people near us were living their last moments. After a few minutes, gigantic, yet silent, fireballs were emerging from the outlines of a small town. A few seconds later, the earth was shaking as in a storm.

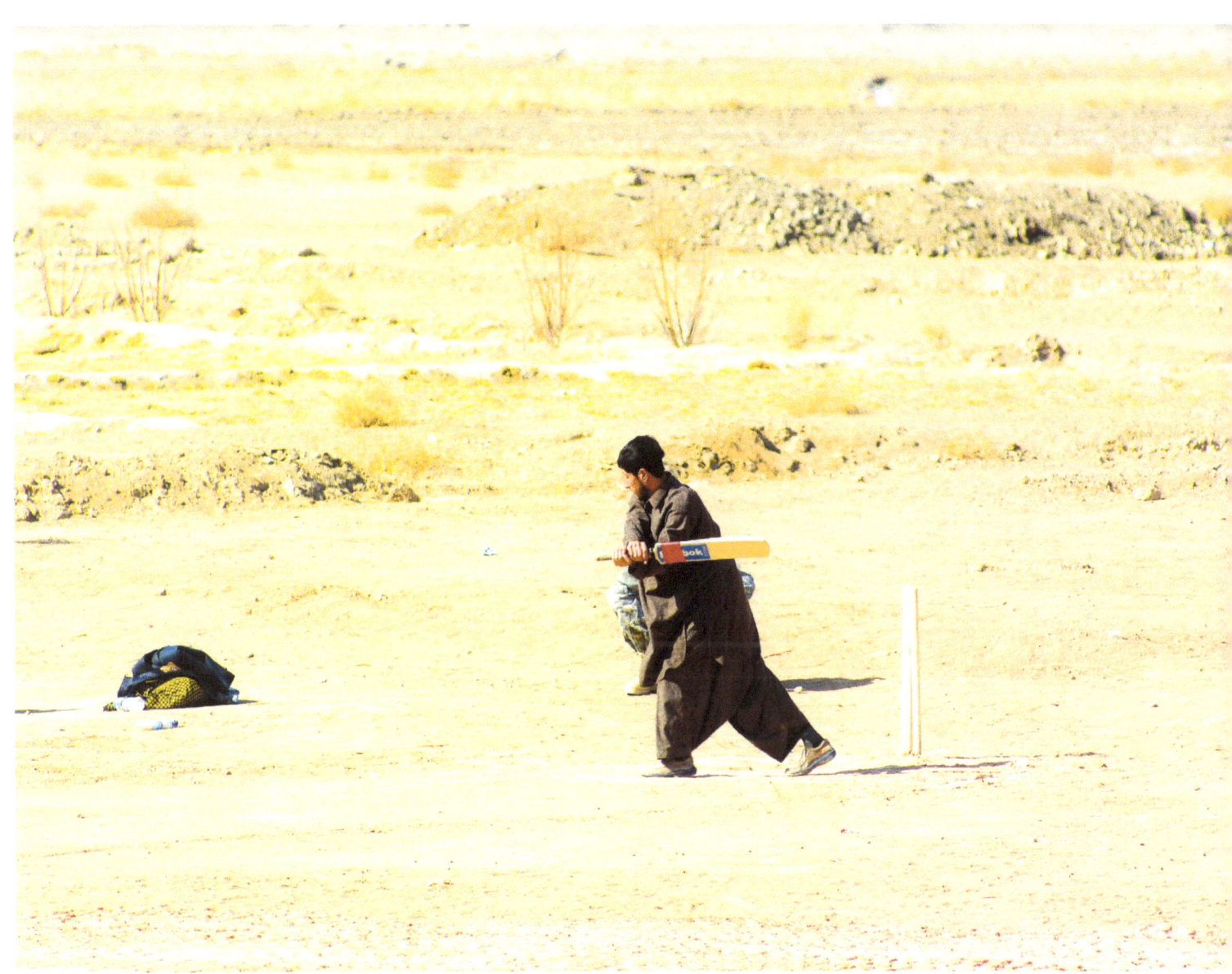

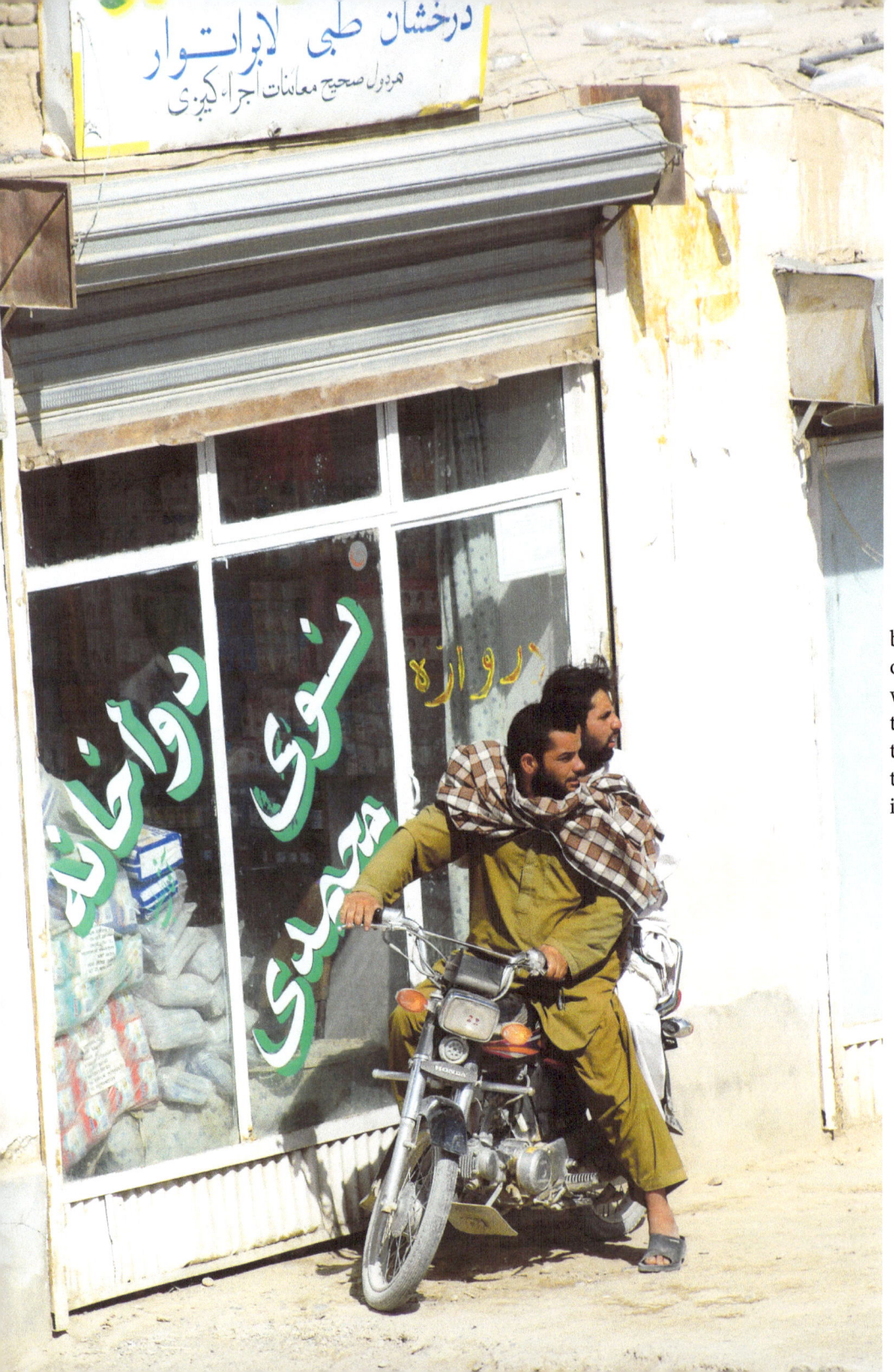

The typical display of a business establishment on the outskirts of Kandahar. In this war, it was nearly impossible to distinguish insurgents from the rest of the population. Were these two men fanatic Taliban or innocent sympathizers?

In the shadows of a small business, two generations were passing the time with what appeared to be a remote-controlled toy. A small antenna could be seen coming out of the hands of the young Afghan. Some of these devices were confiscated by the Taliban, who used them to detonate bombs.

The jars of candy came from an Asian country. China is nearby, and it shares a border with Afghanistan.

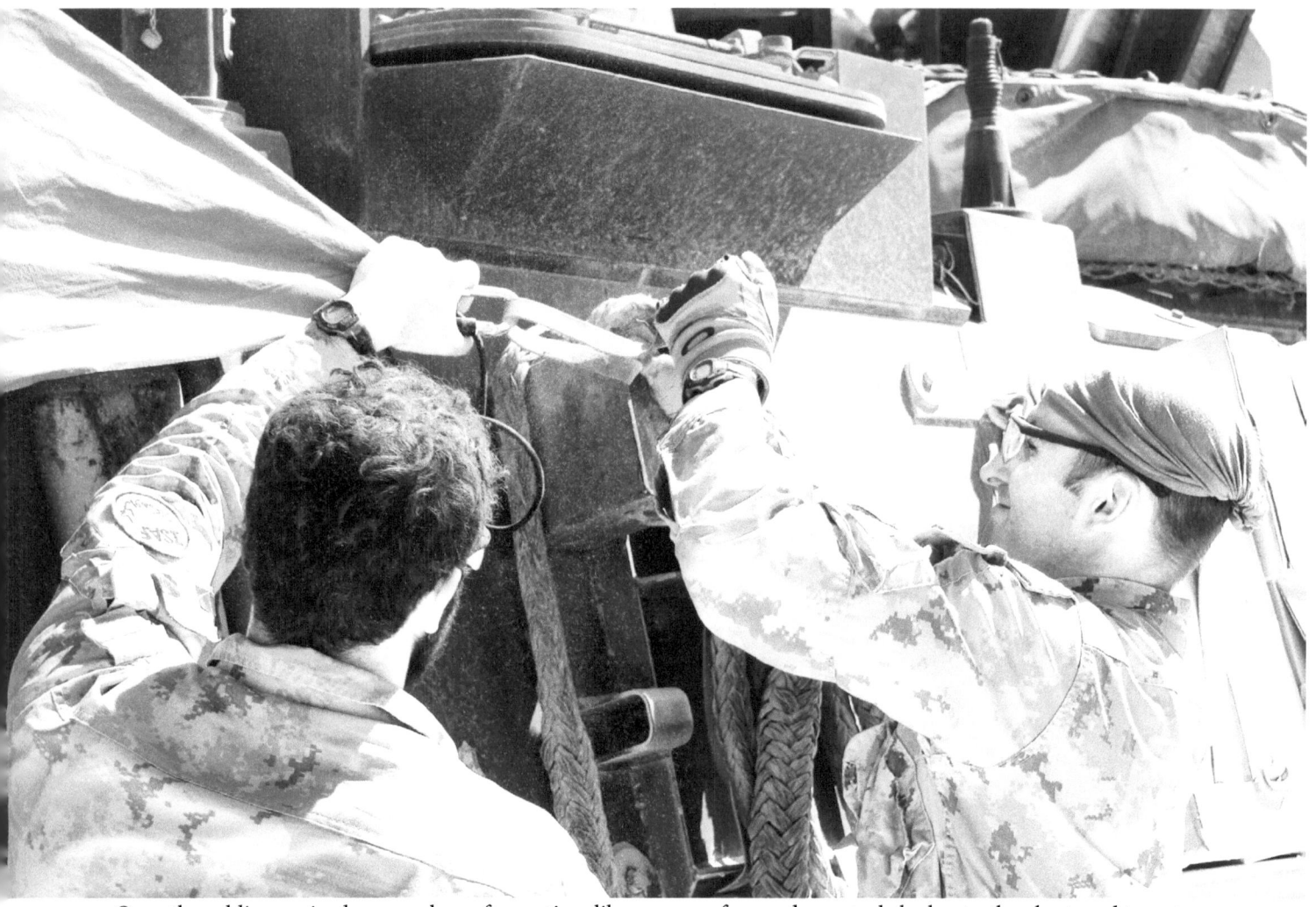

Once the soldiers arrived near a place of operation, like a group of nomads on steel elephants, they hastened to put up tarps behind the vehicles in order to shelter themselves from the hot summer sun.

After the tarps were spread and the trenches dug, we needed to set up our cots. Soldiers unrolled their mattresses on them. They put down their music players in anticipation of their return from the patrol a few hours later.

I was preparing my combat equipment when gunshots could be heard. A motorcycle was rushing toward the parked vehicles. We had only a few seconds to make a decision and react, so soldiers started shooting at this fast-approaching kamikaze. Then the shots suddenly stopped. It was not a kamikaze, but an Afghan police officer who had forgotten to put on his uniform. Fortunately, no bullets had hit him. His good mood also seemed to be intact. The young police officer even seemed to find the incident funny!

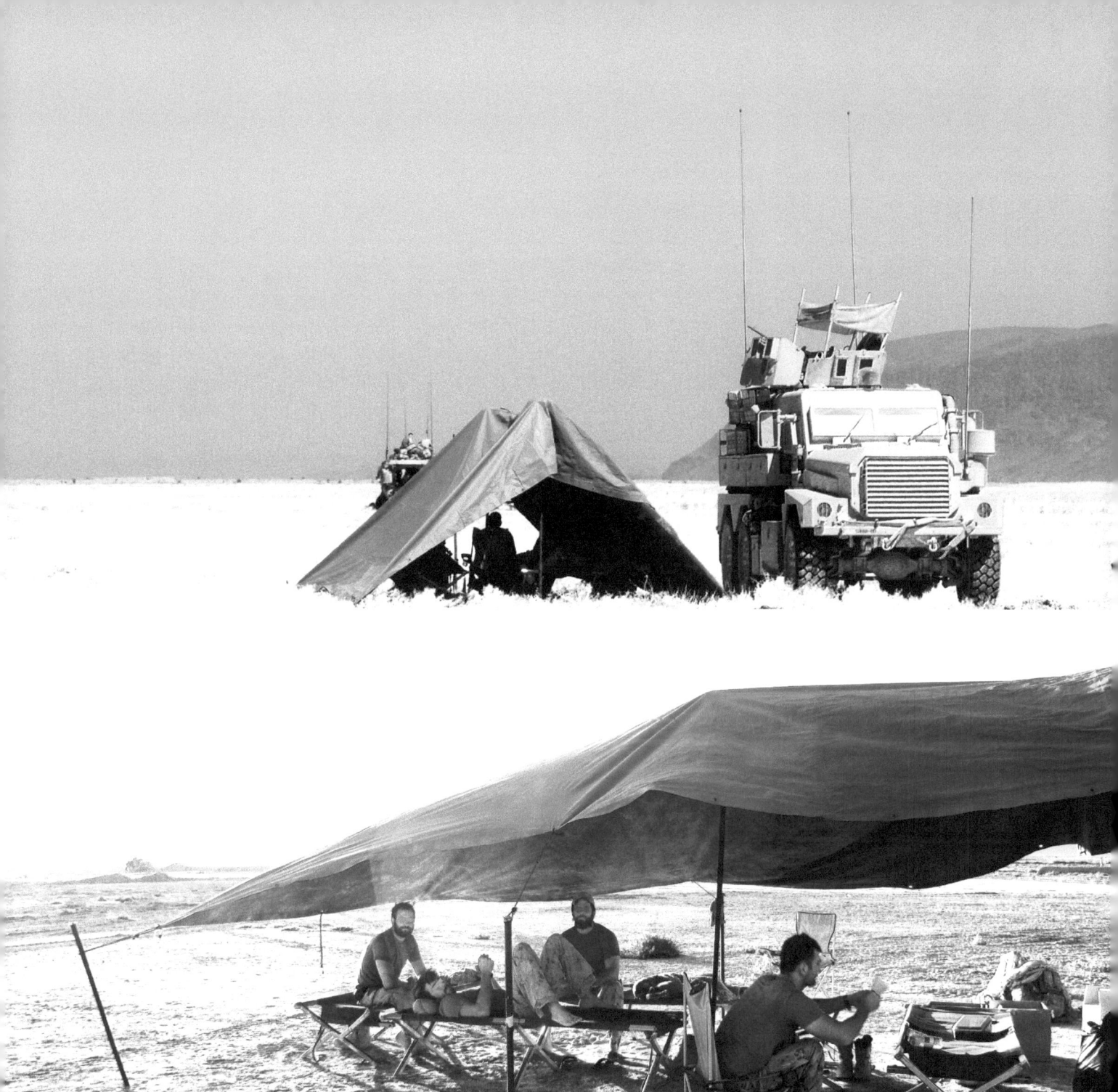

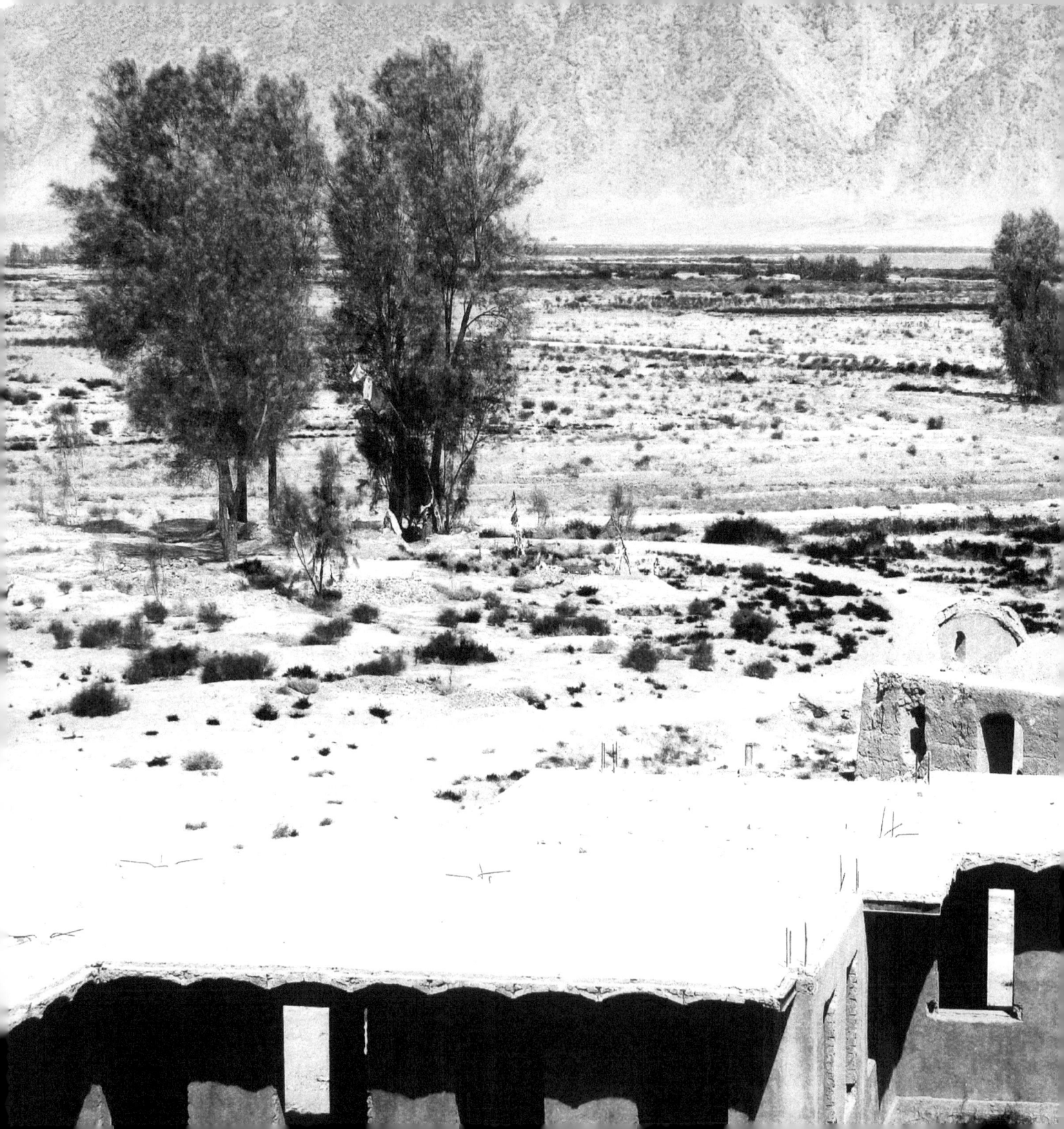

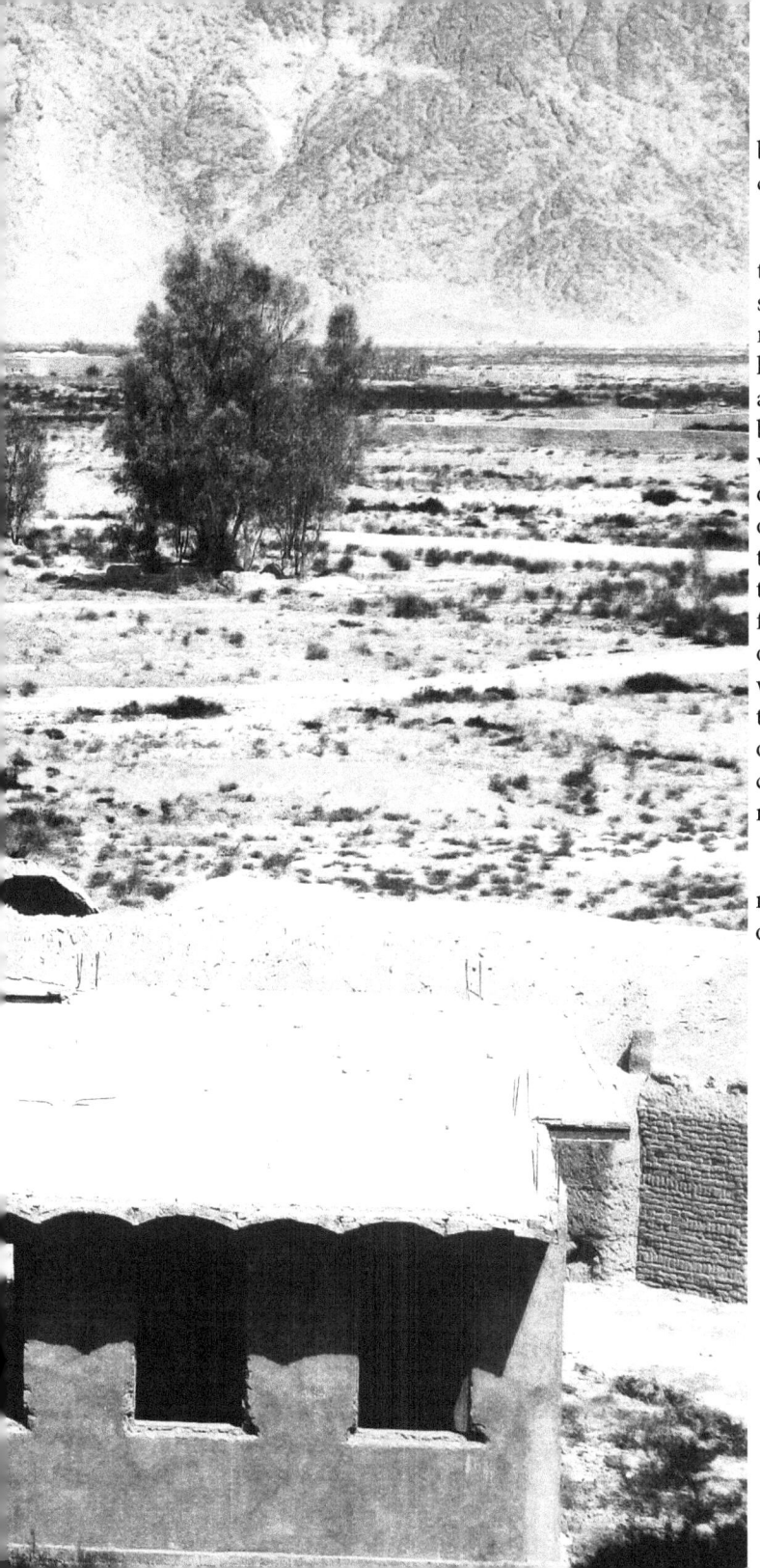

Near the group of vehicles, the remains of a school could be seen. Nearby, flags occupied the undulating shapes of a small cemetery.

The school did not appear to be painted. And yet, defying the arid hues of the landscape, it well and truly held the entire spectrum of colors. The building appeared empty, yet it was not. It was filled with children. In the window on the right, a little one who could have become a doctor. All he knew of the art of healing was comforting his childhood friend with the bloody face. Right next to him, with her elbow resting on the window sill, a little girl with idealistic dreams. In the room on the left, a geography teacher who will never see mountains other than the ones of Kandahar, and who would not be able to find his own country on a map. Right near him, a history teacher who will not recount even his own short life. His friend, an English teacher, will remain mute forever. In the other room, the one with the rounded roof, a blinded artist. He will never uncover the beauties of his region. He will have seen them for only a few years, when he was a child. And finally, fifty other lives farther way, behind the school—a class of curious children. Buried under the mounds of the cemetery, they will remain silent forever.

In Afghanistan, all places are haunted by hopes that were not even born, unfulfilled promises, disappeared lives, and other lives that were never even lived.

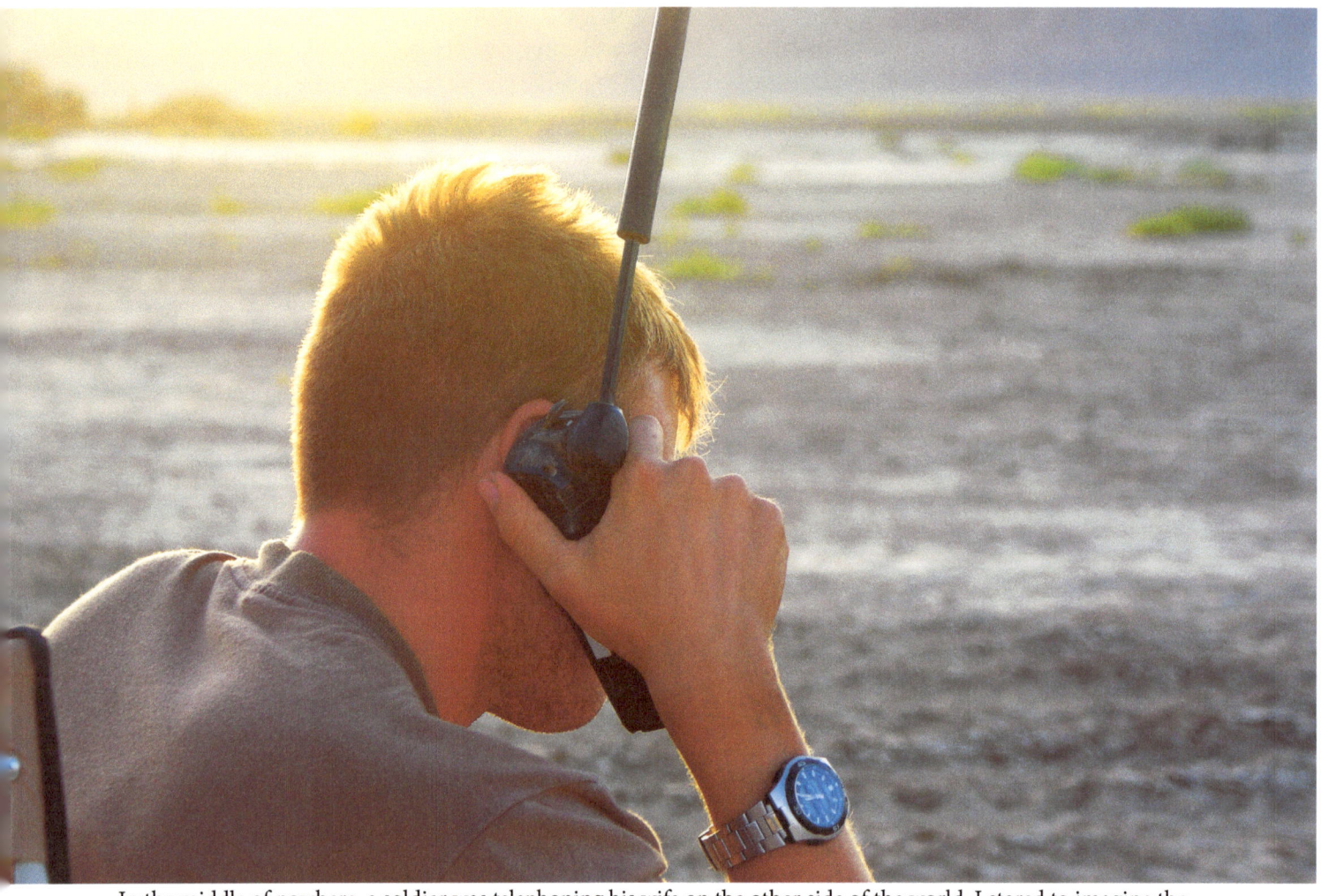

In the middle of nowhere, a soldier was telephoning his wife on the other side of the world. I stared to imagine the conversation:

In Afghanistan, it was evening. At home, the family had just woken up. Over the nearby hum of moving engines, the soldier could hear the laughter of his children, who had just jumped into the swimming pool.

His gaze crossed the expanses of desert sand. For a moment, he was imagining the dew on the cool grass of the fields of his country and listening emotionally to the story he was being told about the vacation at the family cabin. But a rumble was gradually taking the place of the comforting voice. It soon became deafening. Like a flock of birds of ill omen, the passage of helicopters was announcing the approach of death. The soldier was forcing himself to stay connected to the world of peace. Now he could distinguish the familiar voices of a television program. During this time, a few kilometers away, in the world of war, shells that looked like lasers were emerging in slow motion from flying aircraft.

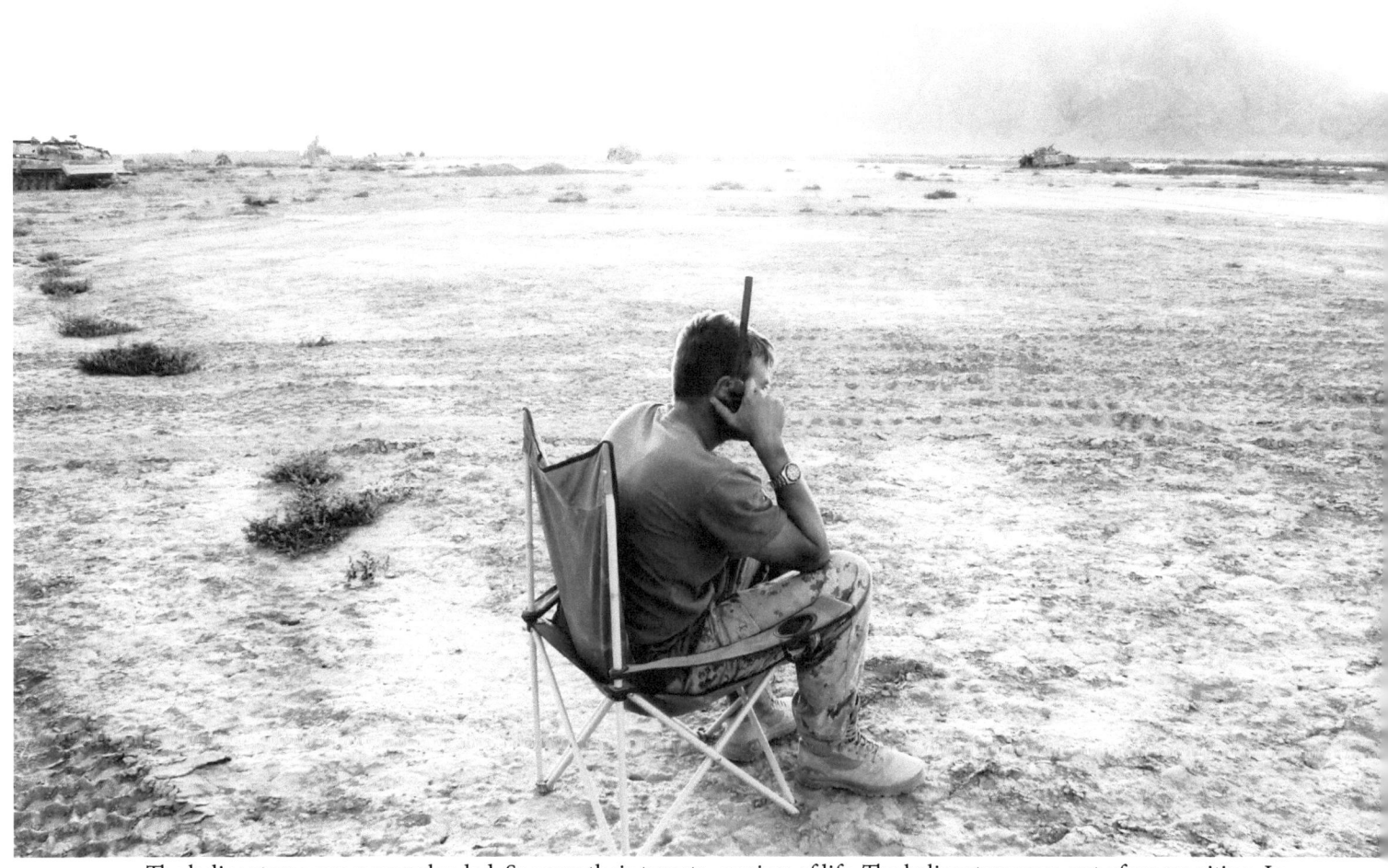

 The helicopters were now unloaded. So were their targets, carriers of life. The helicopters were out of ammunition. In an hour, the pilots would go drink coffee in front of the high-definition television in the break room at the air base.

 The insurgents' bodies were lying on the ground, emptied of breath. Here, blood had flowed. In the soldier's wife's home, it was hot coffee that had flowed. The soldier was grasping on to this morning scene, to the light that was bathing the kitchen, to the smell of toast. He learned with sadness about the first words of his last-born child. "Daddy" was not part of this vocabulary. The child had seen his father only once. This was not the case of his brothers, who every day used the word "Daddy" a lot, especially since a school friend had told them that their father would die. They already knew too much about Afghanistan.

 The sun was between a woman and her husband. The soldier's gaze now turned toward the distant mountains. Above, the setting sun. The conversation was drawing to an end. Here, night was gaining ground. In the Home Country, the day was starting.

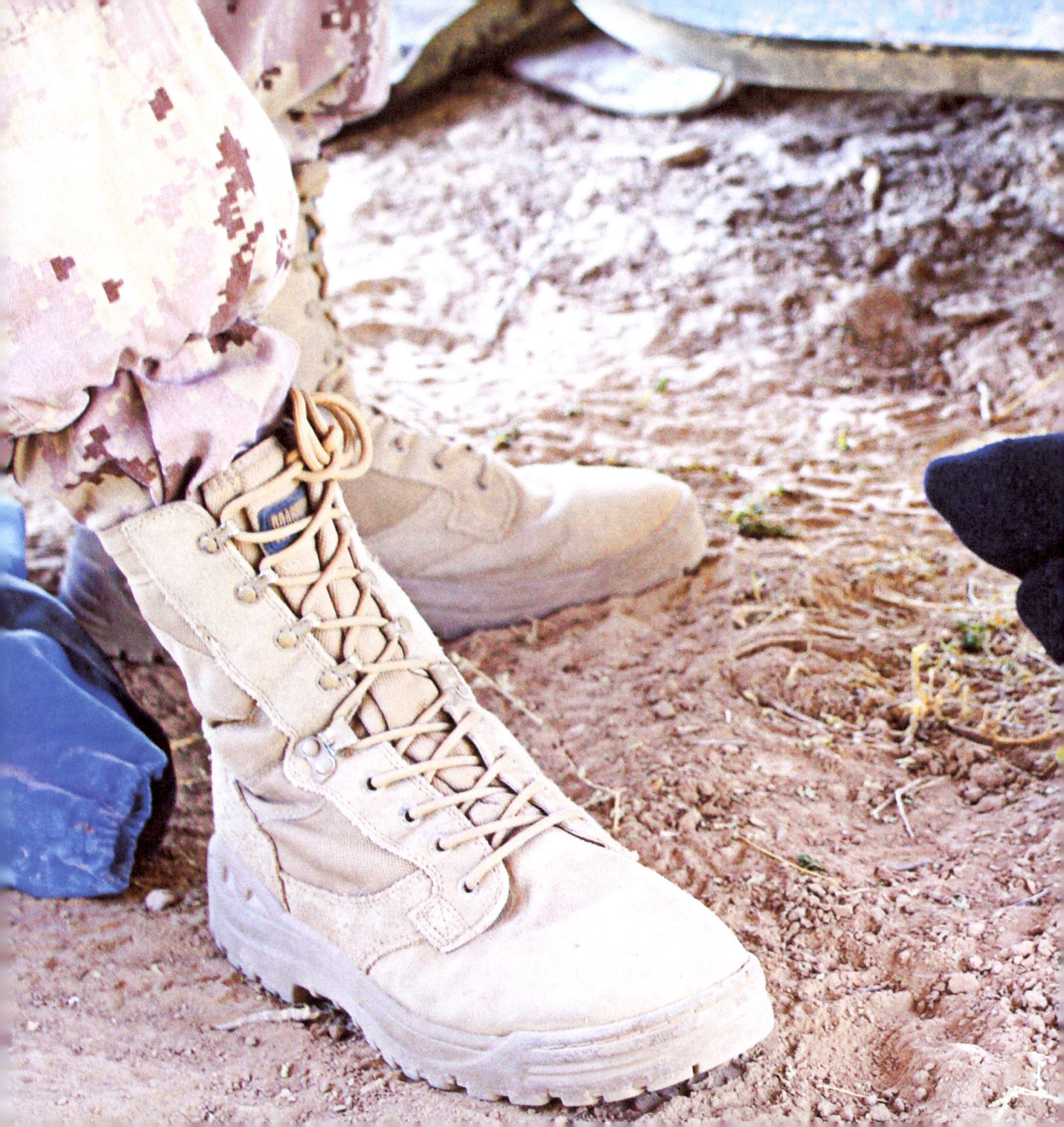

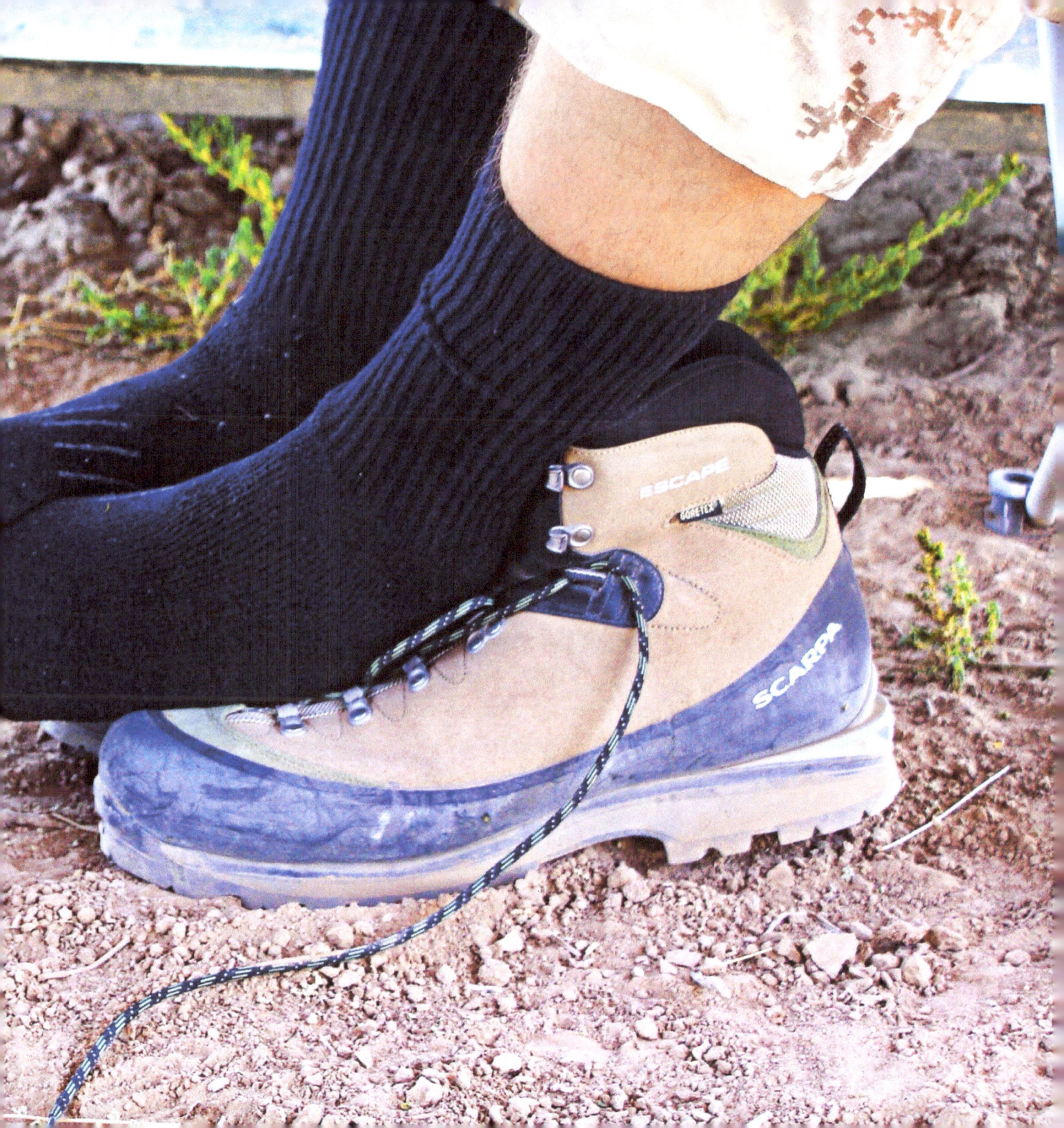

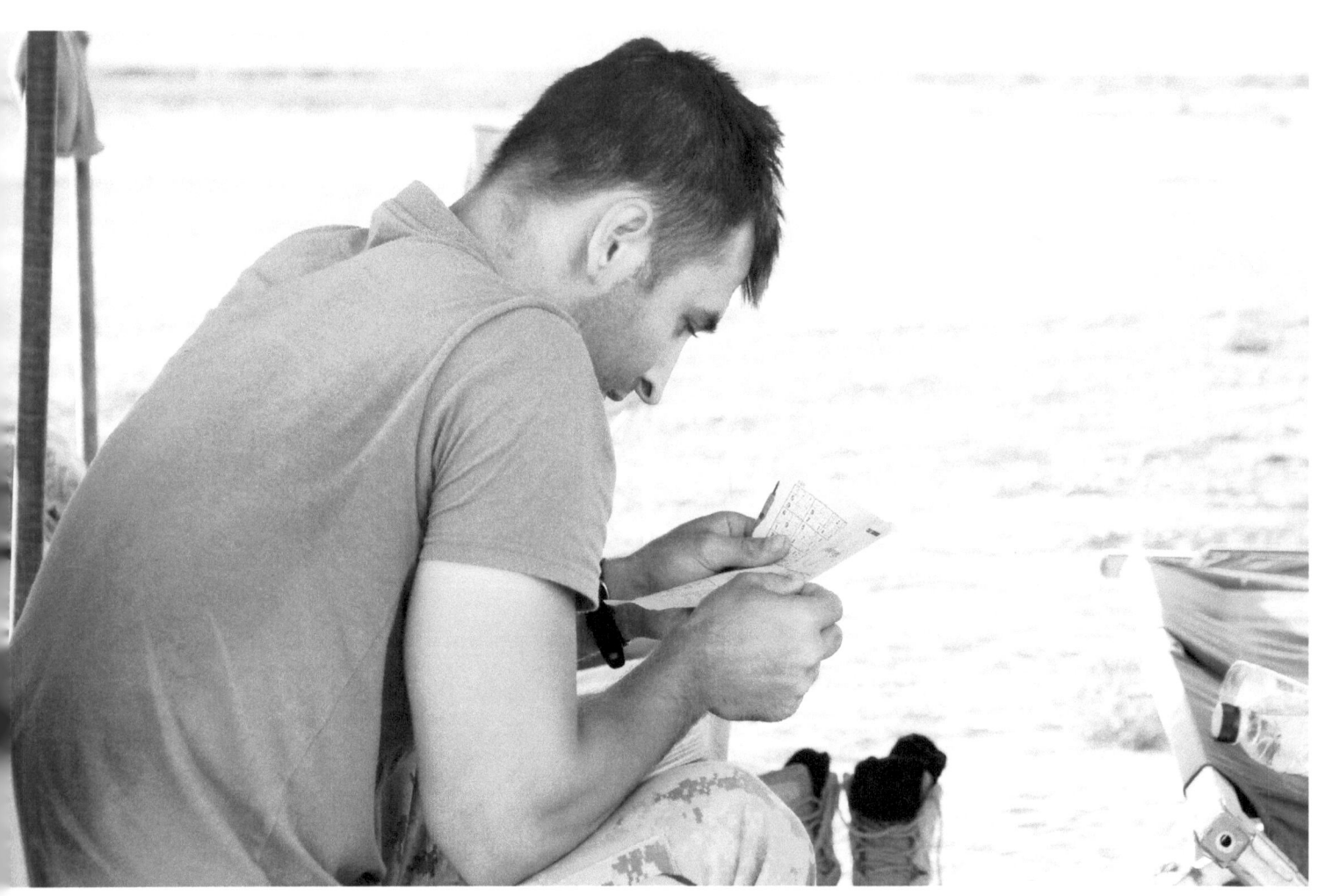

In less than an hour, the soldiers would risk their lives once again. But for now: Sudoku!

The adrenaline of war is like a cigarette. At first, it makes you sick. After some time, you can no longer resist it!

When a soldier returns from the intensity of a conflict zone, ordinary, calm life becomes boring.

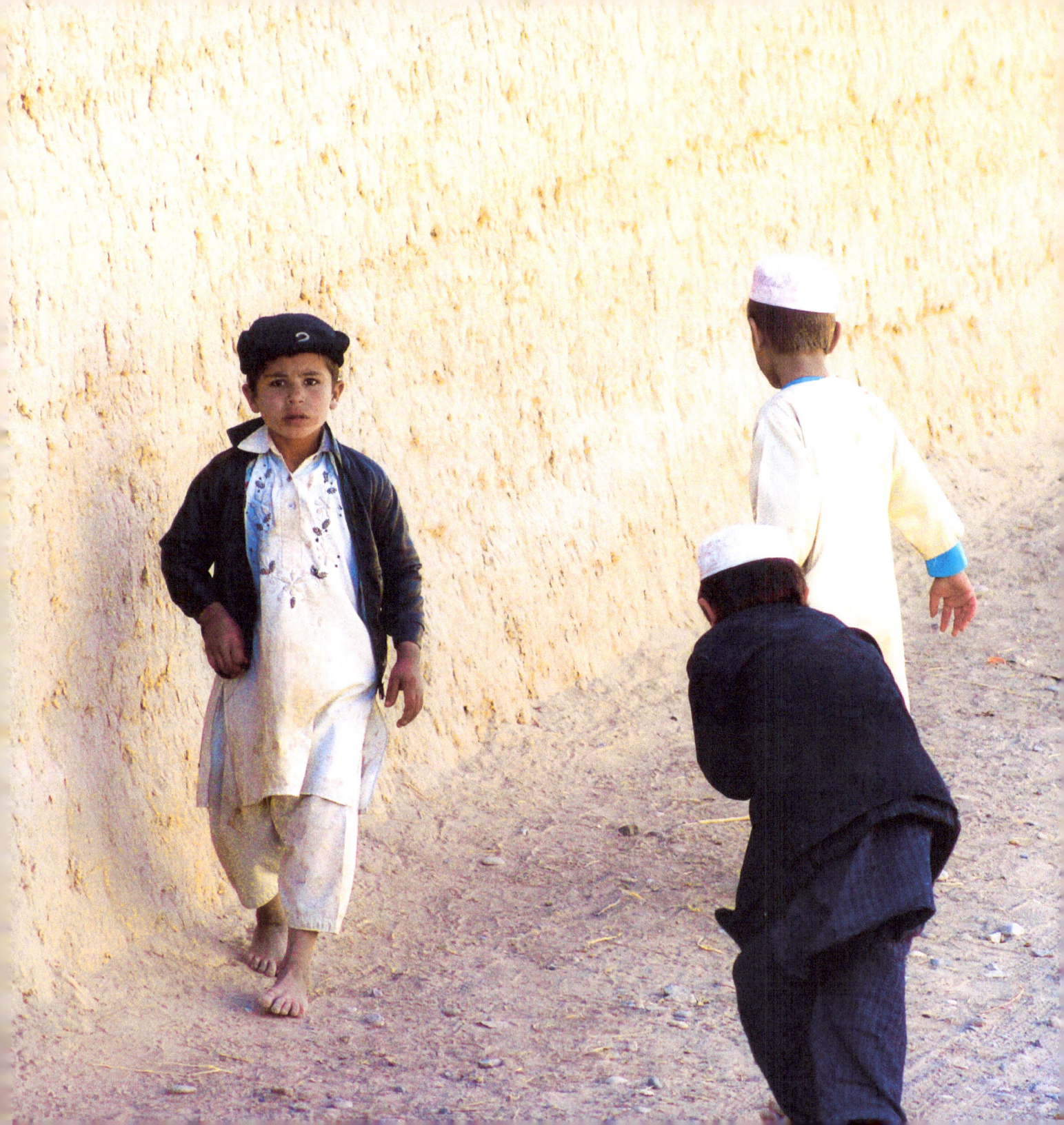

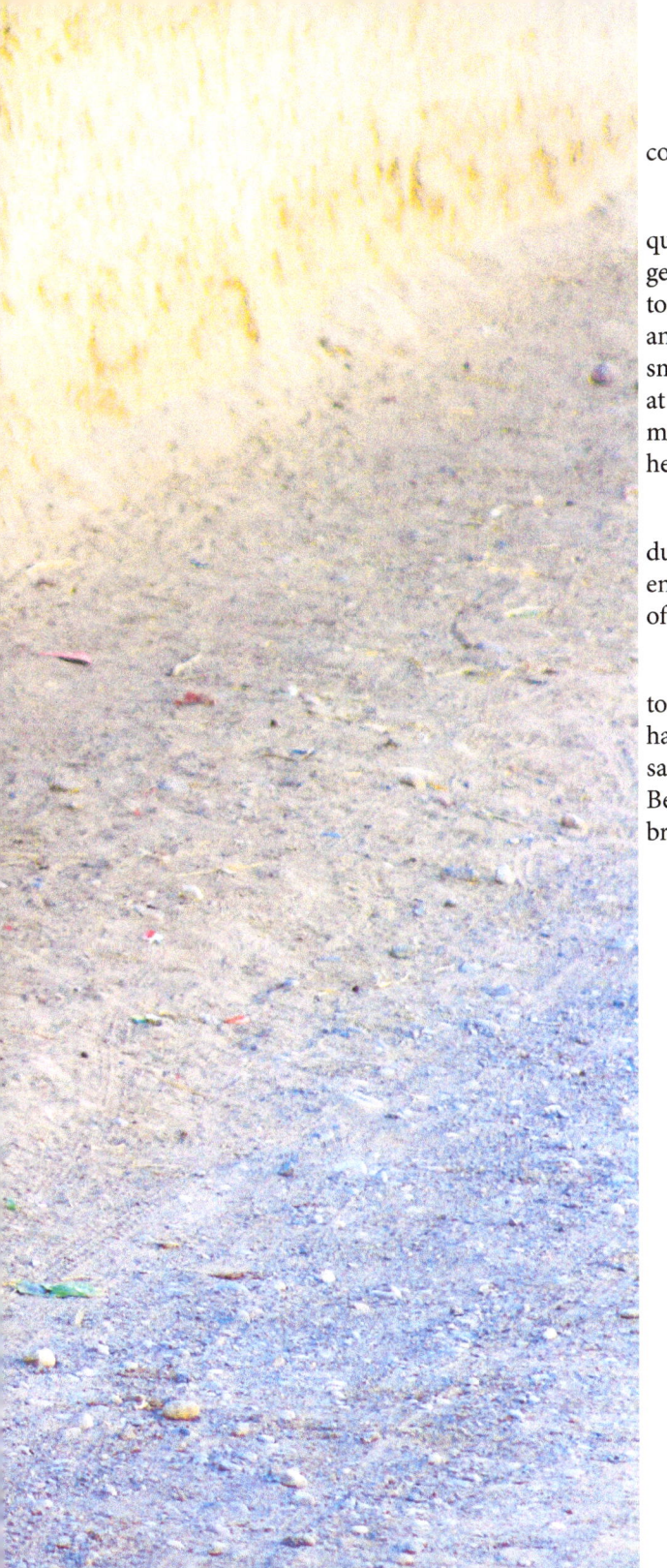

A foot patrol was beginning. Soon thereafter, we entered a pastel-colored village.

In areas that are visited little by the military coalition, a patrol quickly becomes the center of attention and curiosity. I remember once getting out of my vehicle to plot the itinerary of the patrol. I was looking toward the paths we were going to cross when a little girl approached me and grabbed my gloved hand. She looked incredibly serious. She was not smiling. Then, her silent mouth kissed the back of my open hand. I smiled at her and she left the same way she had come. A few moments later, a man came to see me and invited the whole patrol to visit the school where he taught. I was then sure that there were no Taliban in this village.

Things had changed since my first missions. Some people say that during fighting there are always more terrorists, and that they multiply endlessly. I believe the opposite, that over time, there end up being fewer of them.

At the beginning of World War II, Nazi Germany was the planet's top military power. Some governments, believing that the cause was lost, hastened to sign peace treaties with Hitler. Several years later, after the sacrifice of soldiers and their politicians who had initially been criticized, Berlin was occupied by the enemy's cannons and boots. Perseverance brings rewards.

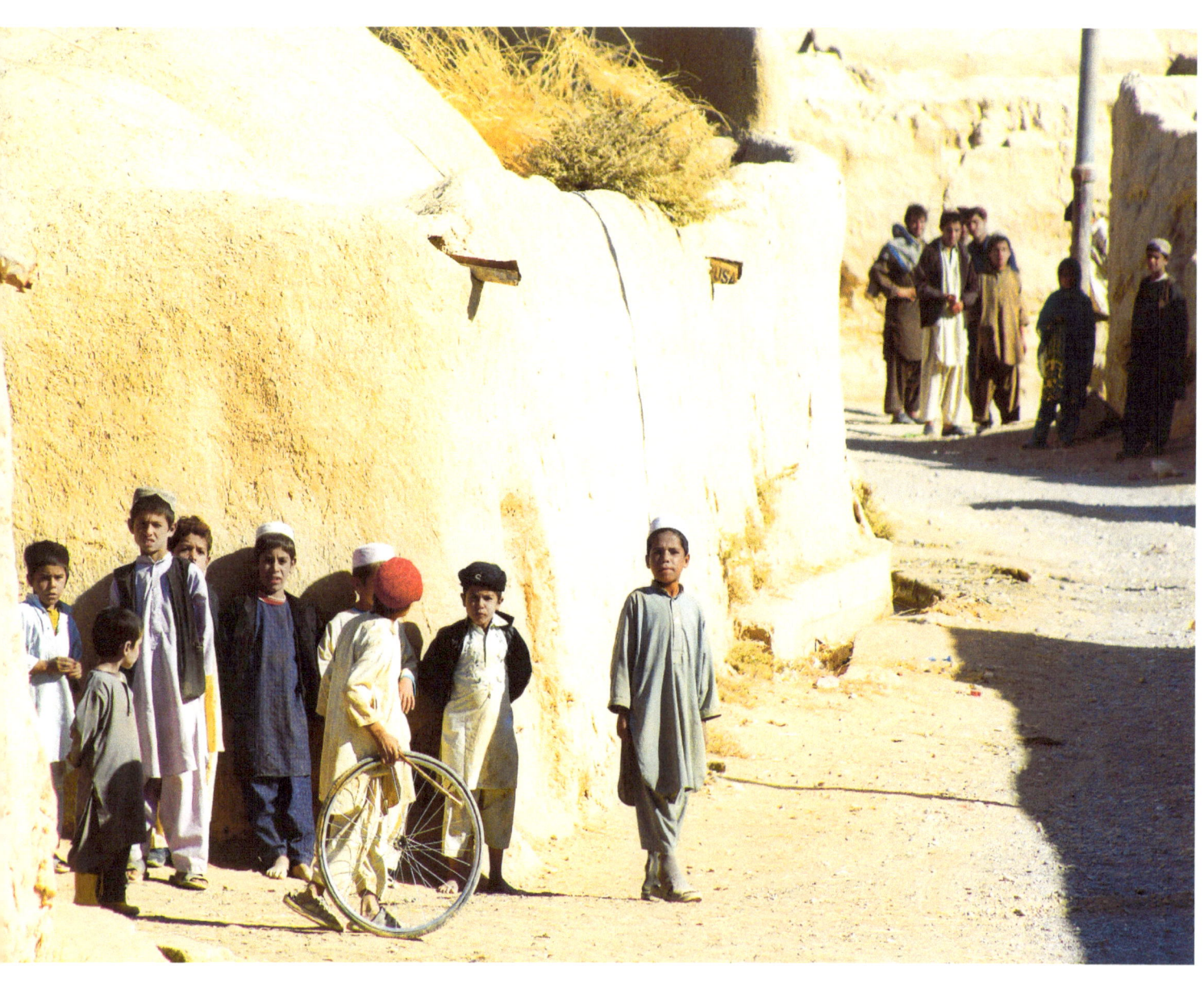

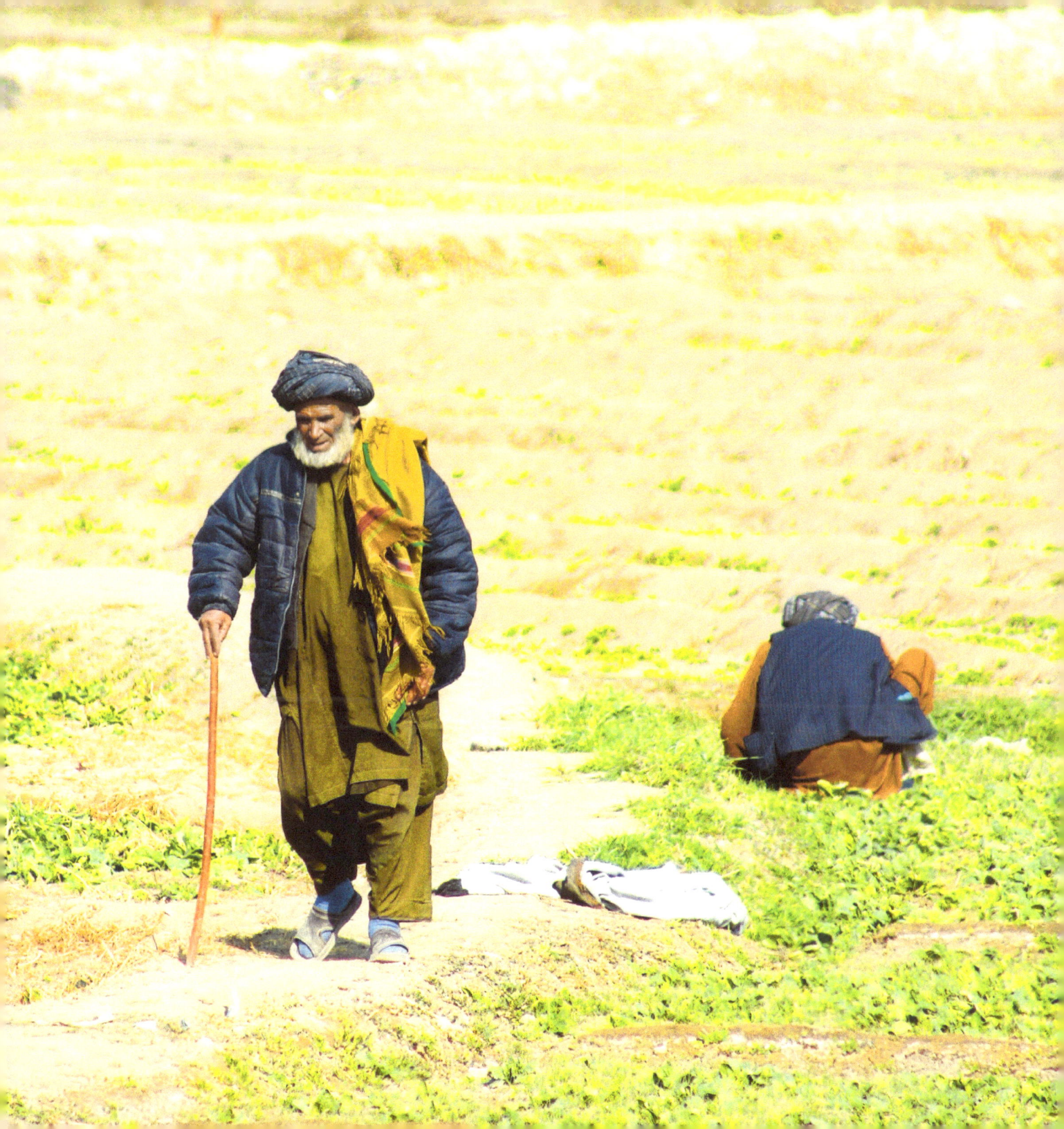

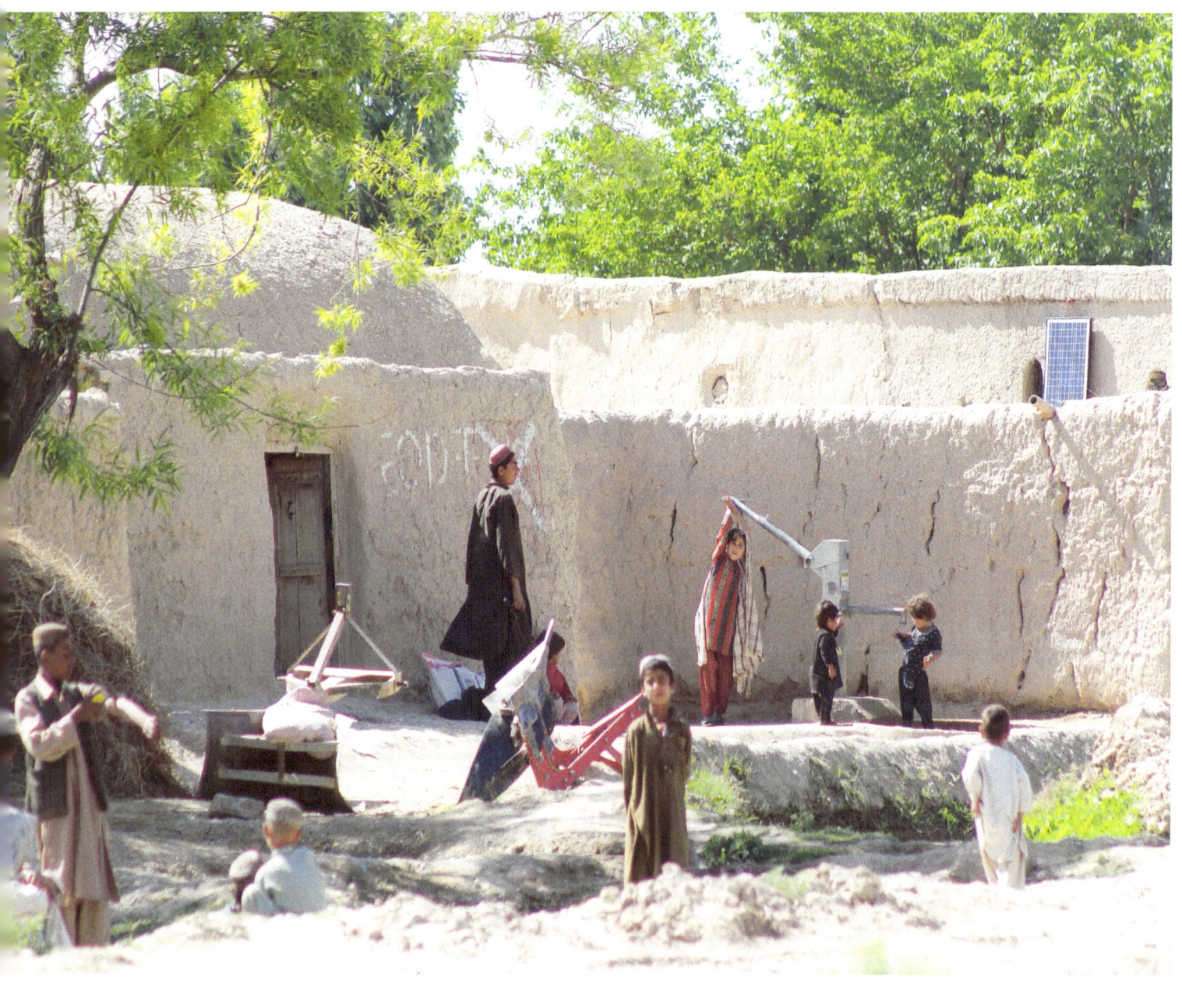

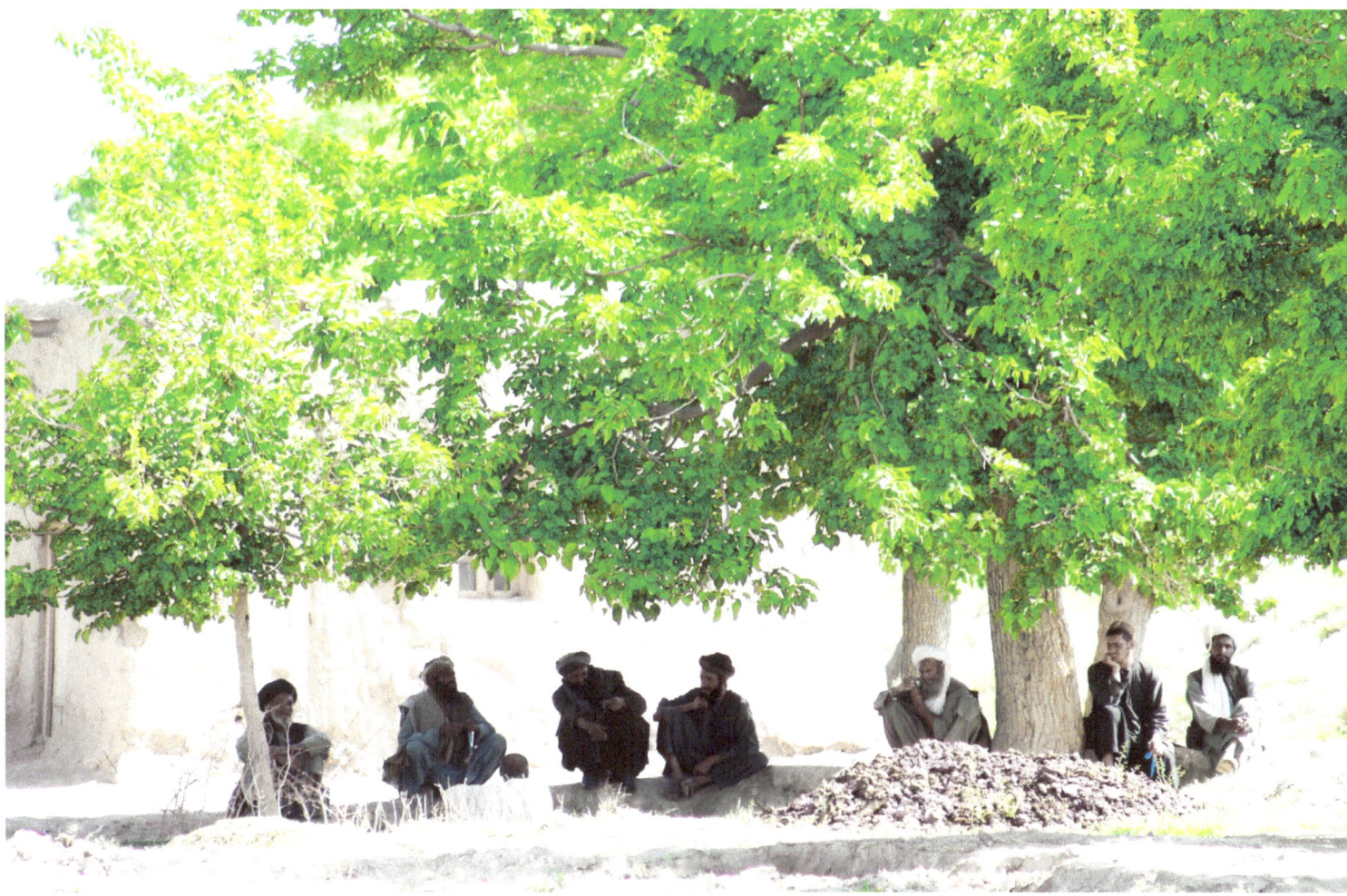

A typical day in a village that was teeming with life. The men were outside, the women inside. In an Afghan village, the mosque and water pump together make up the center of the community.

While patrolling in this replica of Jesus's time, I felt as though I were on a set of a science fiction film about a distant planet. How many times did I see scenes like this one, whether while walking in the heart of villages or from a hiding place in the surrounding mountains, while I was looking through my powerful lenses? For me, Afghanistan is a place that is above all peaceful. It is small villages like this one that will remain engraved in my memory. Not the battles.

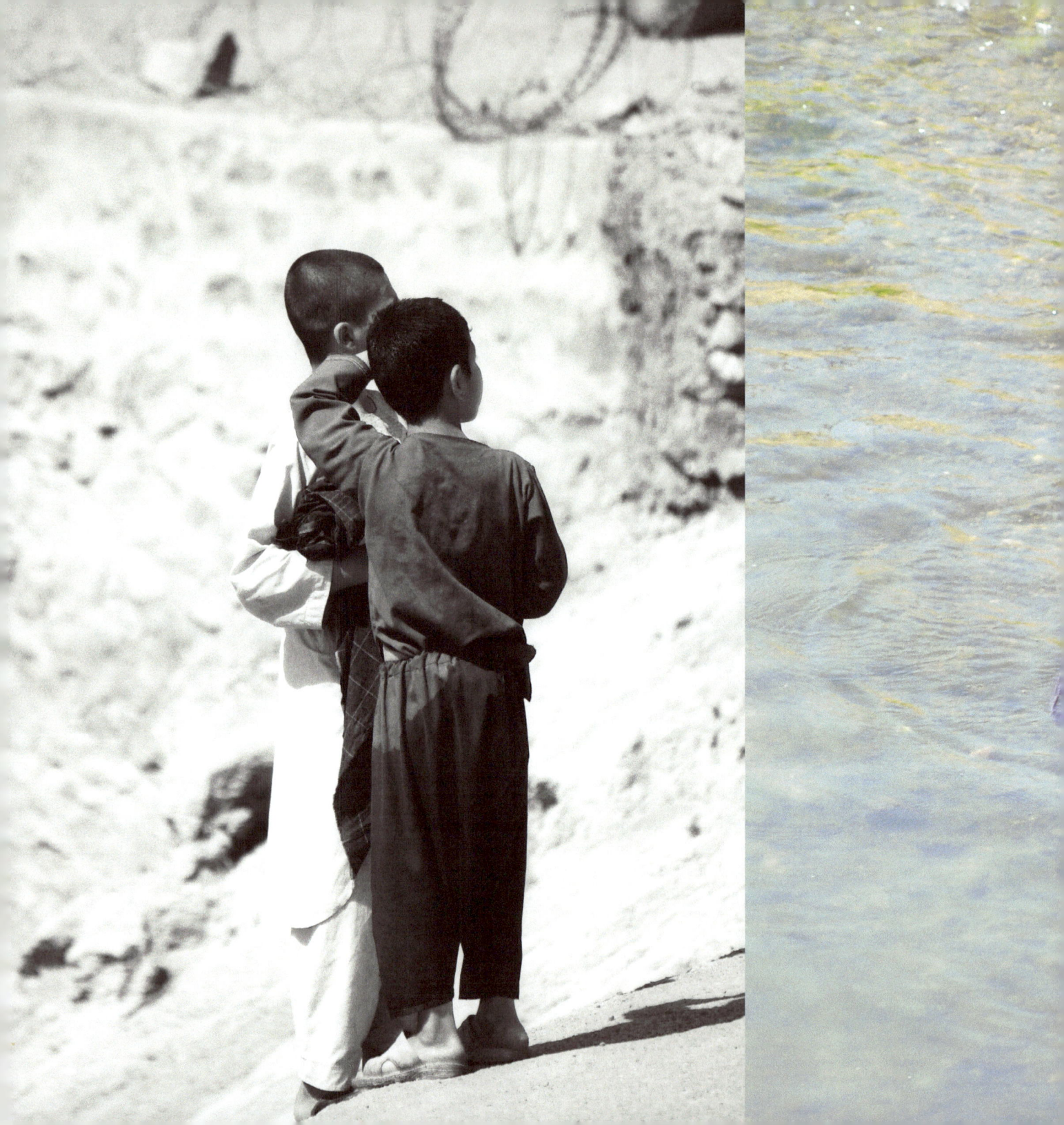

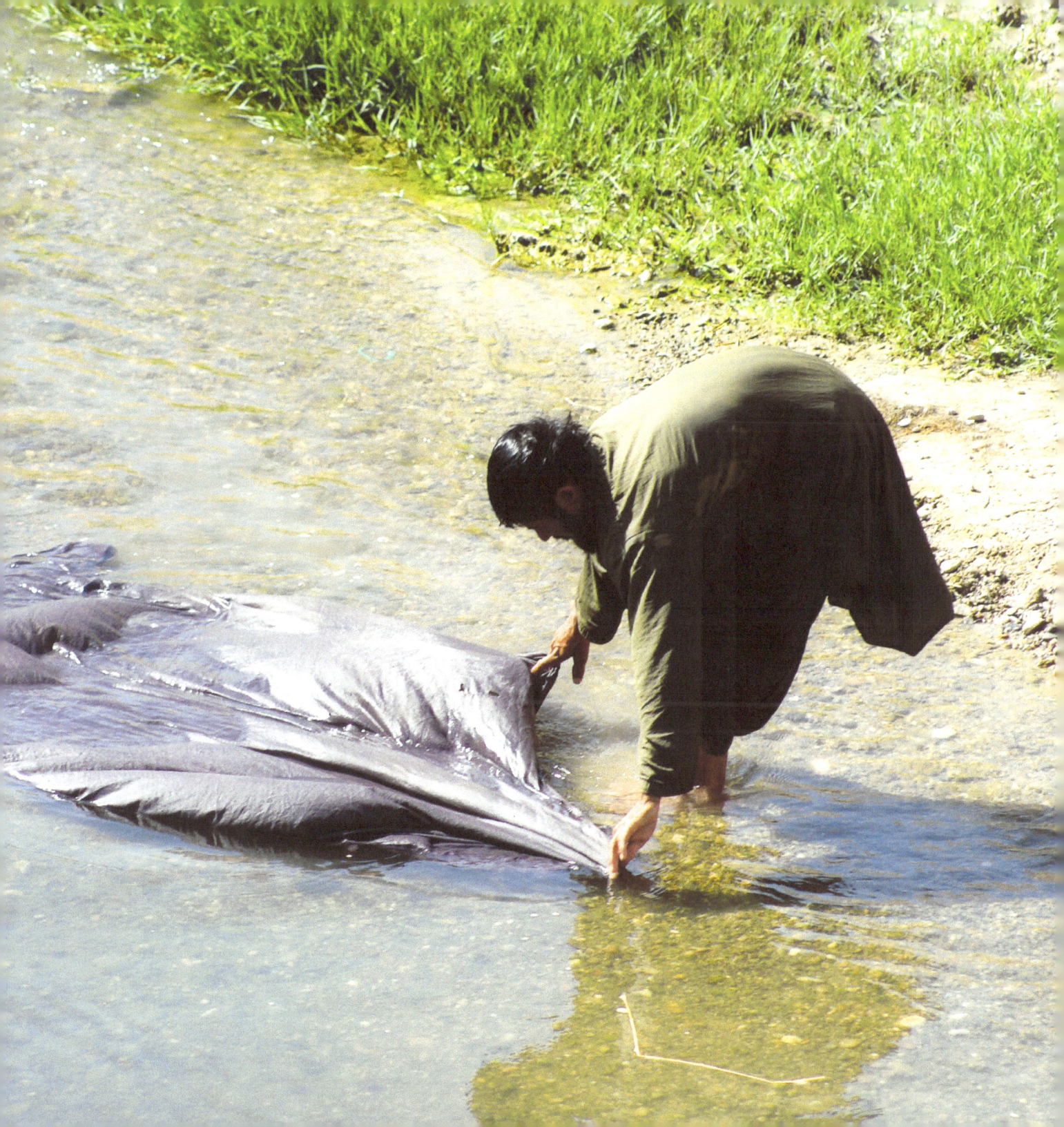

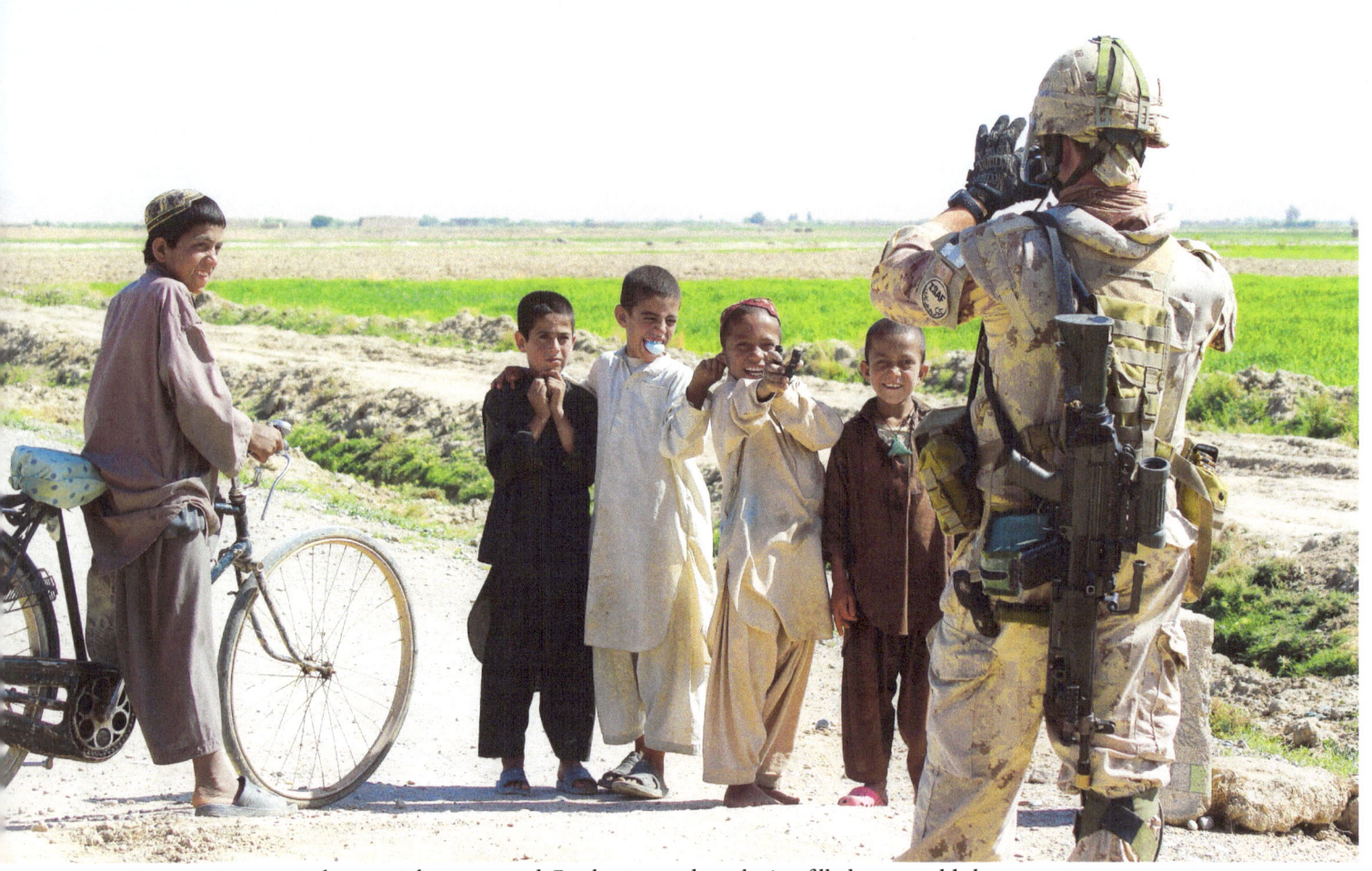

Our mission was to keep watch over a road. Booby-trapped, explosive-filled cars could show up at any moment. Instead of that, young Afghans came to visit us. Aren't children the same everywhere?

During this time, a soldier who was watching over the other direction of the road notified me that intruders were approaching: a brother and sister were walking their second family. The boy appeared suspicious and was clutching the garment of his sister, who, unlike him, appeared unperturbed.

In the distance, the second horizon formed by the desert expanses could be seen. There were certainly nomads there, just like the bodies of their ancestors, who in the past traveled between empires on the Silk Road. The empires of the era have died out. Under the effects of the wind and time, their fortresses and armies have little by little disappeared under the orangey dunes. Nomad peoples are still present in the desert. Their small fabric tents float in the wind, on the desert sand.

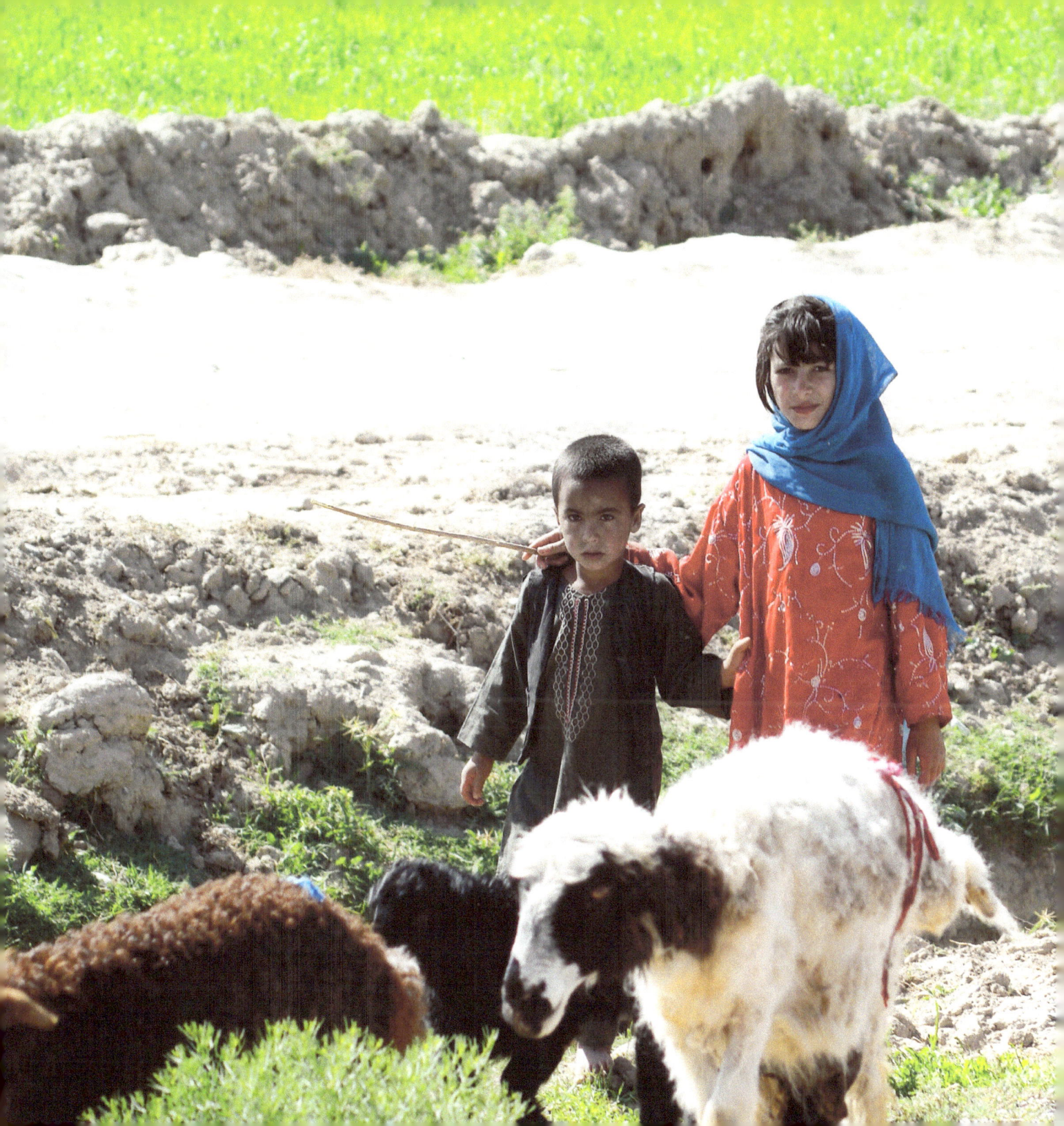

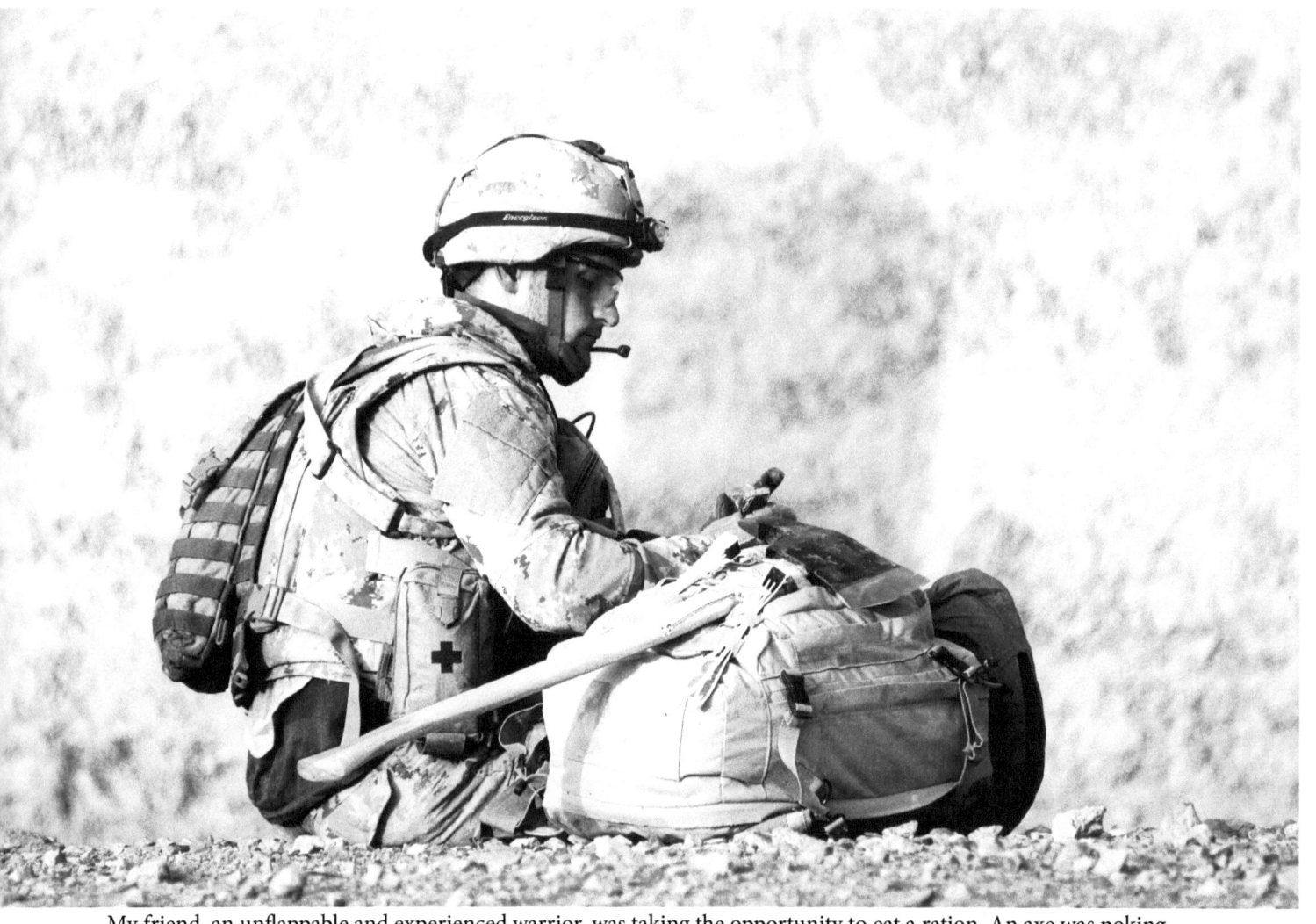

My friend, an unflappable and experienced warrior, was taking the opportunity to eat a ration. An axe was poking through the straps of his bag. This tool, which is unexpected for a soldier, was used to make holes in earthen walls that separated streets. By "digging" our path through the walls, we avoided using a route that could be predicted by the enemy, who undoubtedly would have booby-trapped it.

In the village, we met some Afghan police officers. Afghans have a sixth sense for danger. They are in their country. They were born there. They are familiar with it. So it was reassuring to see them holding a cigarette rather than the handle of their weapon.

Signs that seem insignificant can serve as indicators of a population's state of mind, or of the presence of insurgents in the sector. A seasoned soldier knows how to recognize such indicators. Even if he seems relaxed, a good infantryman is constantly on his guard. A few dozen meters may separate the peaceful encounter with children who come to give us grapes and a meticulously hidden bomb.

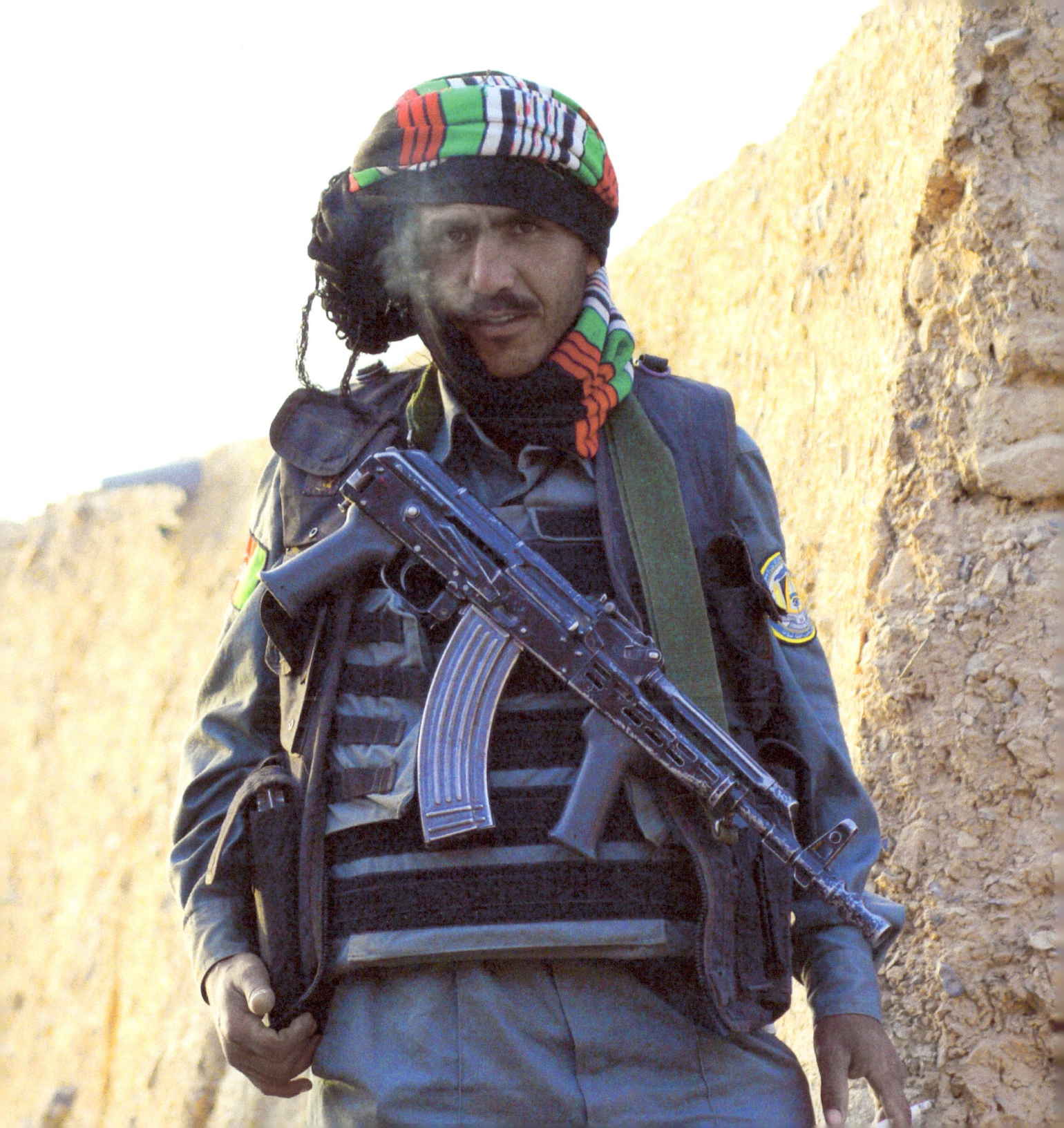

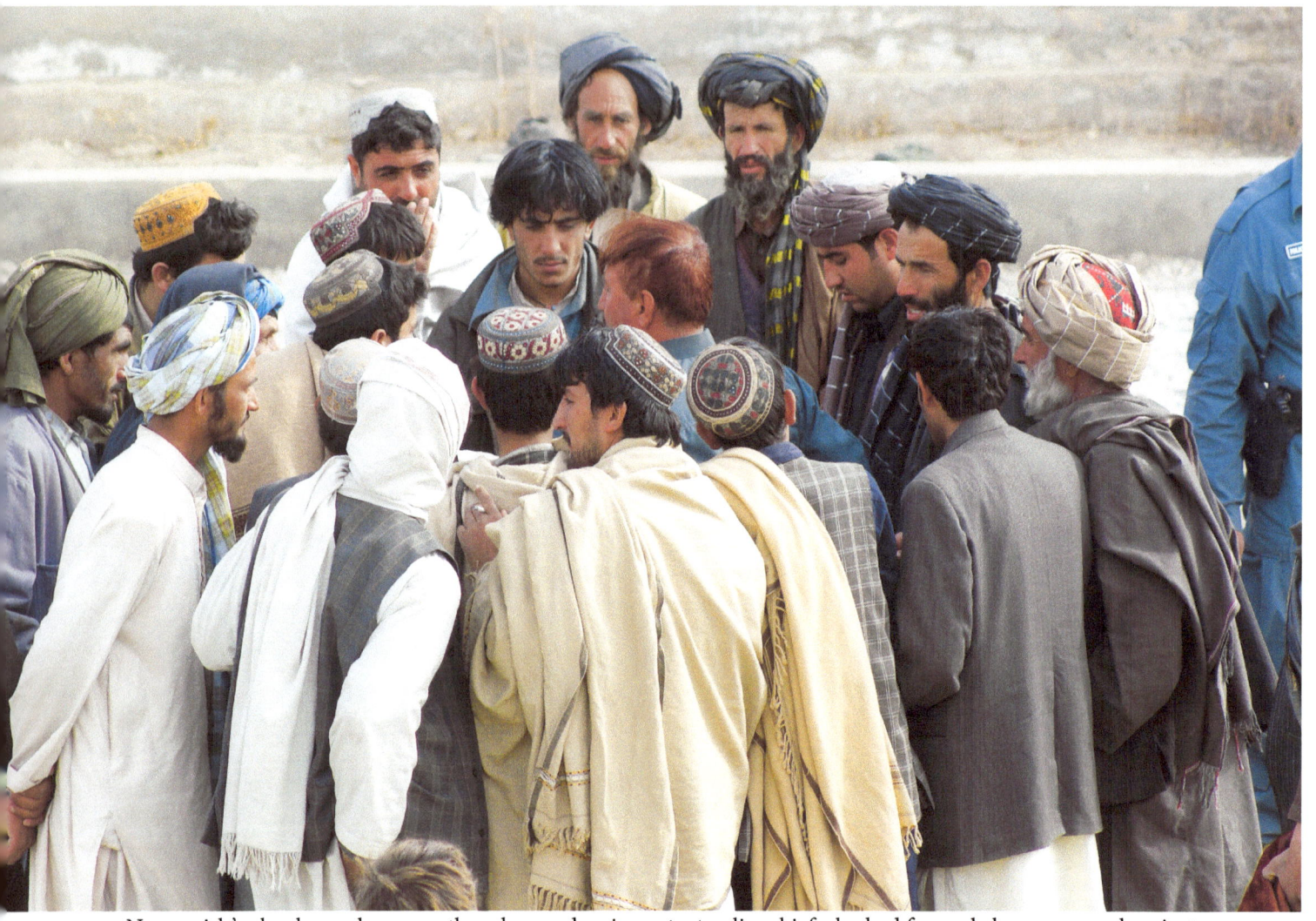

Near a girls' school, people were gathered around an important police chief who had formerly been a general against the Soviets. Afghanistan is a patriarchal society—decisions are made among men.

The villagers were out everywhere in the street. They were watching the patrol pass. Perhaps the young man's shovel had already been used to dig a hole for a bomb? Maybe it had then dug the grave of an insurgent? Or perhaps it had simply been used for work in the fields?

After the patrol stopped, children came up to me. They amused themselves by giving me lessons in religion. To their delight, they had me repeat Muslim prayers. If one can become a Muslim by simply professing one's faith, it can be said that I became a Muslim at least a hundred times that day!

While I was practicing the prayers before the elated children, someone who looked like their older brother came to talk to me. Although he looked like a teenager, he was the father of the boys who were gathered before me.

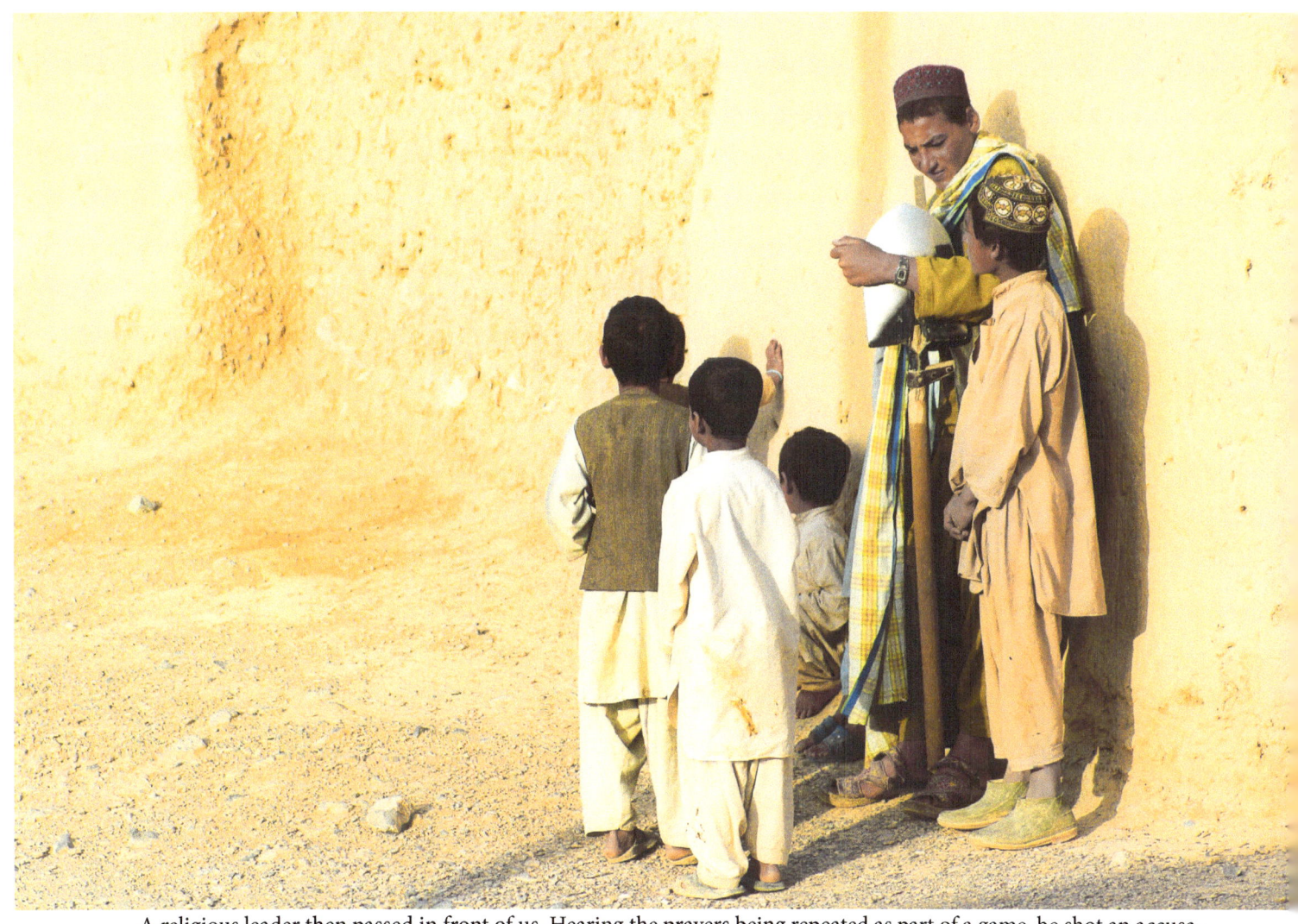

A religious leader then passed in front of us. Hearing the prayers being repeated as part of a game, he shot an accusatory look at the children, but they could not make themselves stop the game. So I continued to repeat the prayers. The man walked away without saying anything, a little smile playing in the corner of his mouth. The children were having a good time with the new mascot I had become.

A man then appeared at the extremity of the patrol. Radio exchanges described the appearance of this new intruder who was determined to infiltrate the group of soldiers. His hands were holding a large metallic object that shone in the sun. We searched him quickly. Then he passed through the middle of the patrol, handing out tea in small glasses with golden decoration. I could not have gotten better service in a luxury hotel! Although the liquid was hot, the beverage of hospitality could not have been more refreshing!

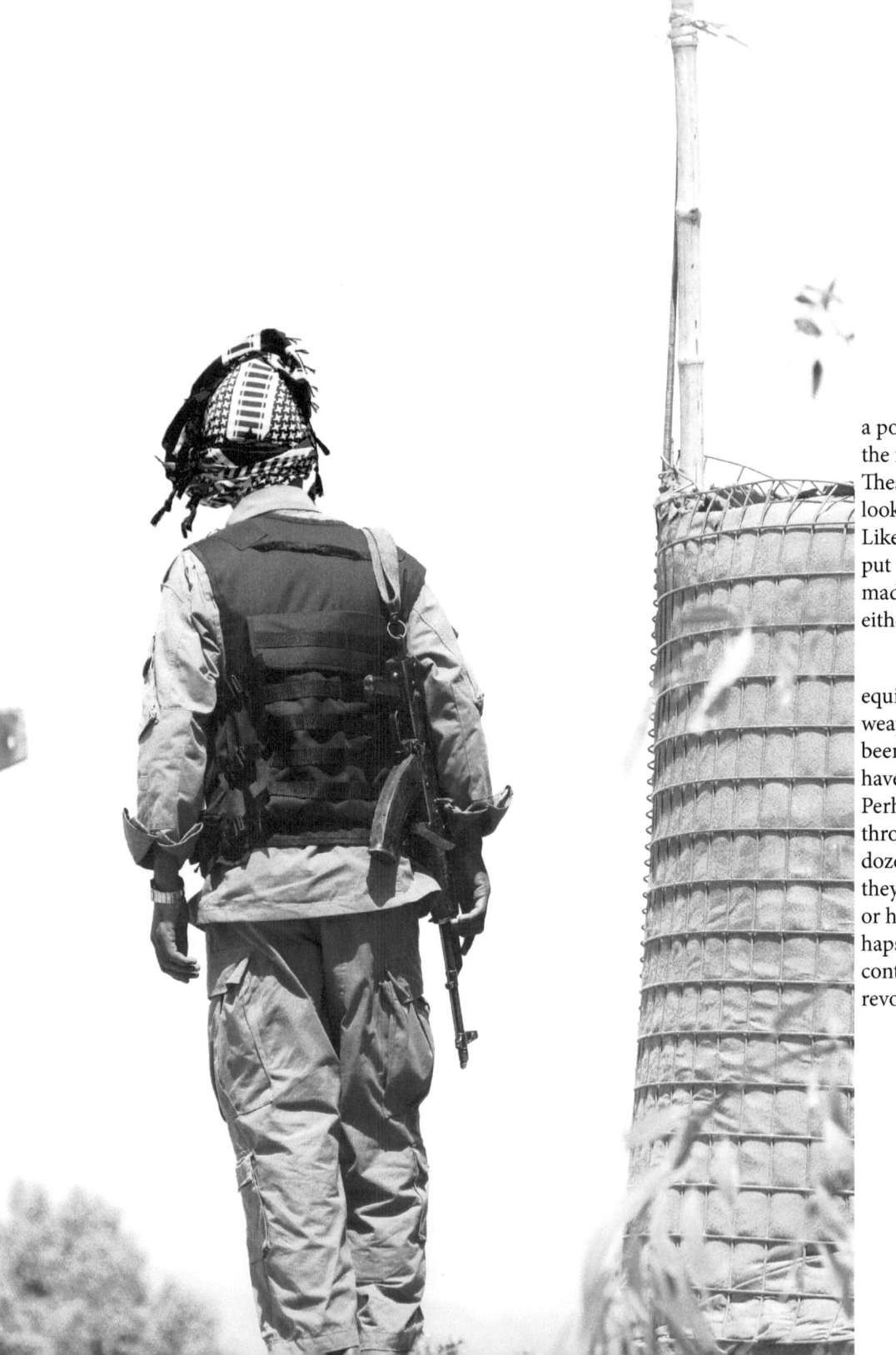

The patrol was approaching a police station. The mesh of the fortifications was visible. These walls were made of what looked like collapsible baskets. Like Lego blocks, once filled, put together, and piled up, they made the base of a fortification, either large or small.

The police officers were equipped with old Soviet weapons. If these weapons had been a living soldier, they would have been covered with medals. Perhaps they had already been through several wars and dozens of shootouts? Perhaps they had already killed Afghans or hardened enemy troops? Perhaps they had fought on several continents, over the course of revolutions and conflicts?

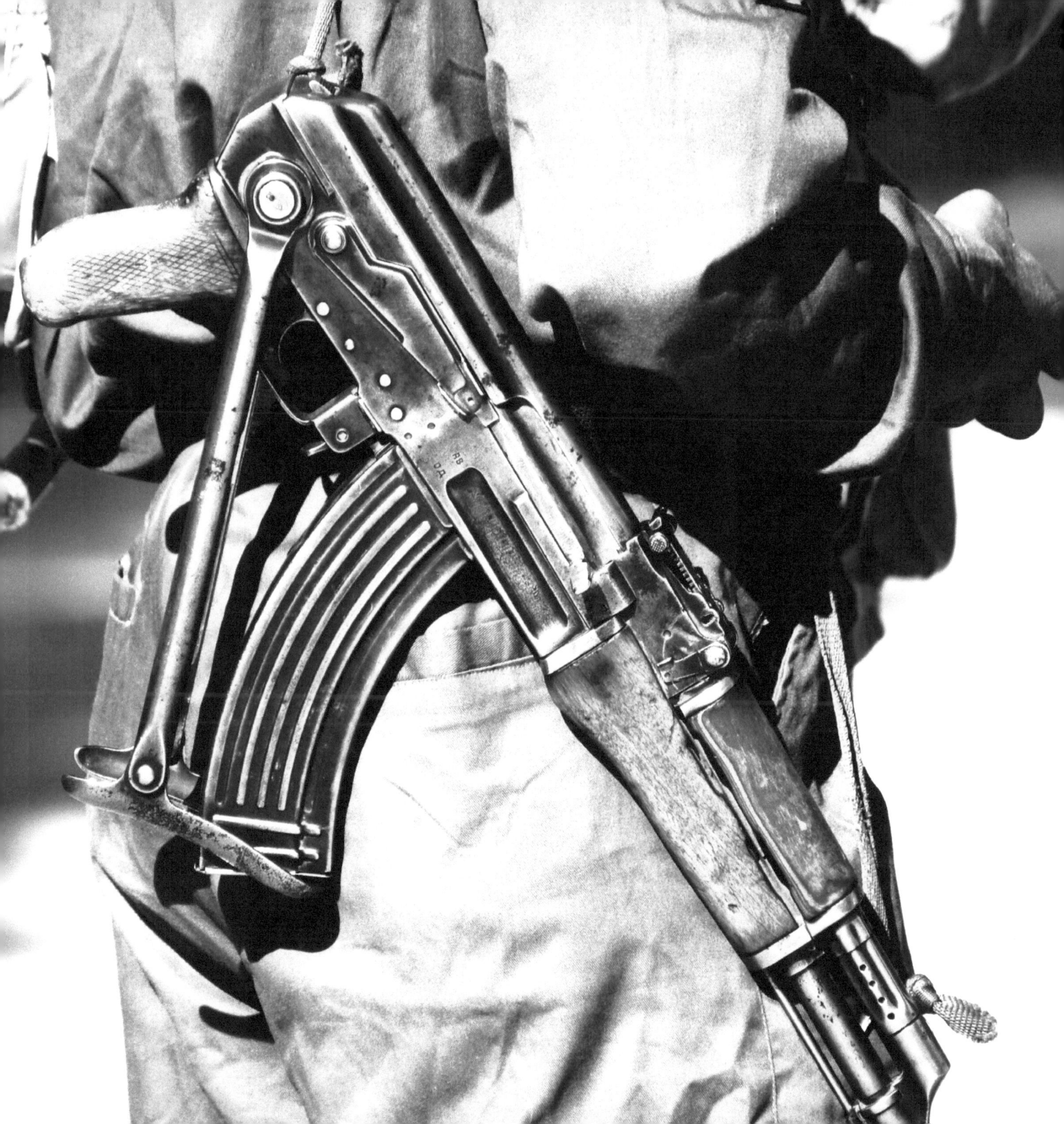

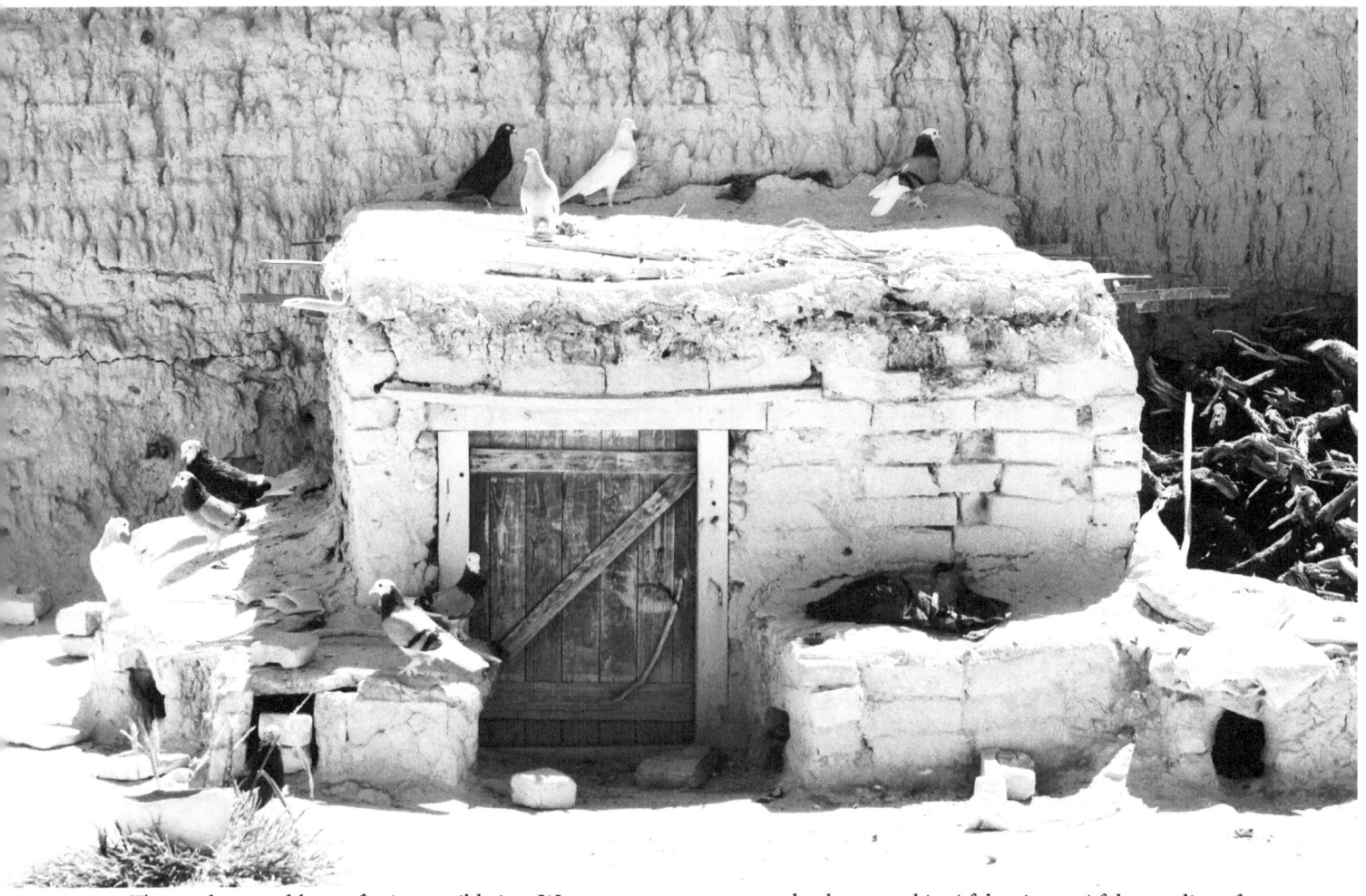

Things that would pass for impossible in a Western country are completely normal in Afghanistan. Afghan police officers had put a dovecote in a police station. I could not resist going to photograph this scene. While I was on my way there, an unpleasant surprise was waiting for me. A dog jumped on me, savagely trying to bite me. Fortunately, I was wearing protective gear. I eventually managed to calm this loyal and effective guard.

According to what the occupants of the site told us, the animal was also used in dogfights. I would bet that the poor thing never collected the benefits of its victories.

The dog probably died a few months later, in a fight against a younger dog. Once it got hurt and became useless, its masters undoubtedly abandoned it in a field or on the side of a road—wasting a precious bullet for this was out of the question. A similar thing had happened to the dog of another police station that we were familiar with. This is how things go in Afghanistan, like in the rest of the world. A person's true character is revealed in his treatment of those who have nothing to give him.

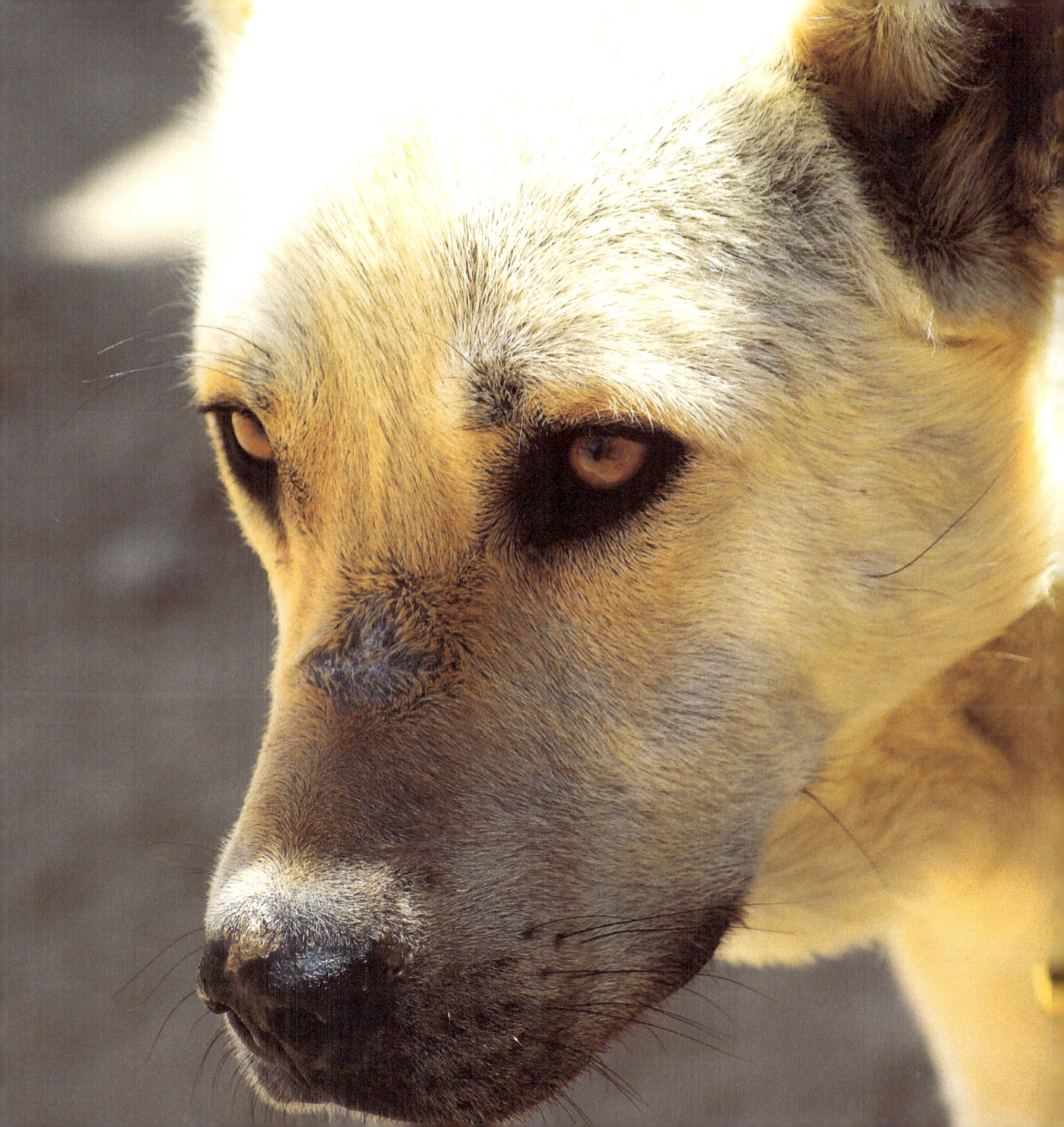

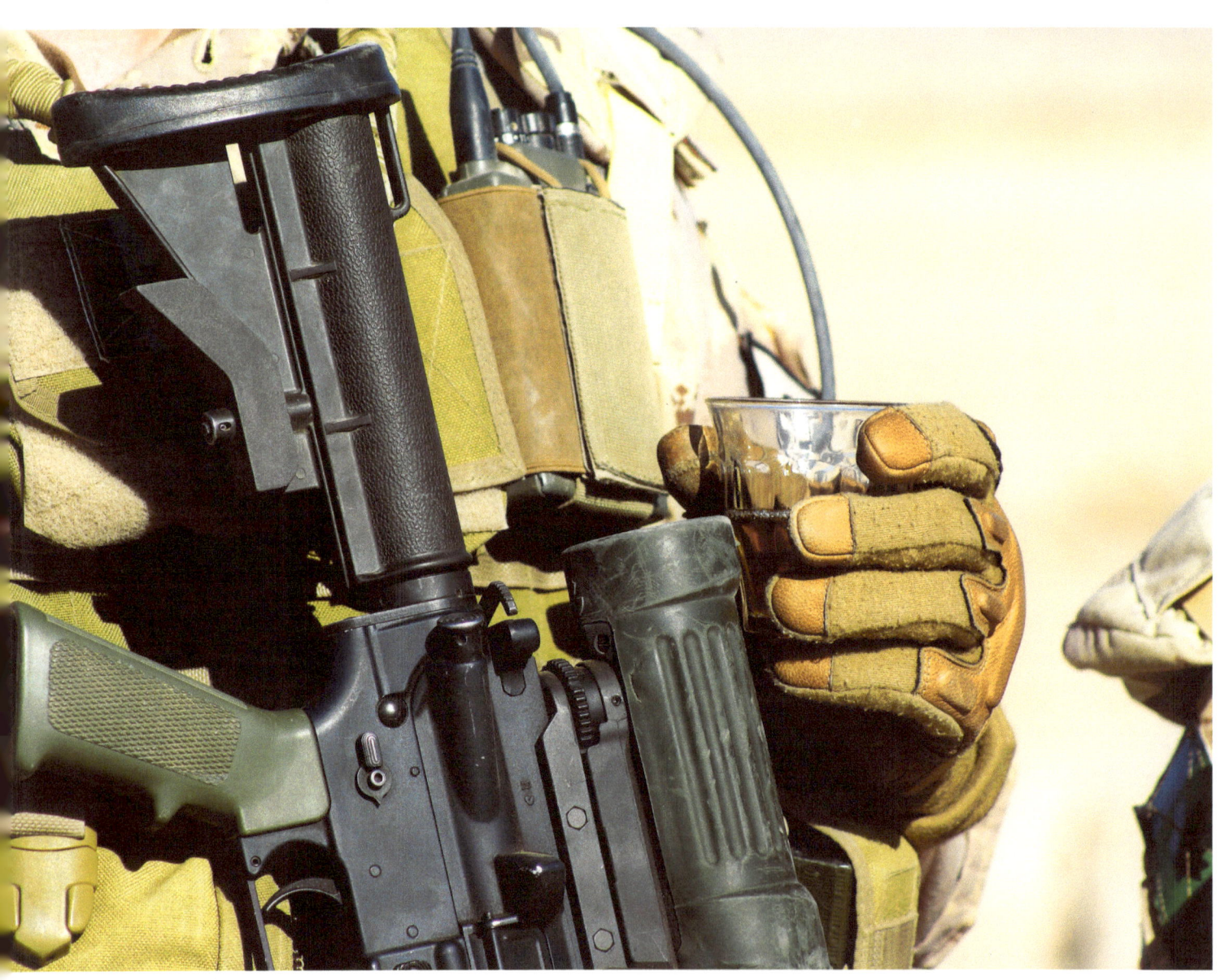

This is how war was won in Afghanistan: a loaded weapon and a brimming cup of tea; a warrior's spirit and gestures of friendship.

At one point I ran into an officer who often worked with the Afghans. I asked him to describe his job for me. He replied, "Tea drinker!"

Because of my appearance and coloring, people in Afghanistan often asked me if I was Muslim. I answered, "I'm neither Christian nor Muslim. Or rather, I'm both Christian and Muslim. I derive wisdom wherever it exists, whether it is in the Bible, Koran, or the simple words of a small child. I have a Koran at home, right next to a candle I like to light on rainy days."

Strangely, people would simply answer, "Thank you!"

In this war-torn country, I met people from different nations: Canada, America, Afghanistan. I talked to Christians and Muslims, but to even more human beings!

I remember how I was once discussing religion with my Afghan interpreter. Over the course of the missions, he had become my friend. He was saying that just like the Koran, the Bible was a sacred writing and that if he saw it, he would kiss it. Smiling, I presented to him a small book that I always carried on patrols, in a pocket to the left of some magazines and grenades. Closing his eyes and without hesitating, he kissed the dusty surface of what he considered a holy book.

I dream about the day when I will go unarmed to drink tea in Afghanistan. We will no longer see fighter planes flying. We will no longer hear combat helicopters whirring. Blood will stop flowing. And teapots will abundantly pour the drink of friendship.

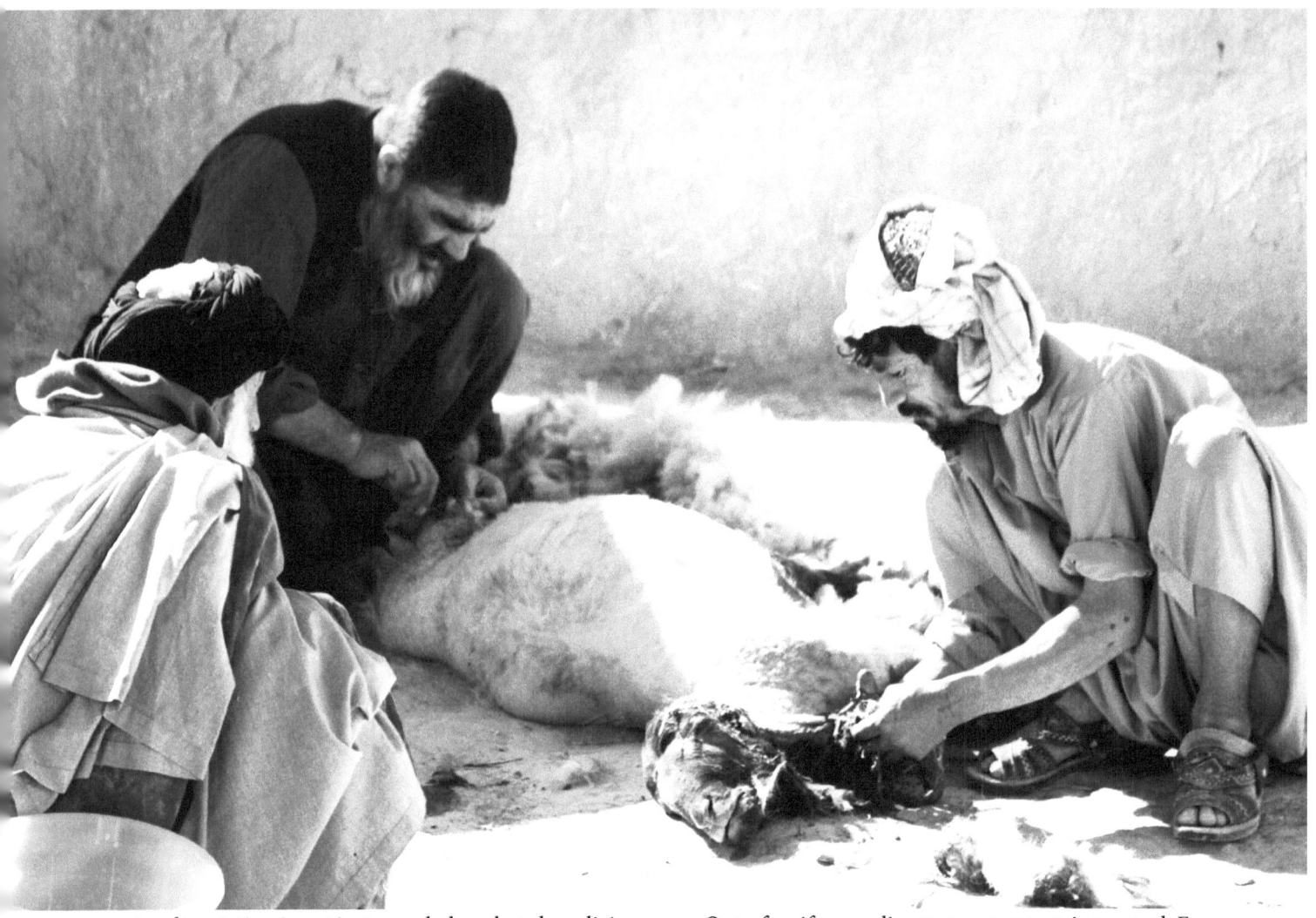

A police station is not just a workplace, but also a living space. Out-of-uniform policemen were preparing a meal. For meat to be considered "halal," that is, acceptable for a Muslim to eat, the criteria are relatively simple: the animal cannot be stunned, it must be facing Mecca, and a prayer must be recited while it is being slaughtered. This ritual is a lot like the one performed by a hunter out of respect for the animal he has just killed.

The police chief of this station liked me. I spoke his language, Pashto. Sometimes we went to his home. I enjoyed talking to him. He always welcomed me with a courteous smile. At the end of my stay in his country, he was imprisoned at our military base. He had changed allegiances, having decided to help the Taliban. To this day, even if I try to hate him, I cannot.

I remember another insurgent who had tried to kill my companions and me with a rocket-propelled grenade. He had missed us by so much that at first I could not believe that he was aiming at us. Perhaps he had poor vision? An American patrol that was passing through the area had managed to capture him. Following procedure, his captors had put a bag

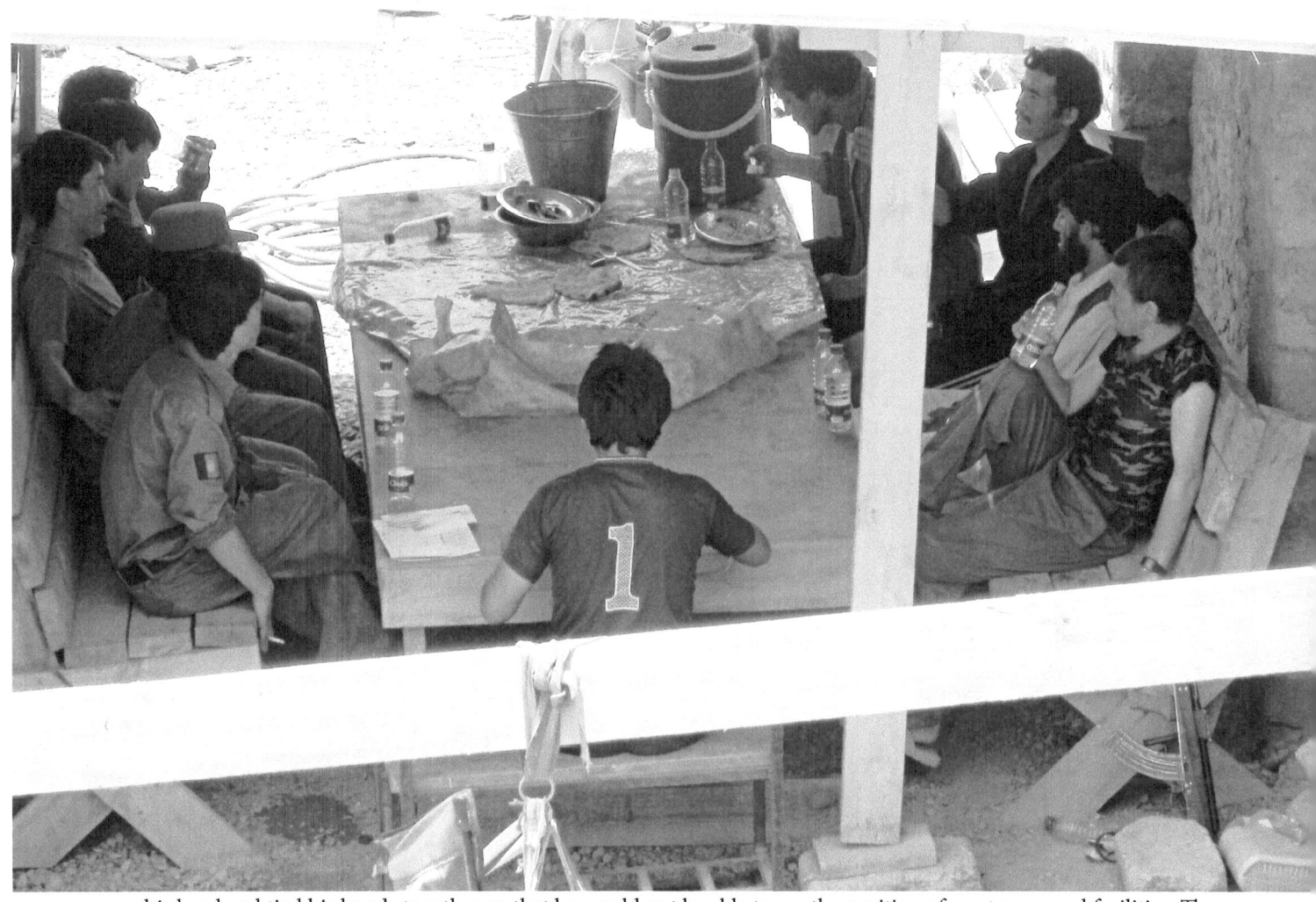

over his head and tied his hands together so that he would not be able to see the position of our troops and facilities. The detainee had then been handed over to an Afghan police station that was on the way back. This was the practice of the American army. The Taliban are treated like criminals who must be turned over to the police.

While we were waiting for the convoy to come pick us up, we were in charge of the security of the small fortified police camp. During that time, below the observation tower and dressed in white stood the man who had tried to kill me a few hours earlier. He was now eating peacefully, protected by soldiers. A bit later, I went down to talk to him. He was praying to his two dwellings to the west. Mecca was far away. His village was only a few kilometers away. Would he see it again?

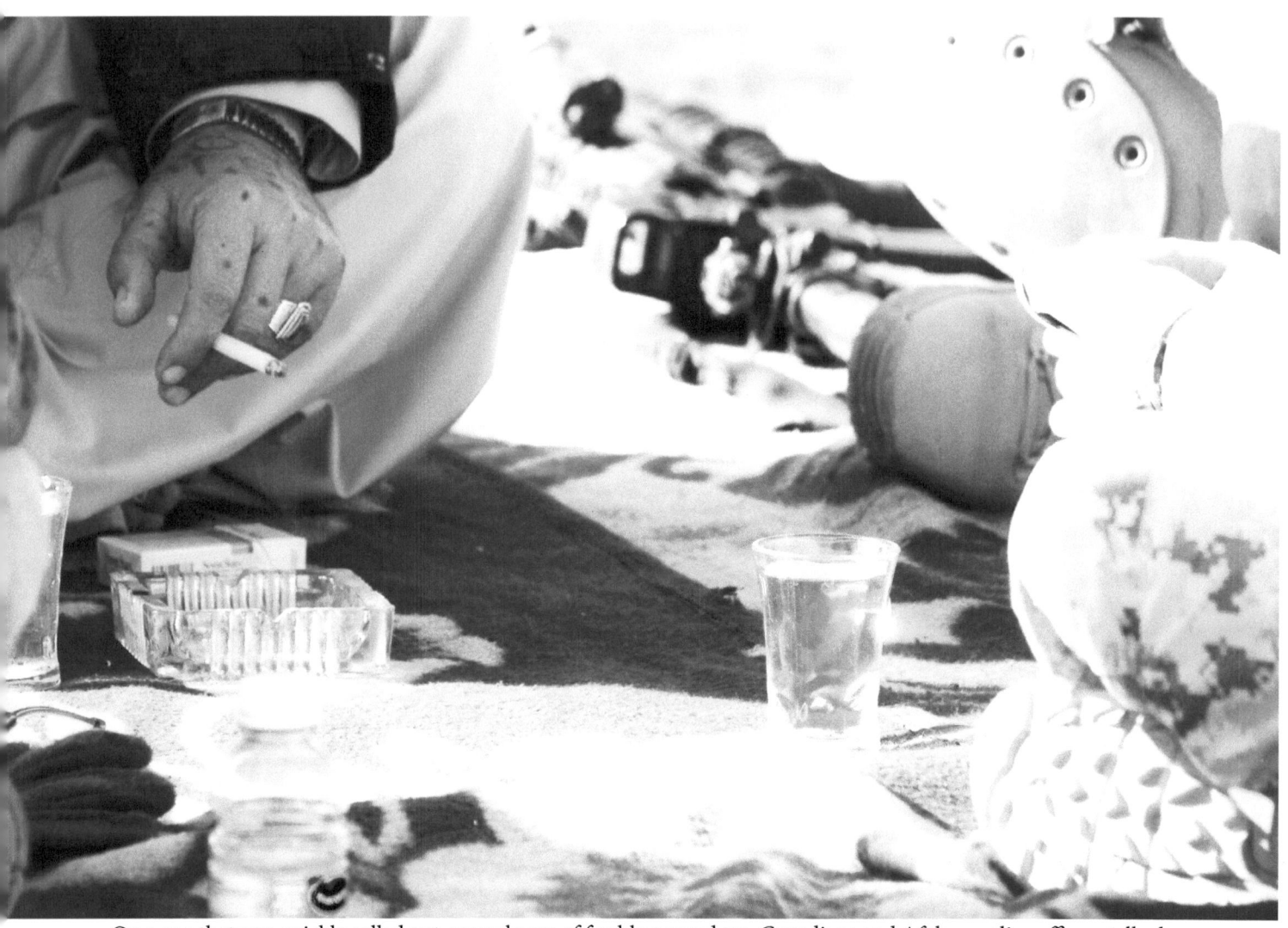

On a rug that was quickly rolled out, over glasses of freshly poured tea, Canadians and Afghan police officers talked. This single photograph reveals the distinct mentalities of two distant countries. On the one hand, a soldier who was avidly taking notes even before drinking the beverage of hospitality. On the other, a police officer who was tranquilly smoking his cigarette. On the right, a soldier who had kept his combat equipment and knee guards on. On the left, a police officer who was hard to ruffle and who had not bothered to put on his uniform.

I remember one particular police officer. He bore the signs of a proud and competent soldier. He always wore his uniform impeccably. His bearing was straight and professional. In front of his police station, he talked to everyone who passed by, meticulously inspecting many vehicles. After a half hour of work before the population, he went back into the police station looking disgruntled. This young police officer came from northern Afghanistan. He said to us, "I hate Afghans from the south. We northerners want to progress."

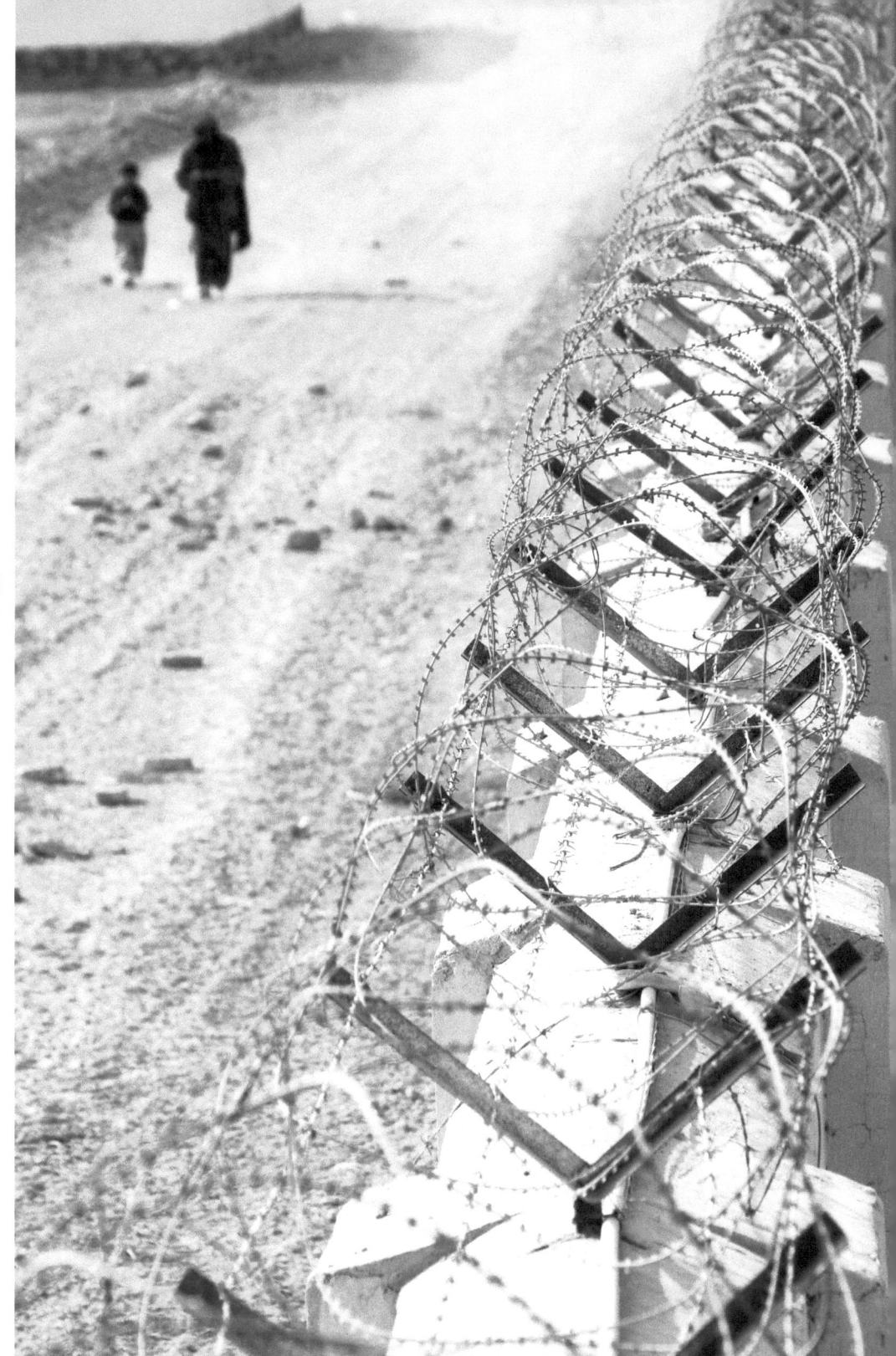

We had to return to our "home away from home." Having arrived at our location near fortified walls, a father and son were walking in peace, accustomed and seemingly indifferent to the military presence.

Inside the base, surprises were awaiting us. Some Afghan cats we had been sheltering were stationed near some spent shells.

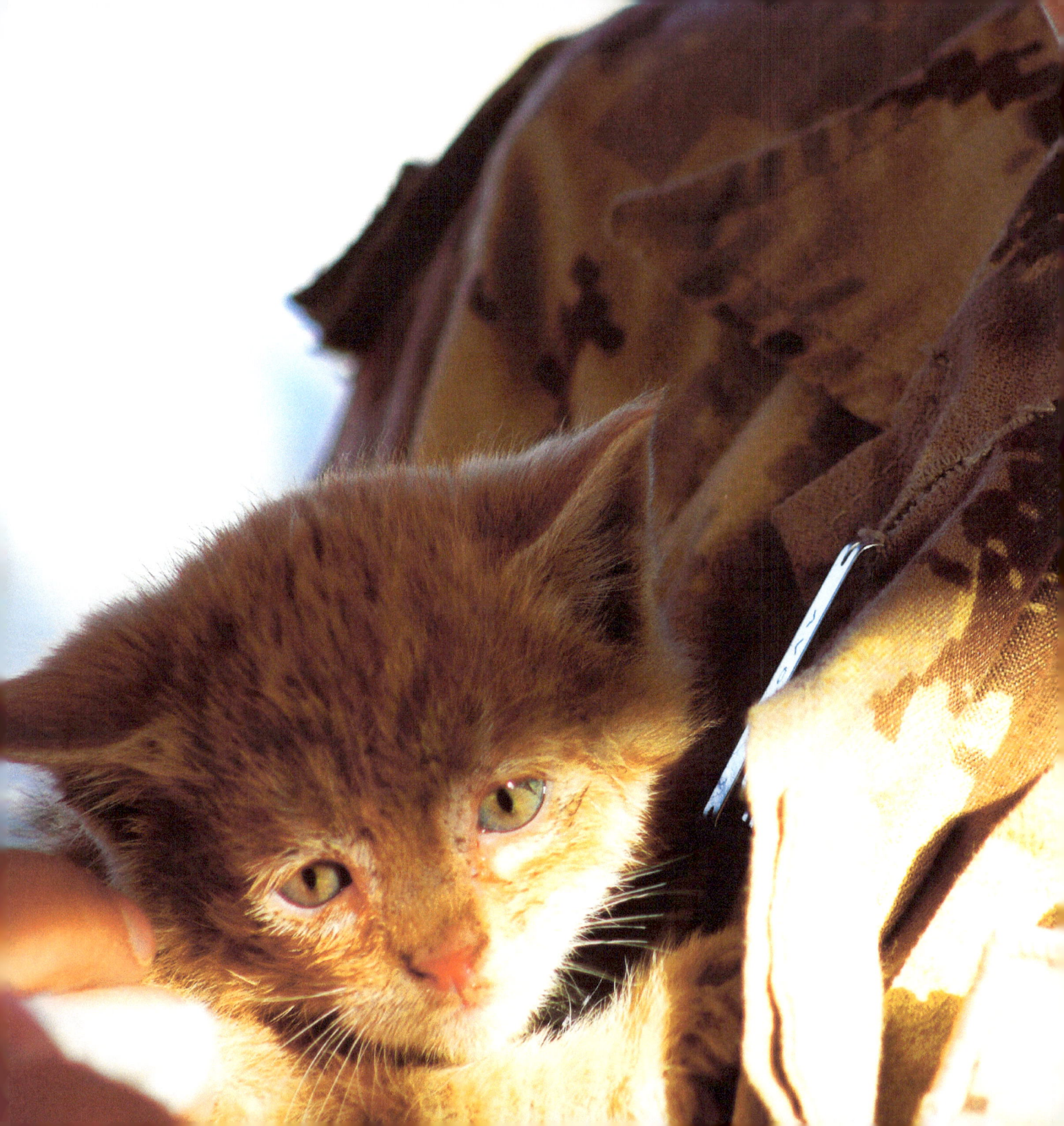

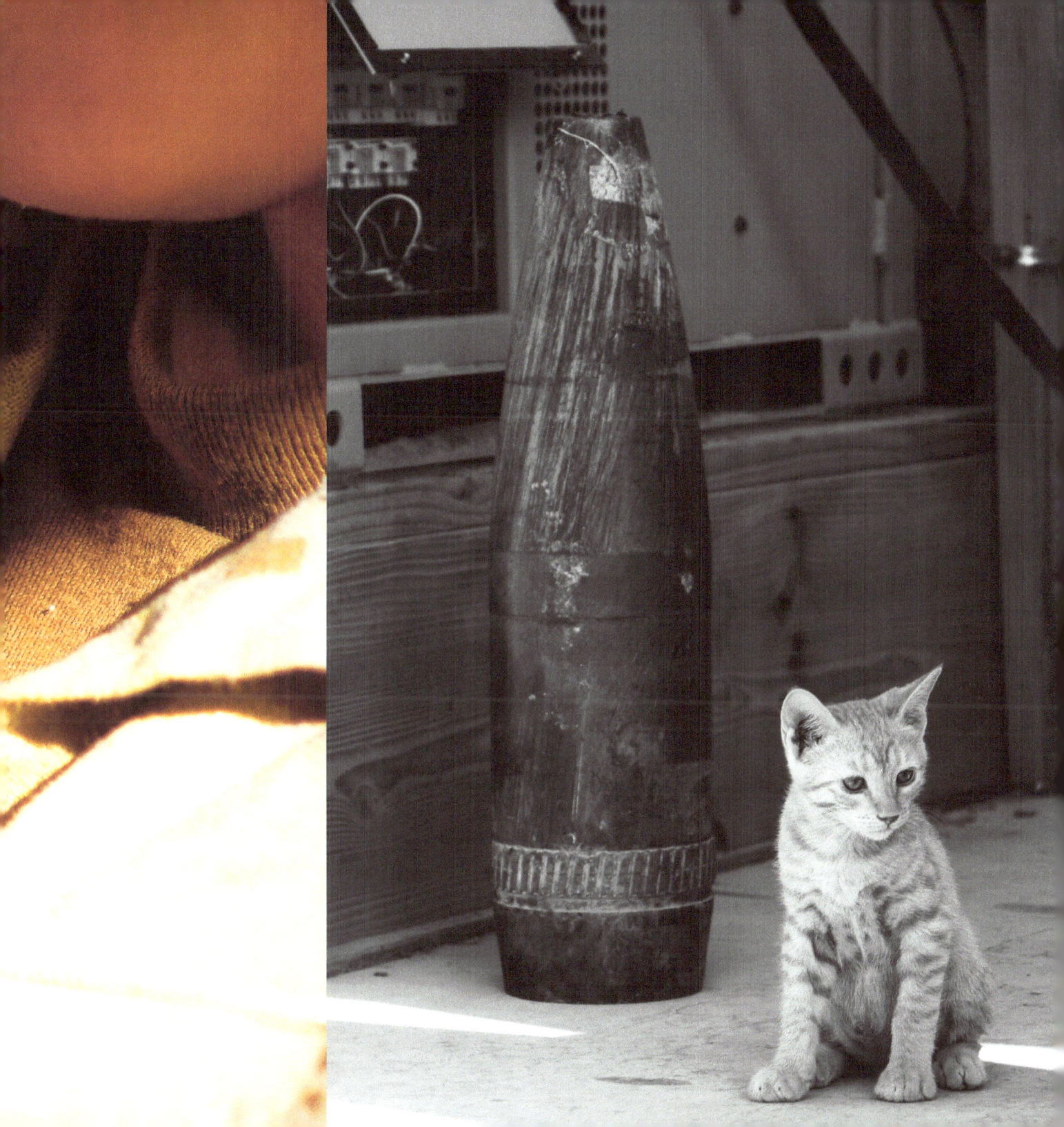

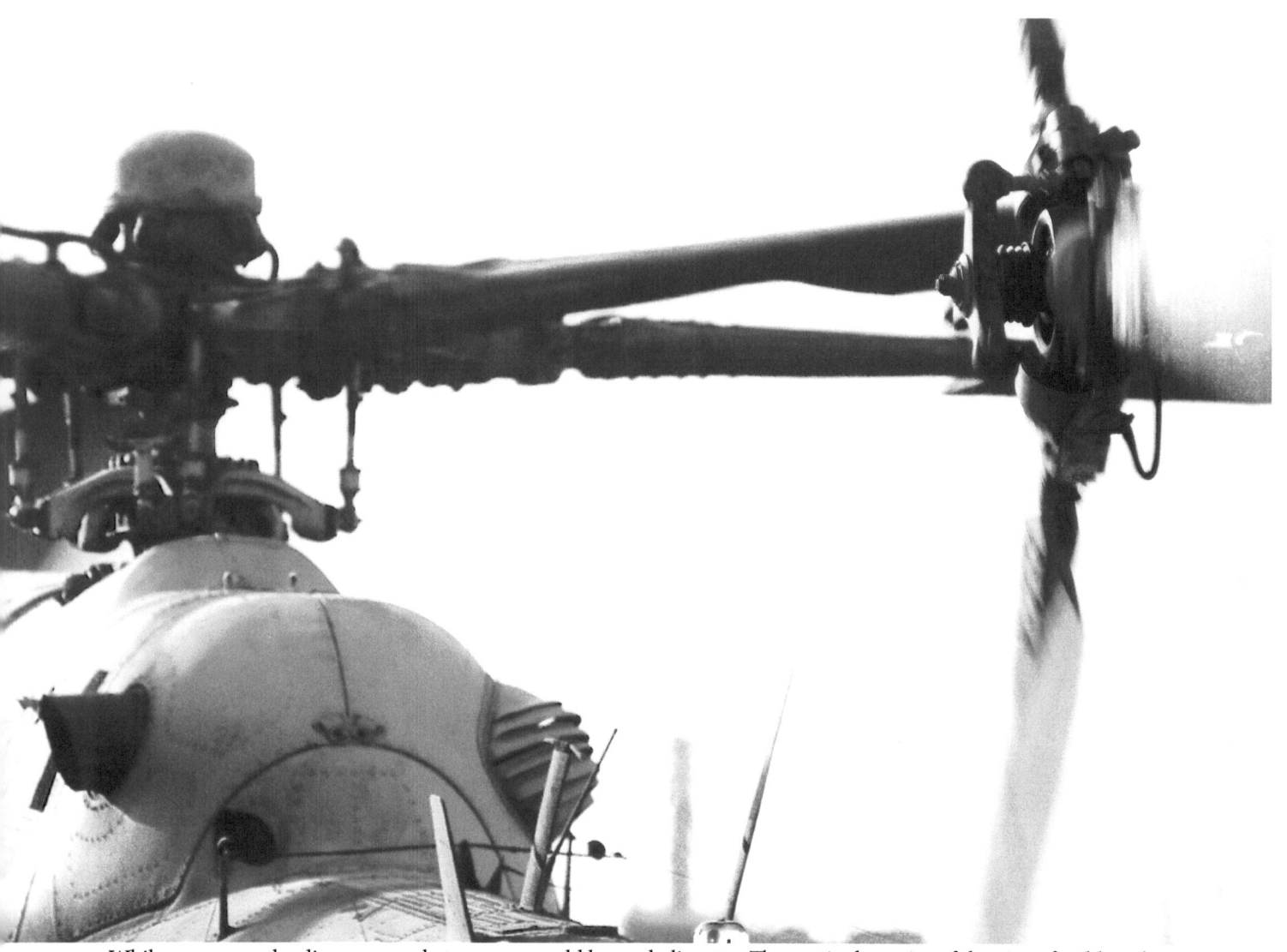

While we were unloading our combat gear, we could hear a helicopter. The particular noise of the aircraft told us that this was a truly unusual helicopter.

It was the mail! Soldiers would soon unwrap and taste candy sent by their families and read letters written by their loved ones. Some would find out about the imminent arrival of their daughter or son, while others would learn of the end of a relationship.

I, however, was waiting for a large package. Weeks earlier, I had arranged for a television to be delivered to me on the other side of the world. After building a small piece of wooden furniture, I set my new toy up in my tent, above a fur that was spread on my bed, under the Christmas lights, and near an Afghan scarf that stood in for a tapestry. My improvised room made more than one soldier jealous.

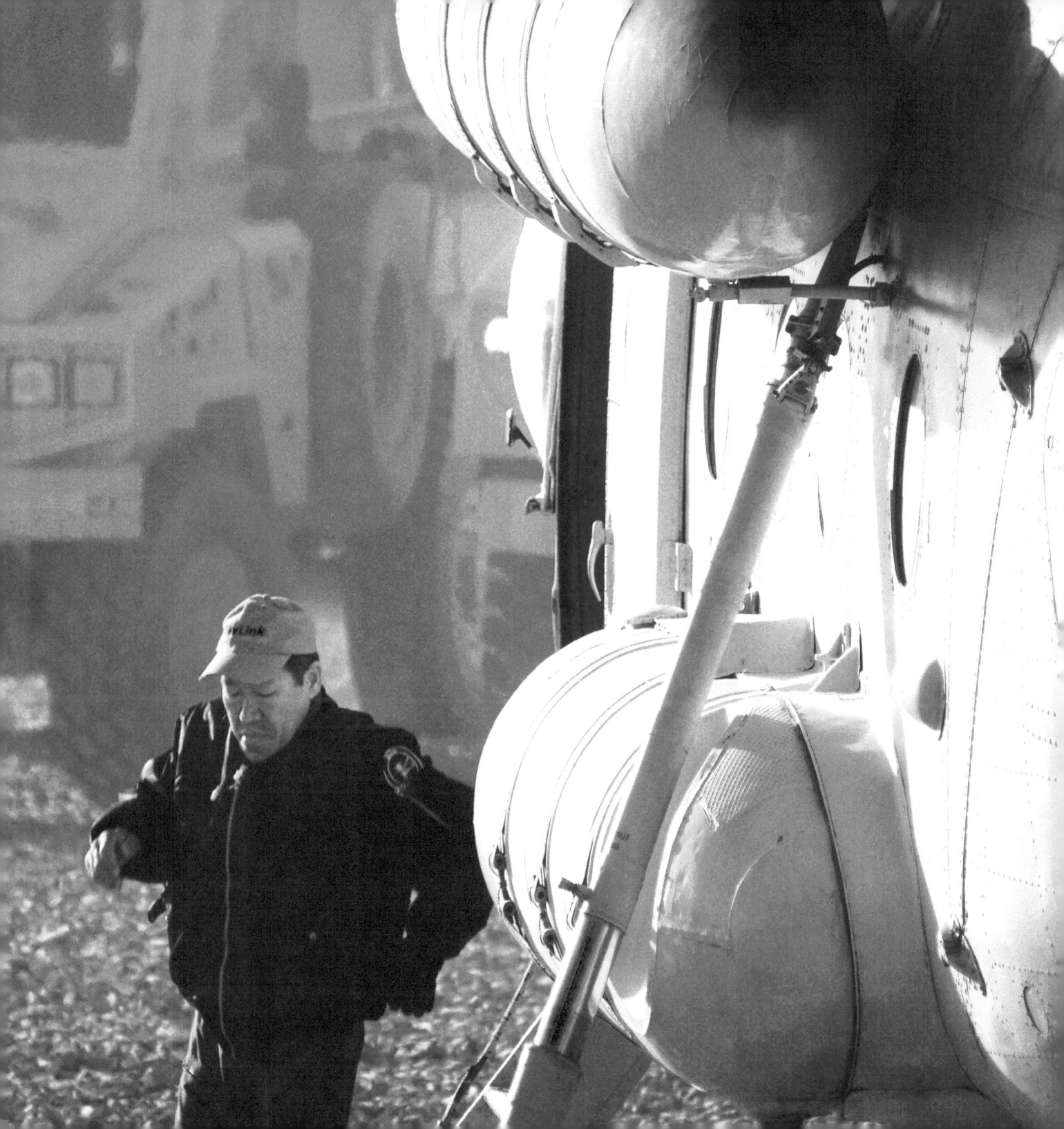

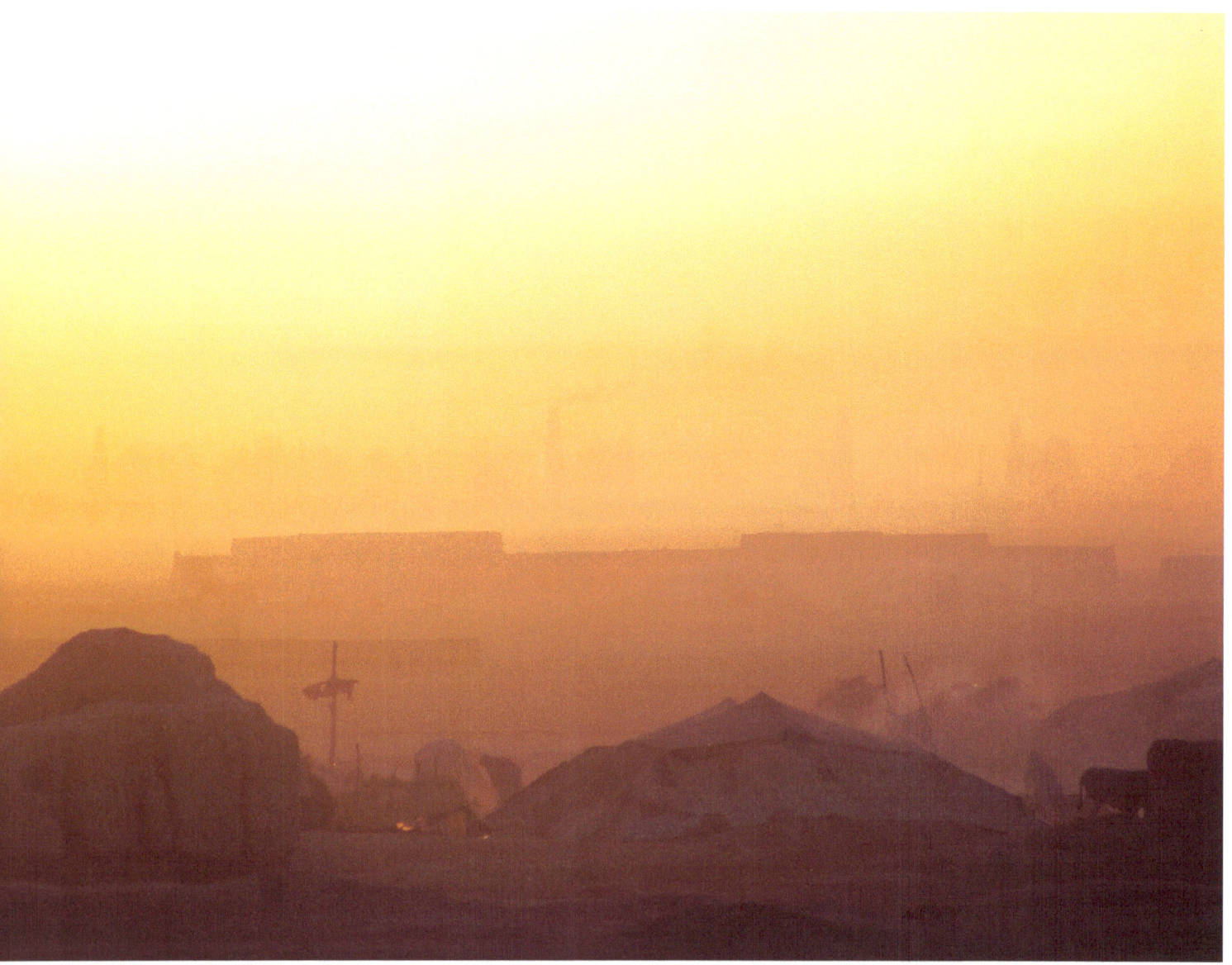

That morning, there was no patrol on the schedule. Nevertheless, we had to take turns guarding the camp. In the winter, mornings are chilly for the soldier on guard. Next to the omnipresent weapon, hot coffee was fortifying. The sound of the prayers that reached us transformed the dawn into a moment of calm and meditation. The smoke that could be seen in the distance came from plastic bottles and other refuse the nomads burned in order to keep warm. While we were trying to get rid of them, a few dozen meters away, people wanted to take possession of them.

I was surprised to find myself jealous of these nomads. I would have liked to live like them for a few months. Their life seemed simple to me! In this war-torn country, everything was imprinted with spirituality.

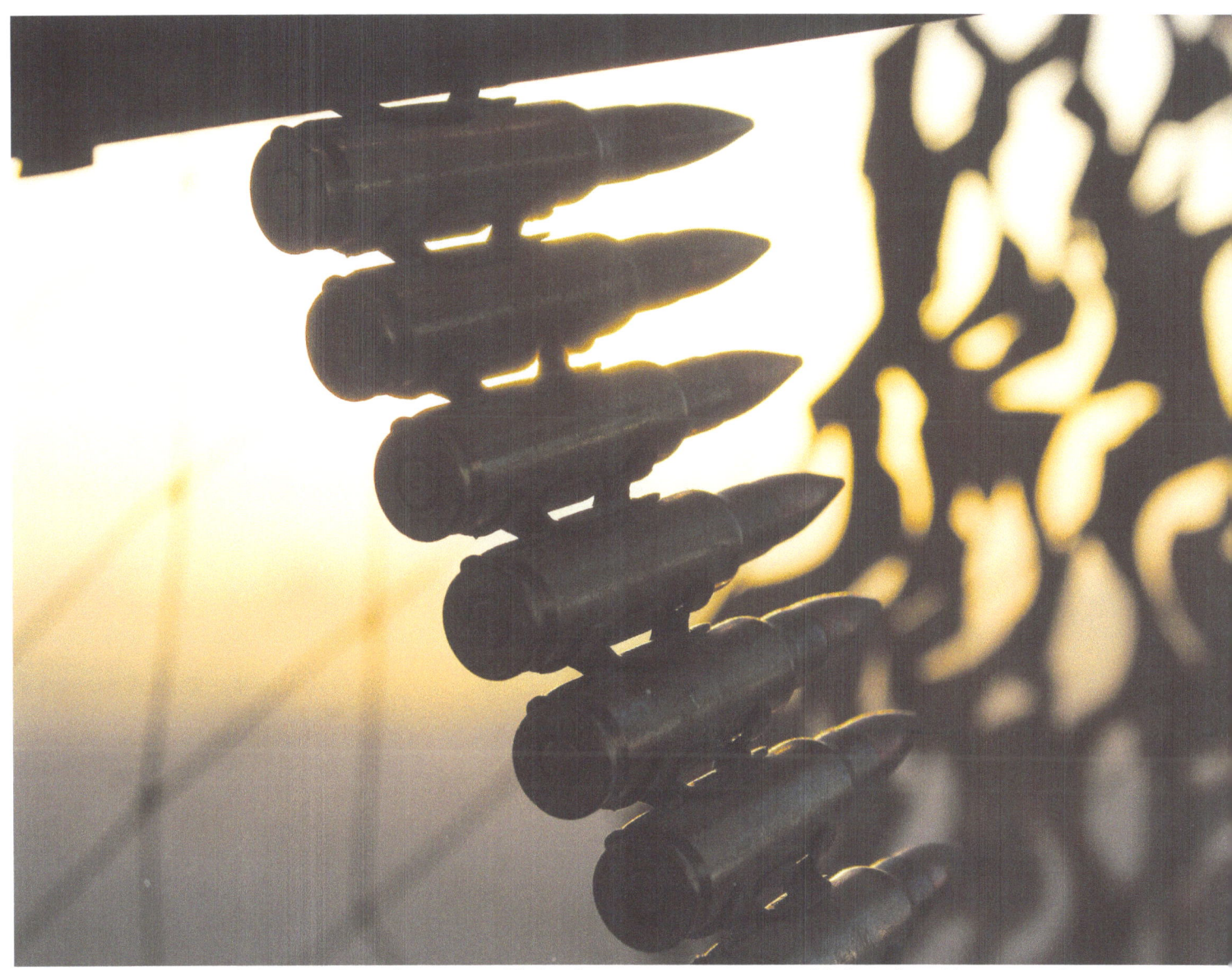

A cartridge belt. Grenades and magazines filled with ammunition are inseparable from the soldier on patrol. In my case, so were the little gifts. I liked giving candy and pencils to children. They were small tokens, but they never missed the mark. The effect was instantaneous: pacifying, disarming!

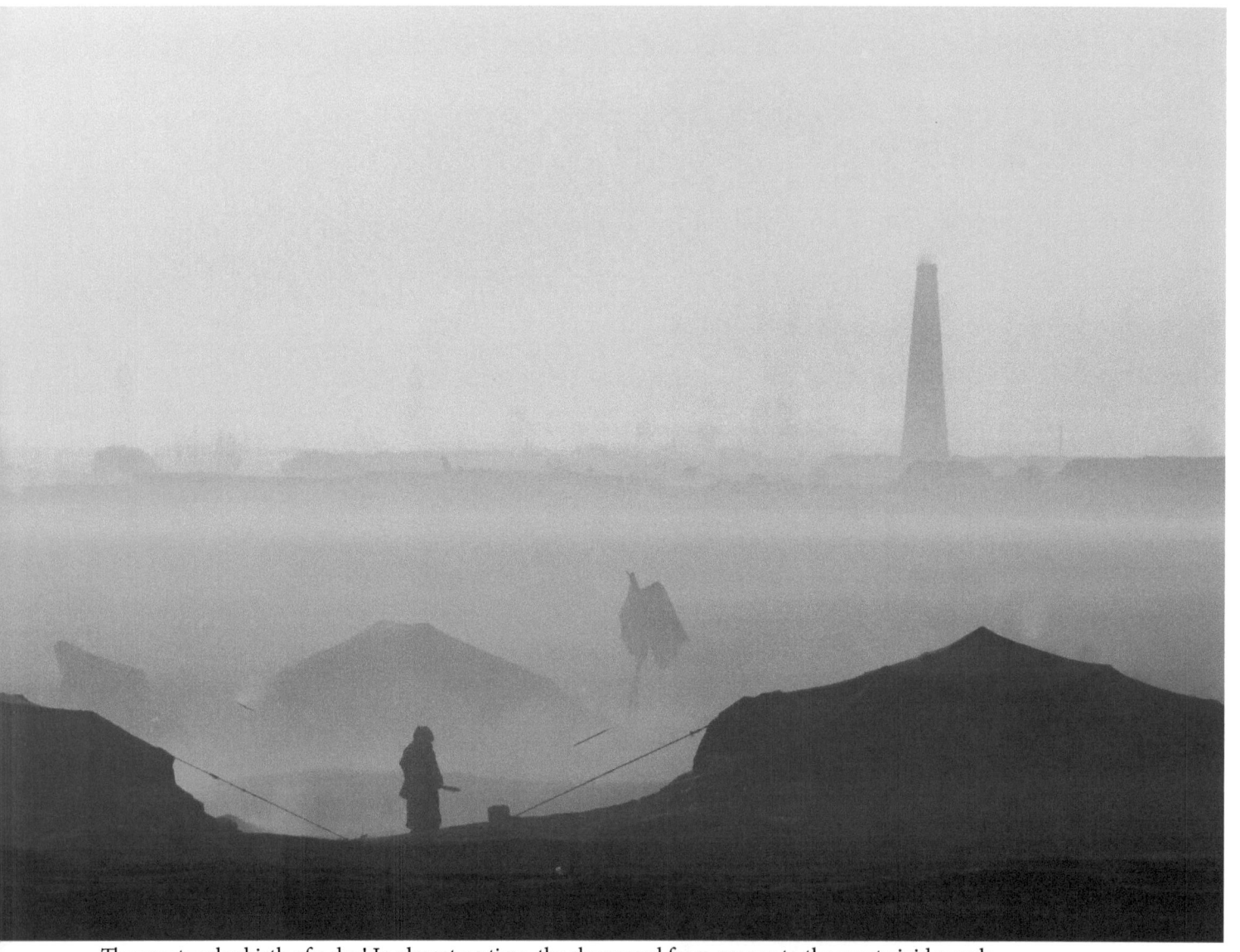

The spectacular birth of a day! In almost no time, the sky passed from orange to the most vivid purple.

The Taliban could not enter the defensive perimeter. I would not have been able to pass unarmed into enemy territory. Fortunately, the morning's beauty had just visited all of us indiscriminately.

As soldiers, our function was to prevent the enemy from intruding and attacking. And yet, an unarmed ginger cat often passed between the edge of the barbed wire, obliviously coming and going between combatants who were trying to kill one another. I dare hope that a few hundred meters from my observation post, a Taliban was also feeding a young cat, all the while admiring the beauty of the rising sun. As long as people are able to recognize beauty, there will be hope for humanity.

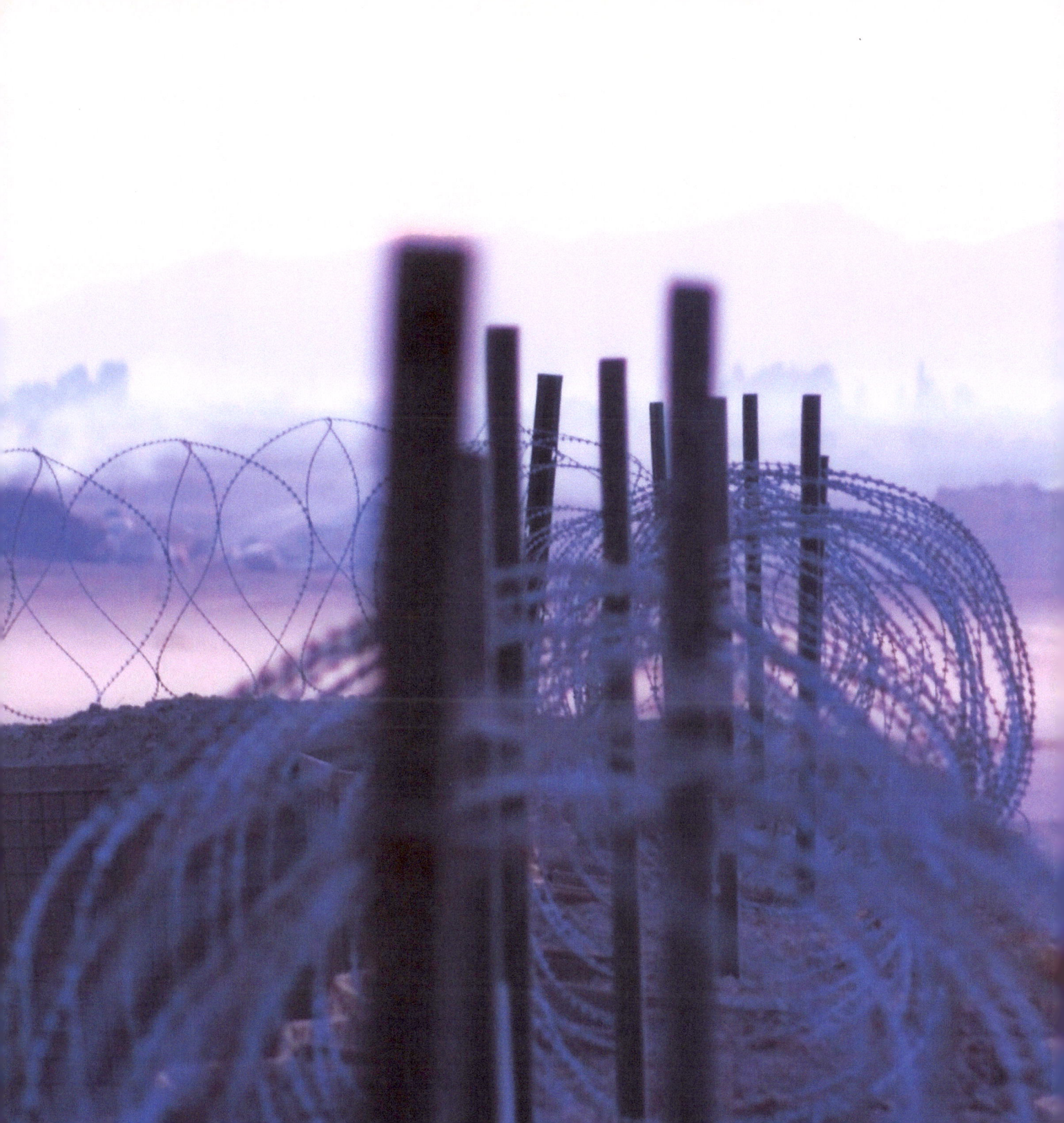

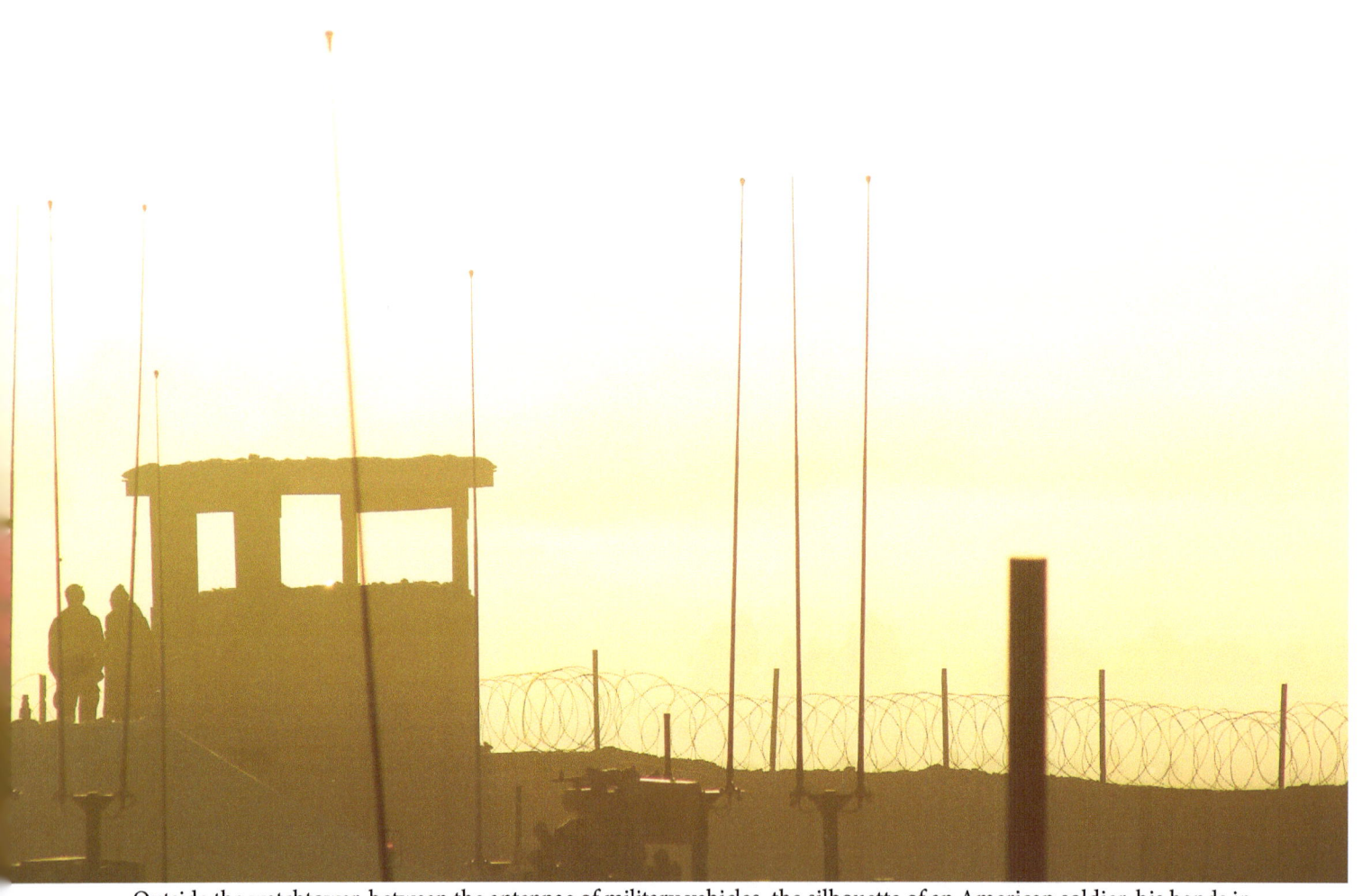

Outside the watchtower, between the antennae of military vehicles, the silhouette of an American soldier, his hands in his pockets, and that of an Afghan soldier wrapped in a blanket. They were talking to a shepherd who was passing near the fortified walls.

A few moments later, an Afghan police officer brought the first tea of the day. On the Thermos, between the silver glints, I could discern the German colors. How had this object ended up in the hands of this police officer? Was it a story of business, war, or friendship? I would never know. I could only imagine!

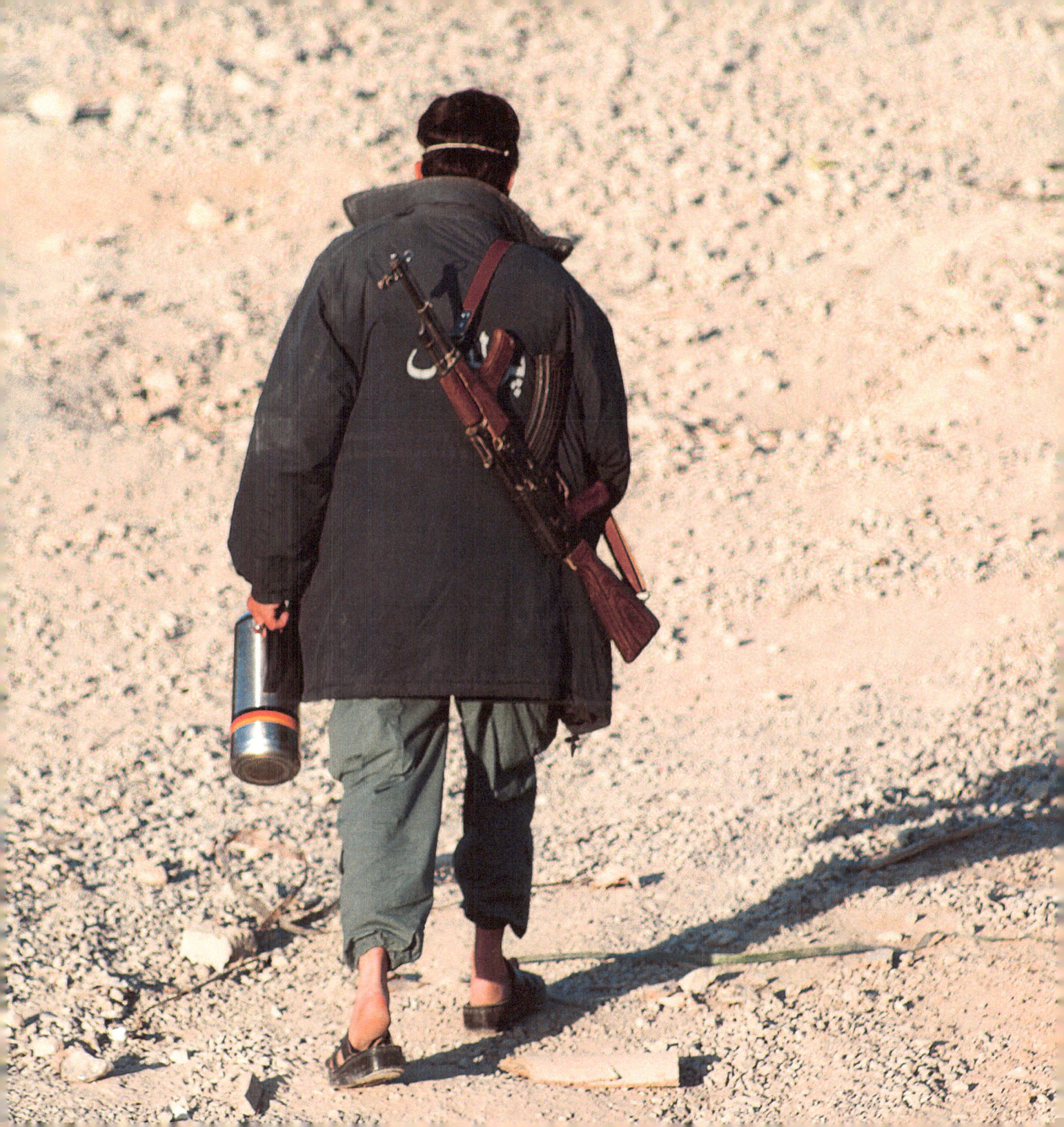

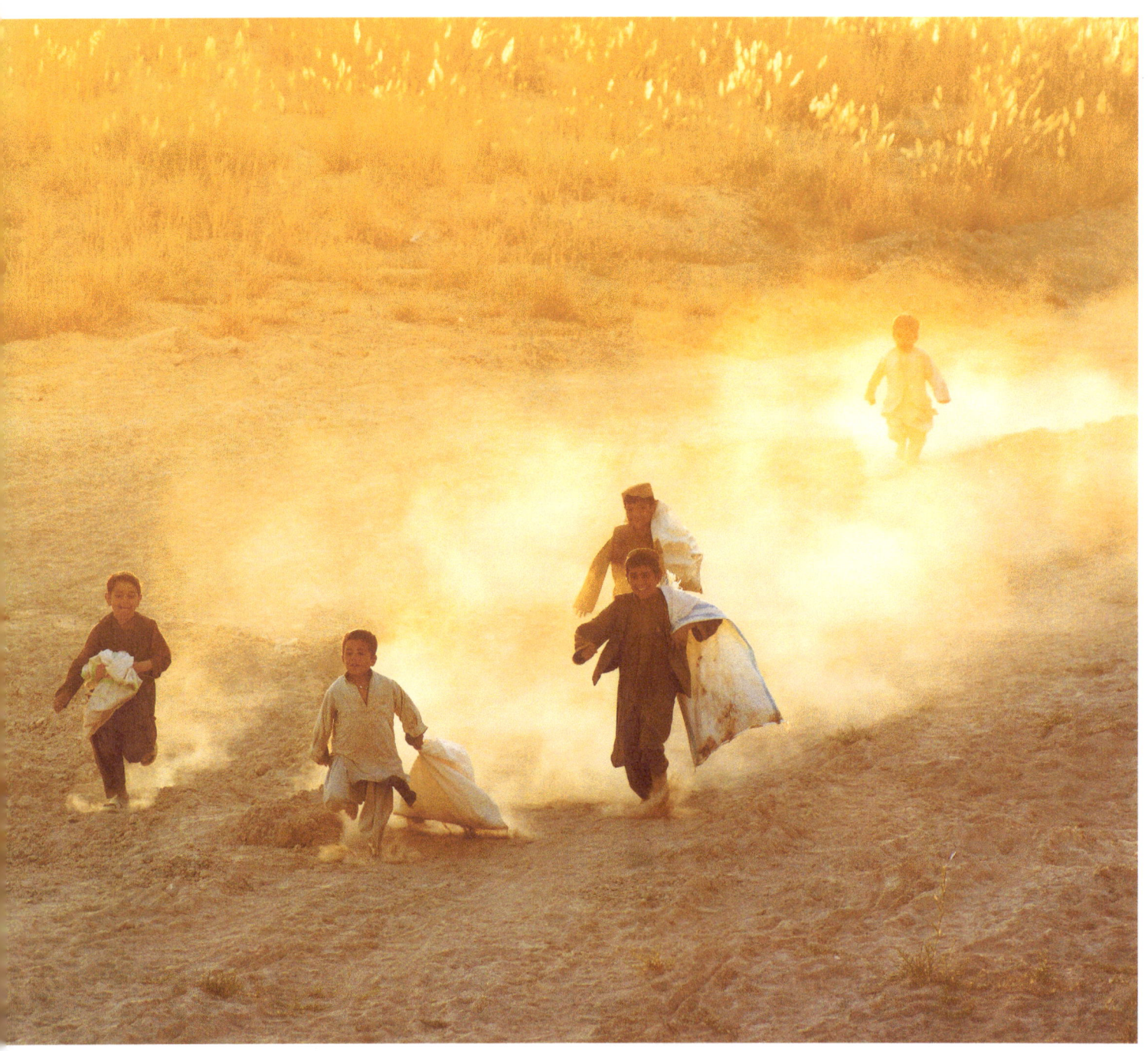

On a calm autumn evening, I was relaxing on top of the fortified ramparts of my camp. Looking toward the setting sun, I noticed a group of children emerging from the light of a fine dust cloud. My heart, moved, contracted before the beauty of the scene. My eye, open and alert, saw the exquisite photo that would soon vanish forever. I did not have my camera! A sniper trains to shoot at distant targets. I had just missed a close one. My hands were empty, but my wrist was encircled by the rosary of every good soldier. This sacred bracelet held not words, but numbers. It was a watch. I took note of the time, vowing to return the next day.

I had secretly arranged things so I would not have any tasks at that time. So just like a soldier awaiting a perfect ambush, the next day I was at my post. My camera was open and loaded. My finger was already crushing the dust on the trigger. A ray of orange light was crossing the focused lens. The stage was illuminated. The spectator, solitary and impatient, stood waiting from the solitary location of the raised platforms. The only thing missing was the stars, who I hoped would soon be lit by the largest of spotlights, the sun.

The ambushing soldier was awaiting the appearance of the beloved and coveted targets. As the sun continued to recede, they arrived! The objects were not enemies , but young children. I serenely raised my arms. I aimed. I pressed. I smiled. From their perspective, I must have looked like an archer aiming from the top of a castle wall. Like infantrymen taking me by storm, when they spotted me they ran toward me with smiles on their faces. I responded with a flurry of photos.

The sun could set now. As if the whole world had waited for the end of this little show, the light of the sky ultimately disappeared under the distant horizon. I descended from the walls. Another village was starting to pray. I too praised the heavens and its beauties. My day had been a success. I too could go to sleep.

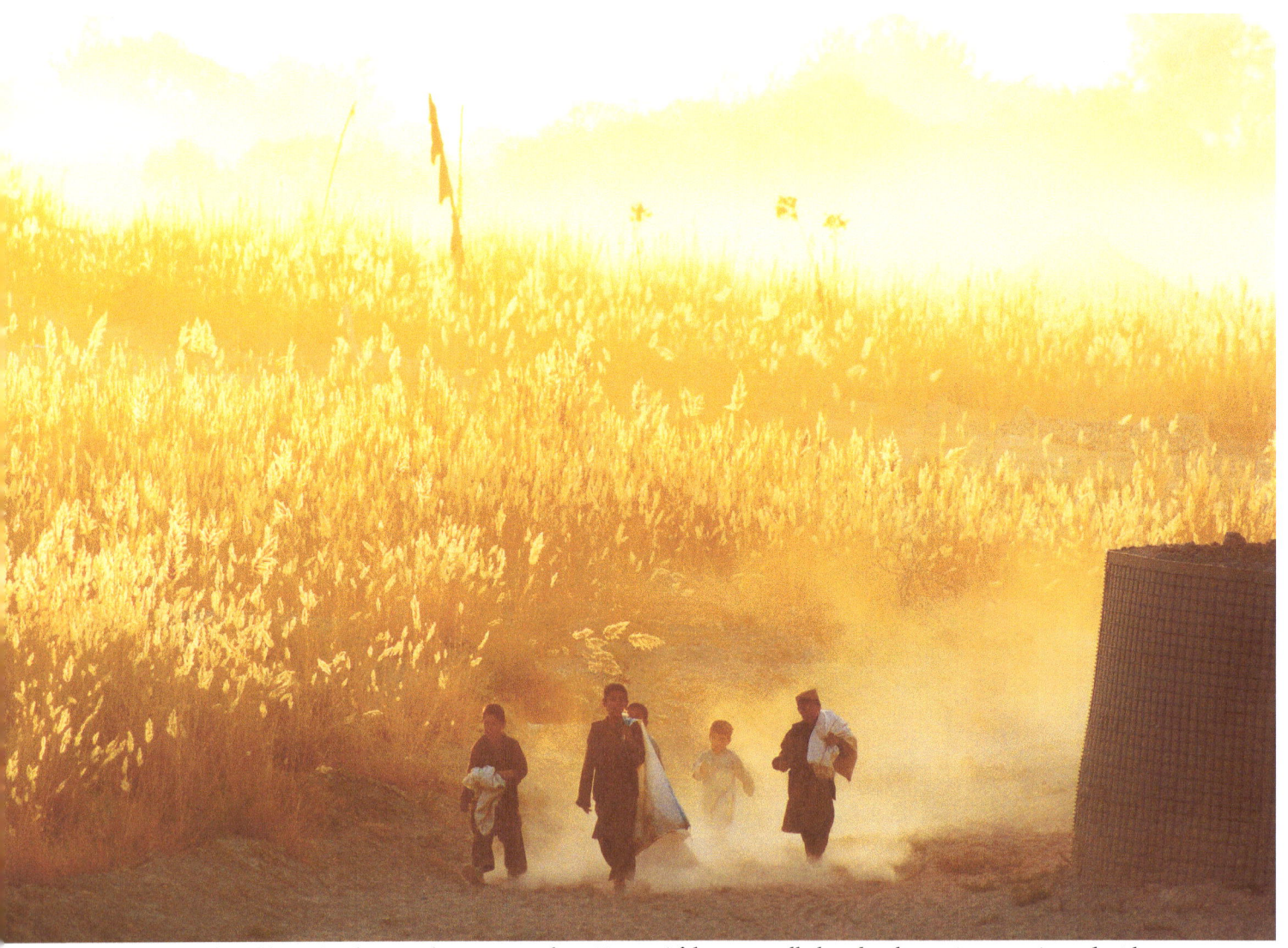

The City of Children: the day was drawing to a close. Young Afghans patrolled under the setting sun. Armed with bags, they were looking for any object that could be useful to them. Did they know that the golden brush concealed a cemetery filled with children?

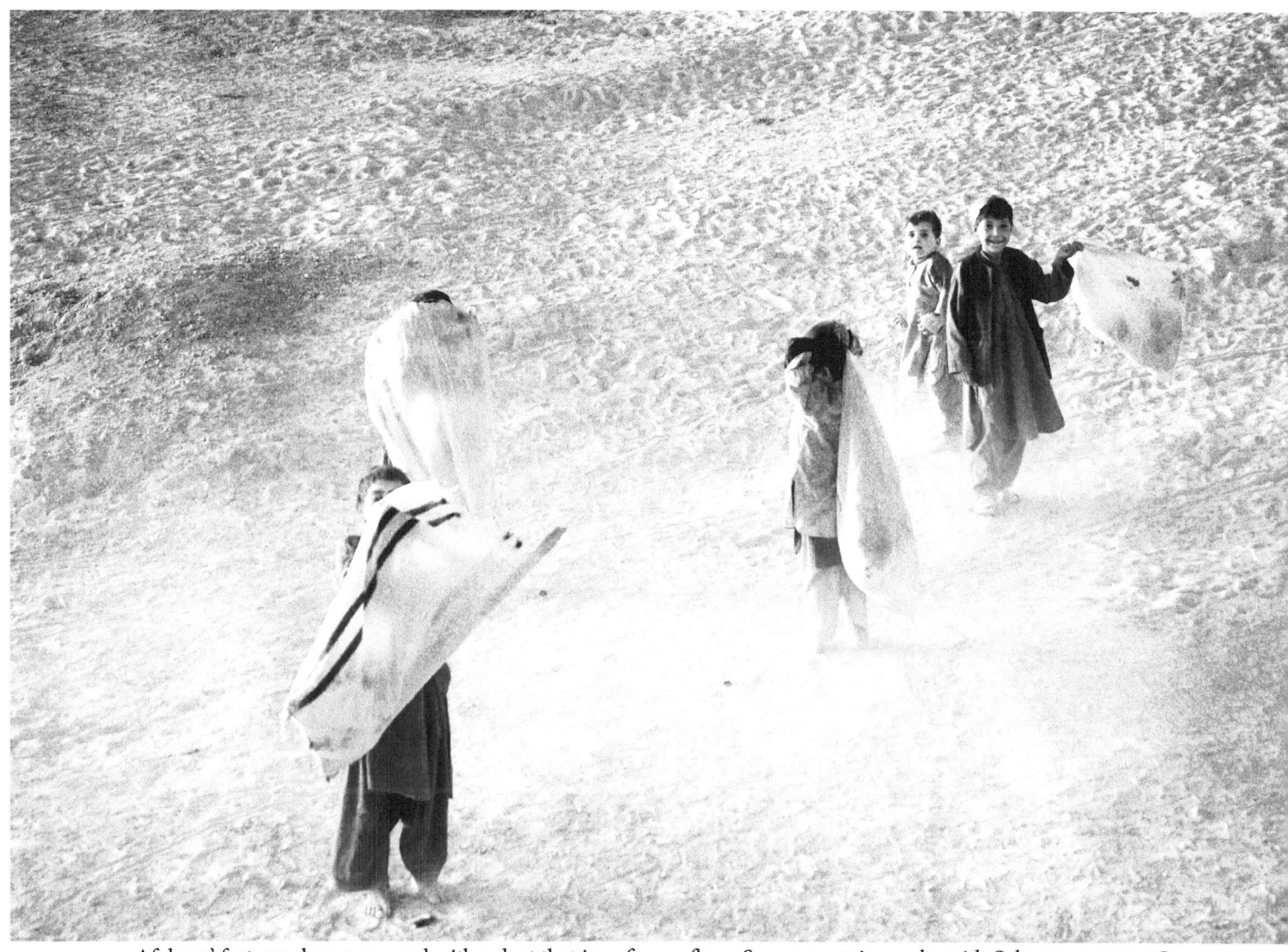

Afghans' feet are always covered with a dust that is as fine as flour. Some countries are humid. Others are snowy. In Afghanistan, it is the dust that is omnipresent.

I had the experience of helping out with a film set that was reproducing the Kandahar region. The property master took out a jar that had cost a lot of money. It was filled with fake dust. In Afghanistan, dust was everywhere. People worked hard to be rid of it. And yet, on a film set, people paid to get an imitation of it. Incredible! It goes to show that some ordinary things gain value when they are far from us.

In the same way, I witnessed many soldiers who, once they returned to their home countries, missed their military adventures. They would have paid a lot of money to return to Afghanistan. Some of them did indeed return. Others stayed there. They paid dearly for this return.

As in many Third World countries, dogs are everywhere in Afghanistan. With no masters but hunger and cold, they prowl in packs. Unfortunately, it seems to be a national sport to throw stones at them. It is the same for donkeys, whose daily cries of suffering mingle with the piety of the calls to prayer. Despite its beauties, Afghanistan is still a cruel country. The strong strike the weak, and the weak strike the weaker. But if one thinks about it, is this situation truly unique to Afghanistan?

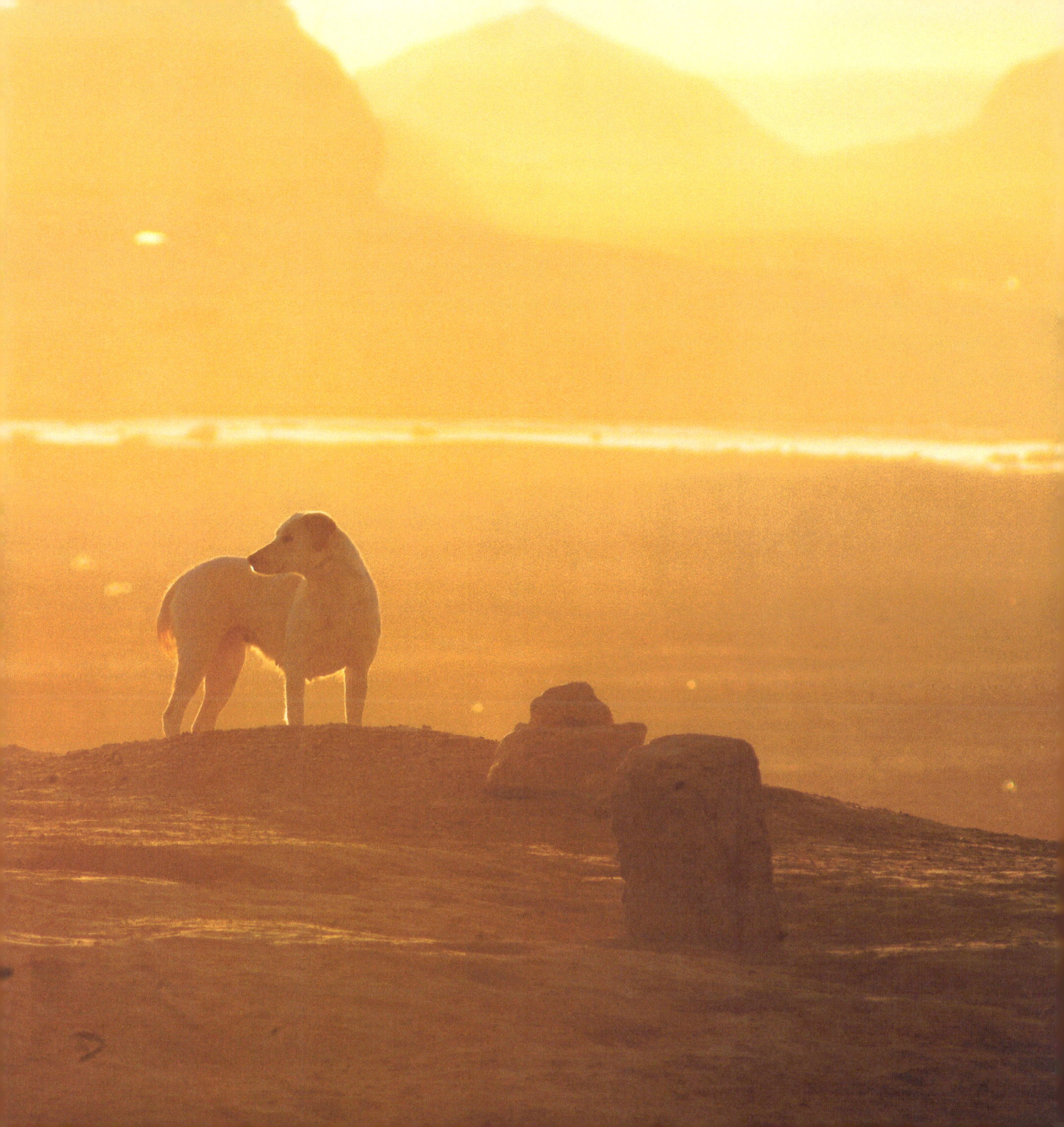

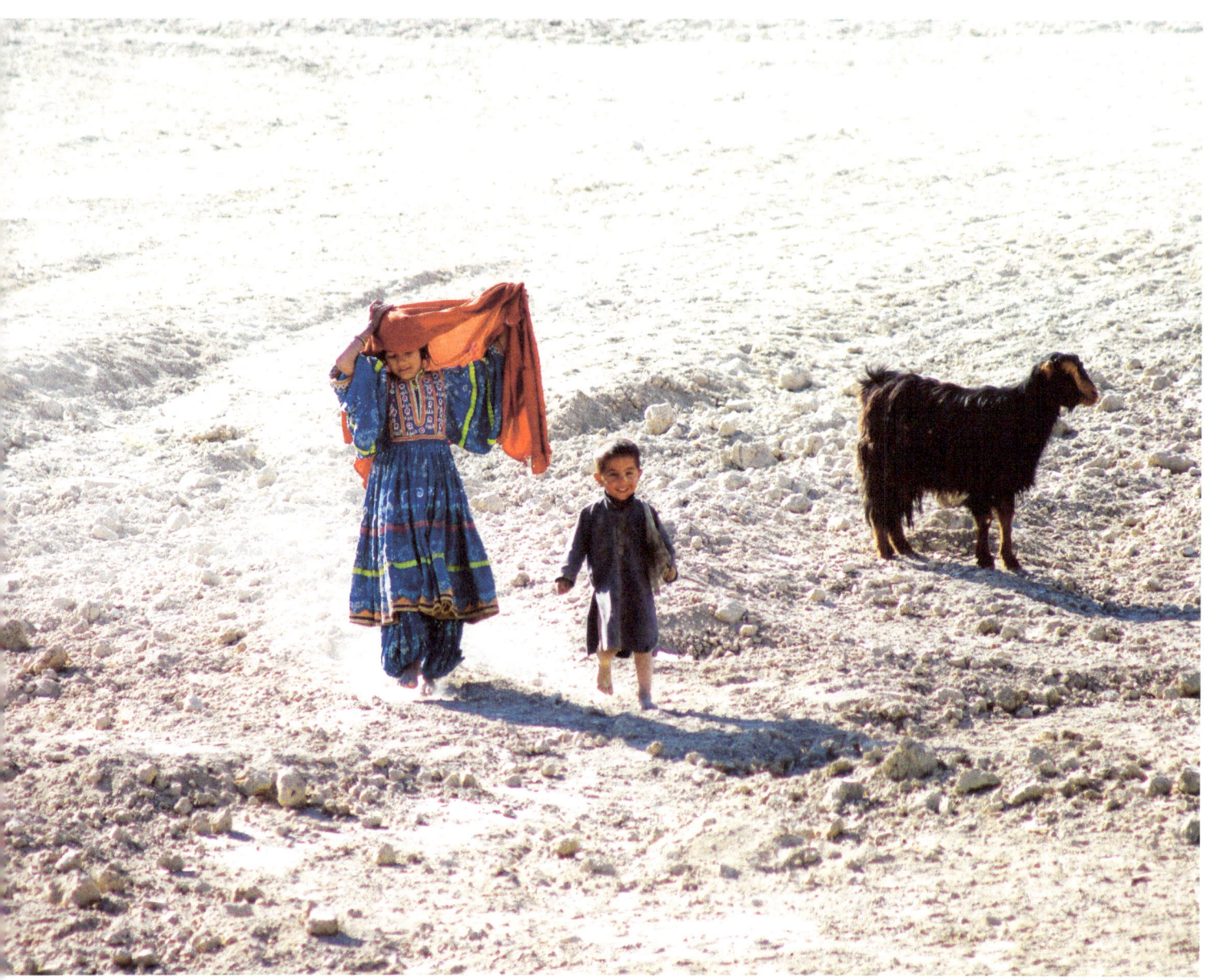

This young nomad girl is one of the few children I saw share what was given to her. She first approached hesitantly, took the drink I offered her, then went to sit down with her younger brothers to make sure they shared fairly. An oasis had sprung up right in the middle of the war!

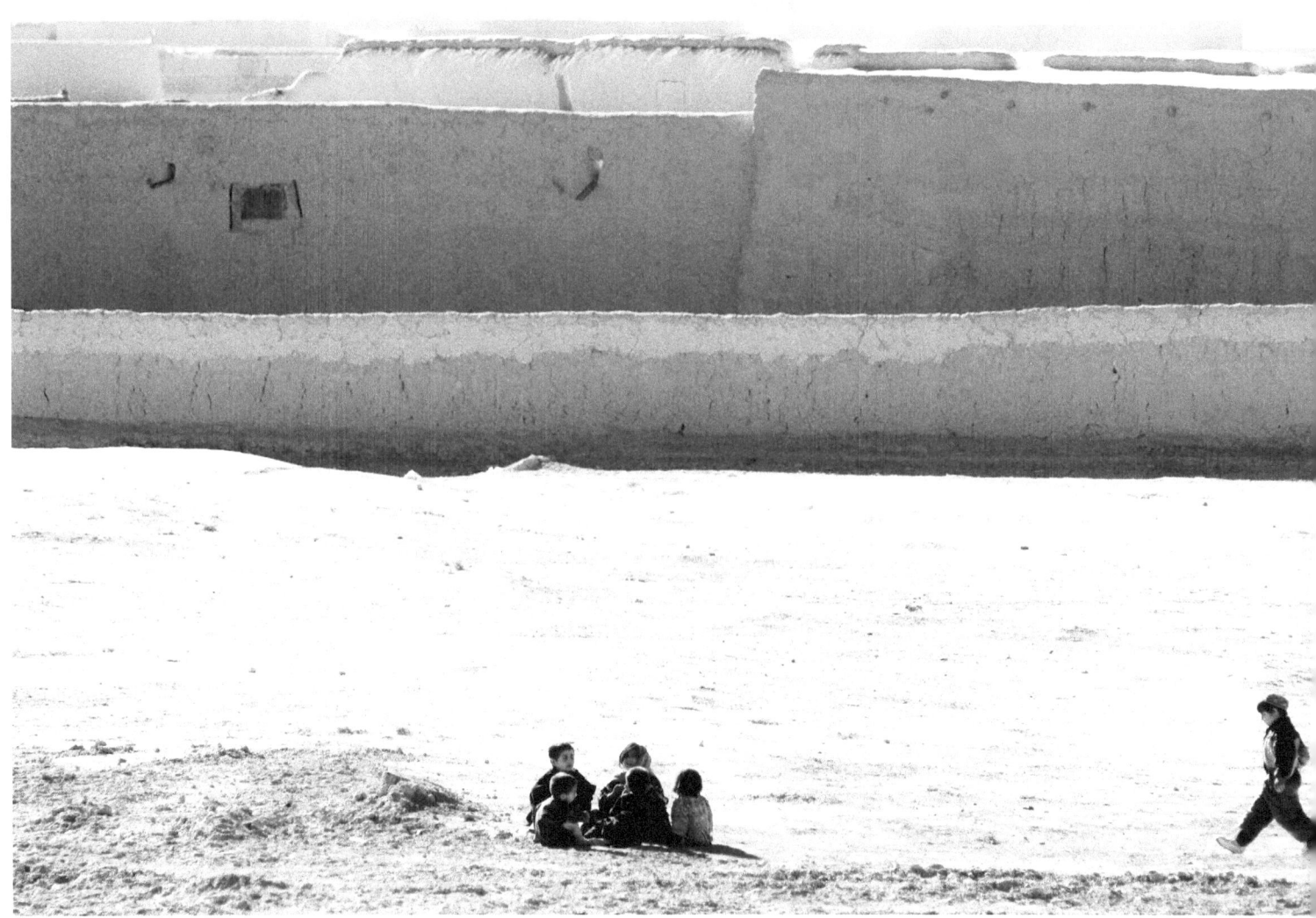

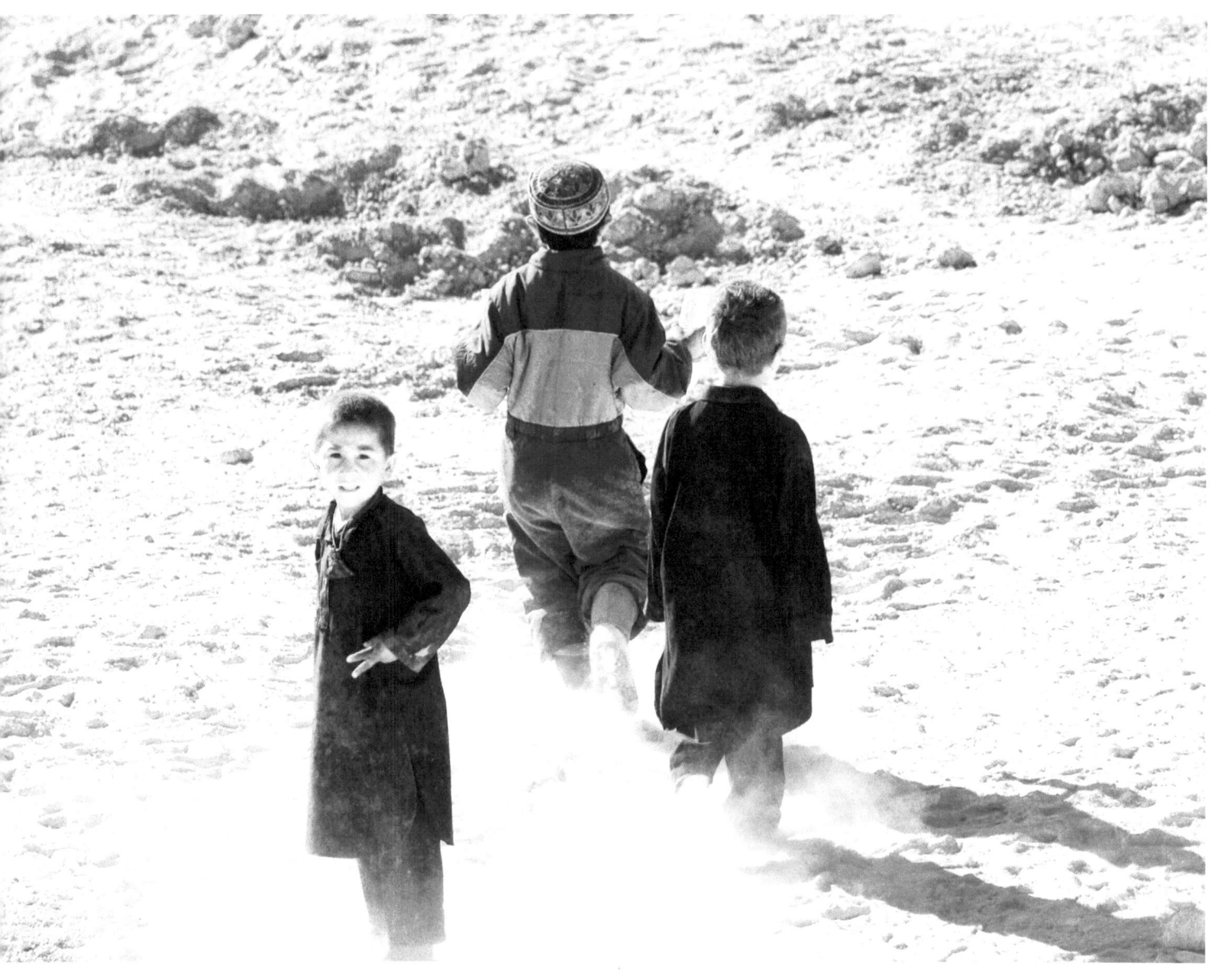

The curious gaze of a child on what must have looked to him like an extraterrestrial dressed in a bizarre outfit: me!

Through the lens of his telescope, the astronomer travels in universes that are billions of light years away. Light travels at a speed equivalent to seven times the Earth's circumference. However, on the galactic scale, light travels slowly. The image of the stars reaches us with a delay of billions of years. Some stars therefore show us what they were like in the caveman era and even earlier. To look at the sky is to travel in time; it is to witness the phenomenon of the beginning of the universe.

With my camera, even if what I was looking at was close, I too was traveling in the past. In Afghanistan, being on the periphery of a military camp is truly to be situated between two worlds, two dimensions. Behind me were satellite antennae and frequency-hopping communication equipment. A few dozen meters in front of me, nomads were walking with their goats between tents made out of sewn trimmings. Behind, zealous soldiers were doing sit-ups on a plastic mat. In the view reflected by my observation equipment, a man was positioning a small rug toward Mecca in order to engage in private prayer.

Closer to me, a group of young people were entertaining themselves by manipulating the joysticks of an electronic game while a nervous soldier was calling his wife for the tenth time that week. And just below a white cloud that had formed some distance in front of the camp, Afghans were gathering at the call to prayer.

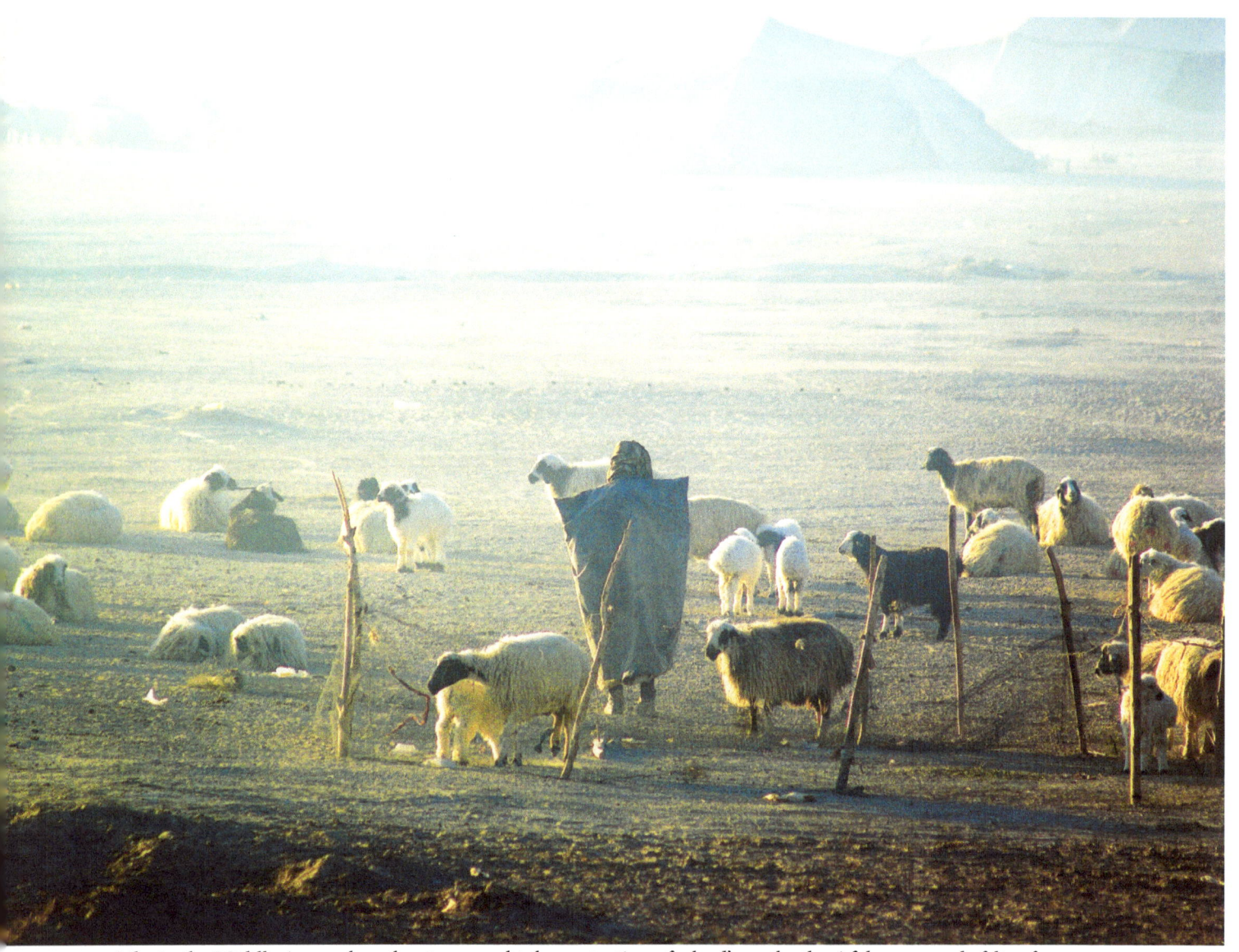

Like in the Middle Ages, when the stags sought the protection of a lord's castle, the Afghan nomads felt safe near a military base. They would come set up their tents there.

That morning, a shepherd was watching his animals in the coolness of a November dawn. I was watching the landscape, keeping an eye out for armed insurgents. Not finding any, I took the opportunity to engage in a photo shoot.

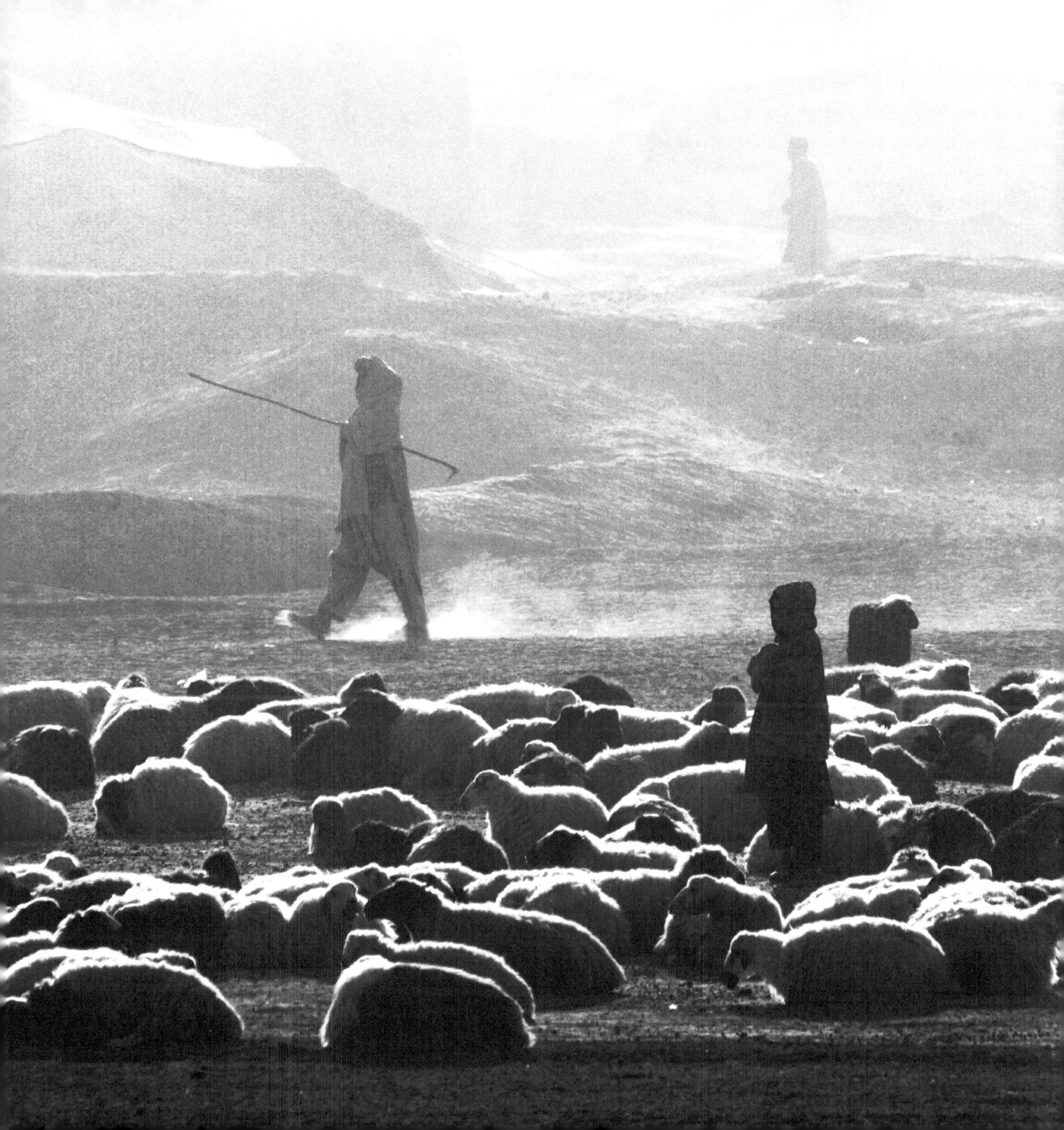

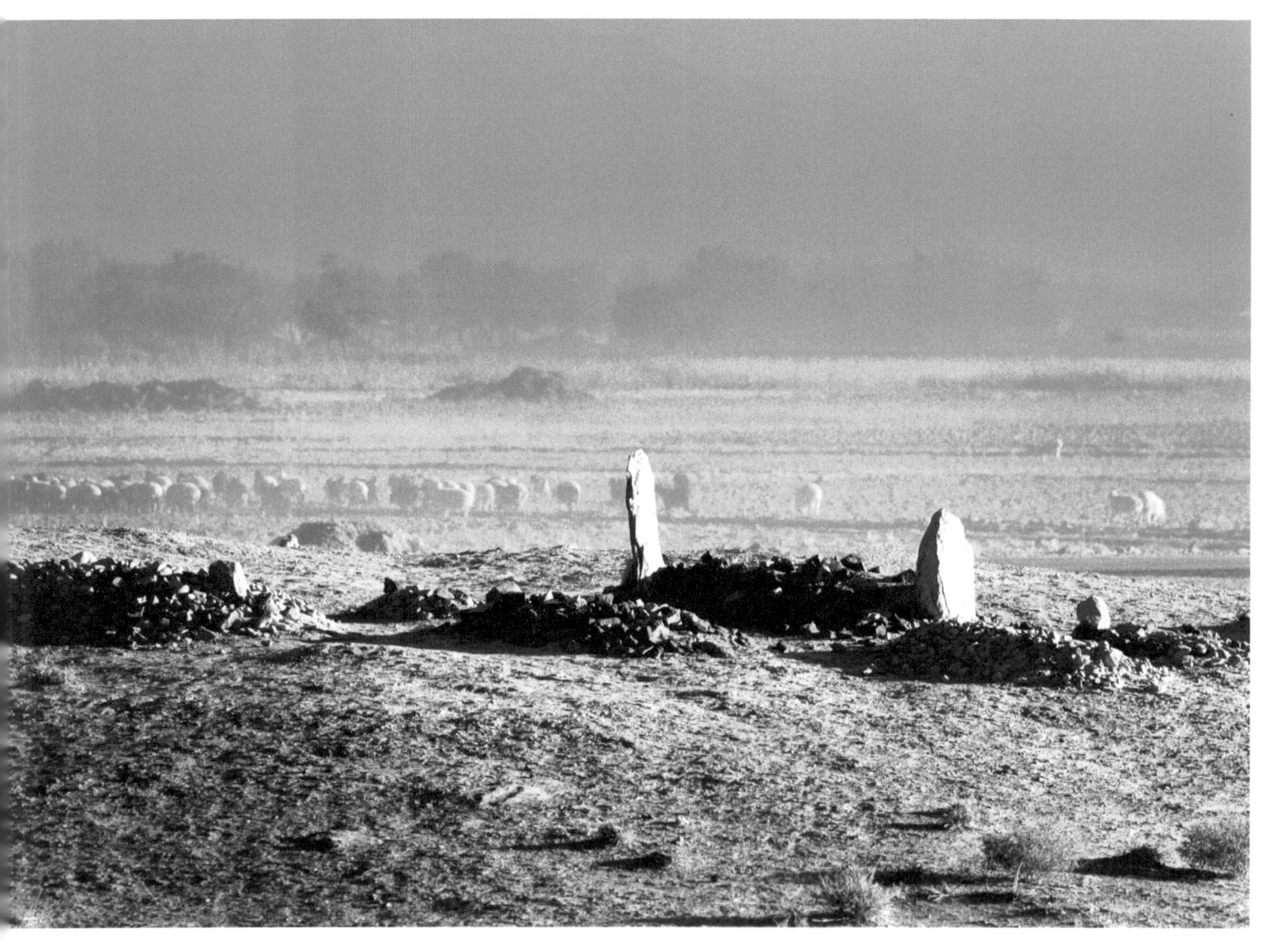

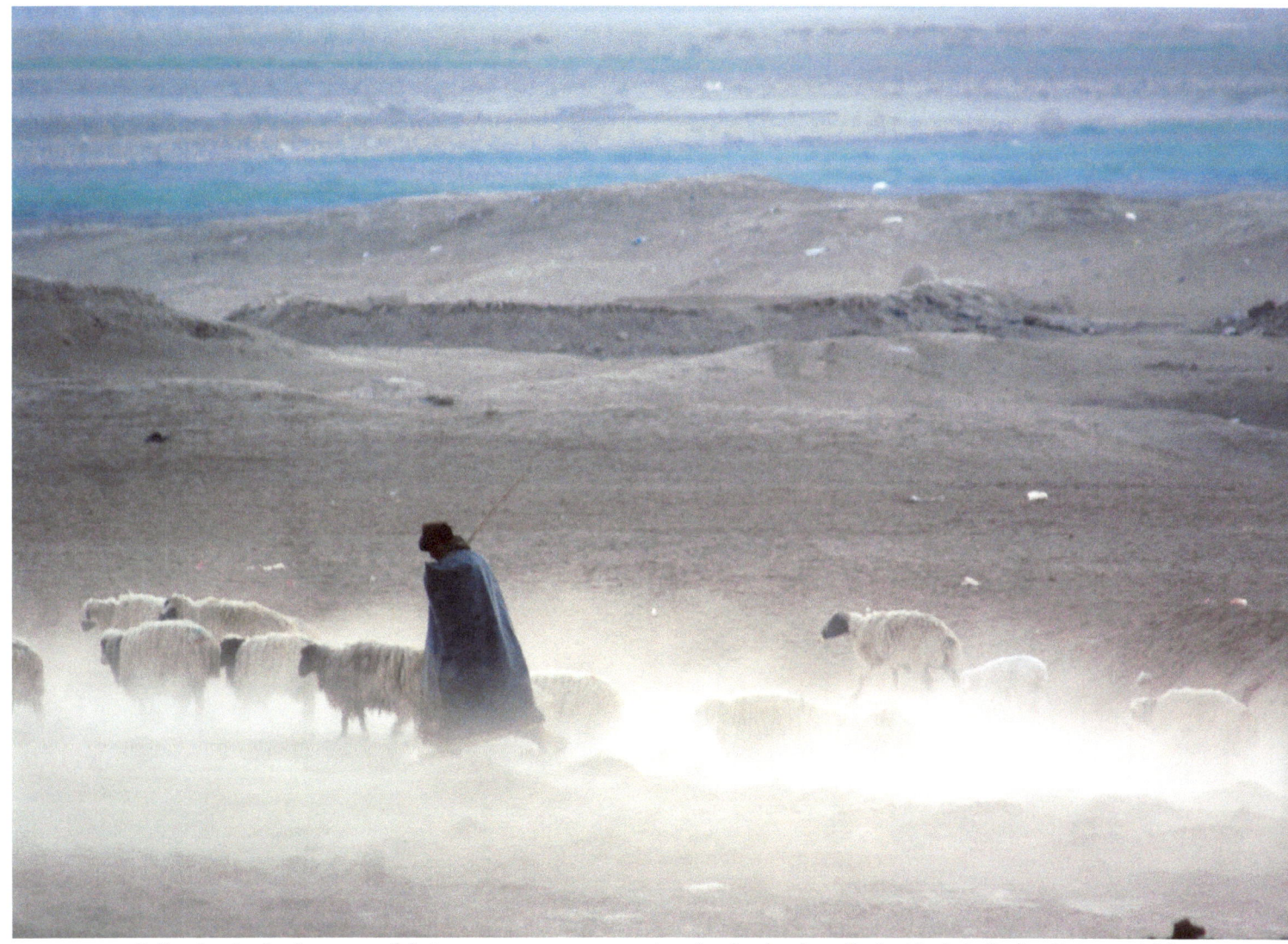

Following in the footsteps of their ancestors, every morning the shepherds walked with their flocks. Going to Afghanistan is a bit like traveling through time—both into the future and into the past. What happened a thousand years ago will undoubtedly be the same in five hundred years, but with the hope that only war will have disappeared.

That day, a shepherd came over to me. I offered him a cigar. After smoking it silently, he left me to lead his flock farther away. He did not know that his image would circulate around the world. He did not know that he would enter our homes. I too was getting ready to leave Afghanistan…

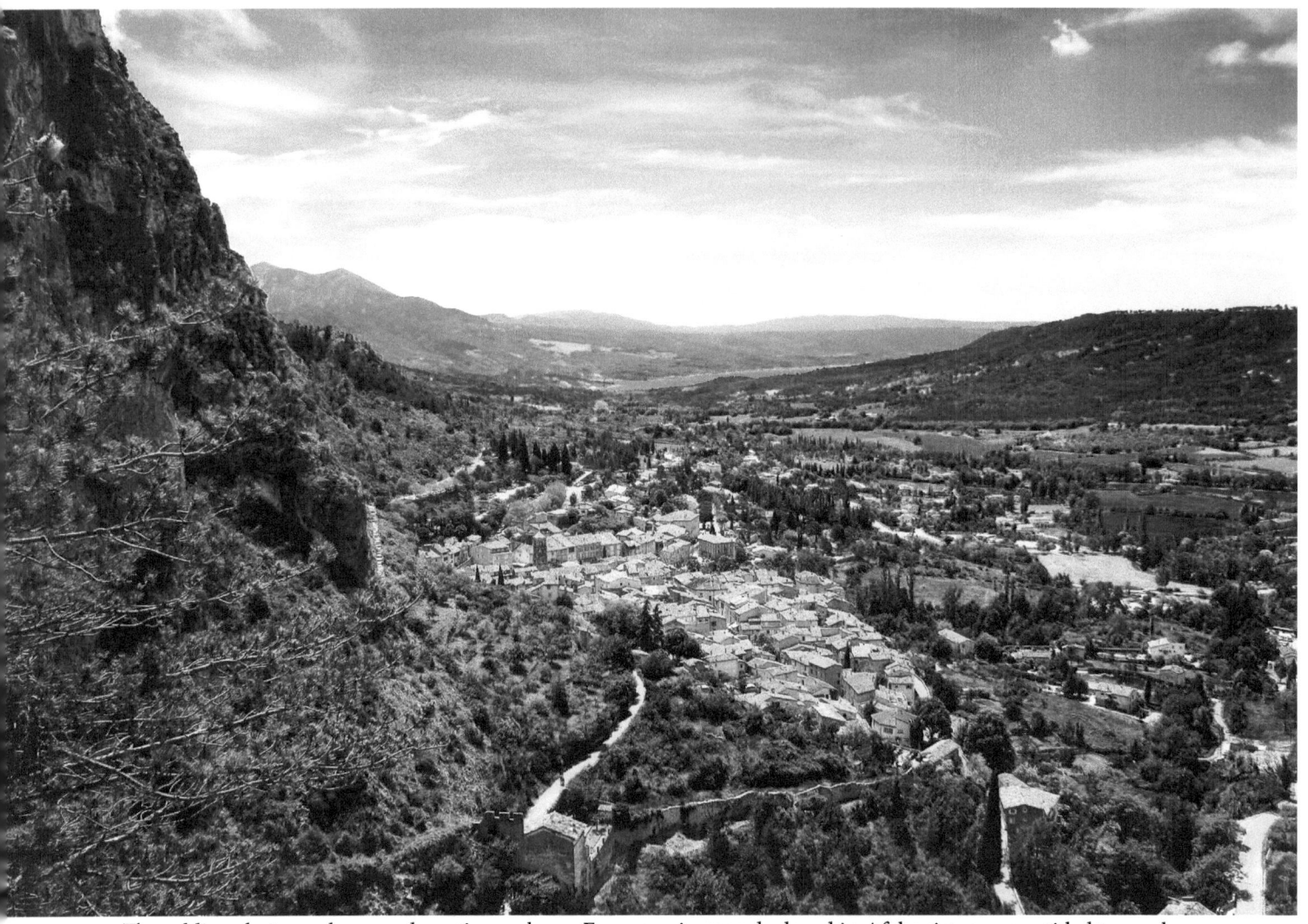

The soldier-photographer was departing on leave. Every serviceman deployed in Afghanistan was entitled to one leave during his mission. He could go home or to an international destination, such as Provence, as I did.

Like Afghanistan, France endured wars for millennia. But today, it is a magnificent country that yesterday's enemies can visit and admire. These enemies do not need armies or strategic maneuvers to take possession of a city and its splendors. All they need to do is go there and look.

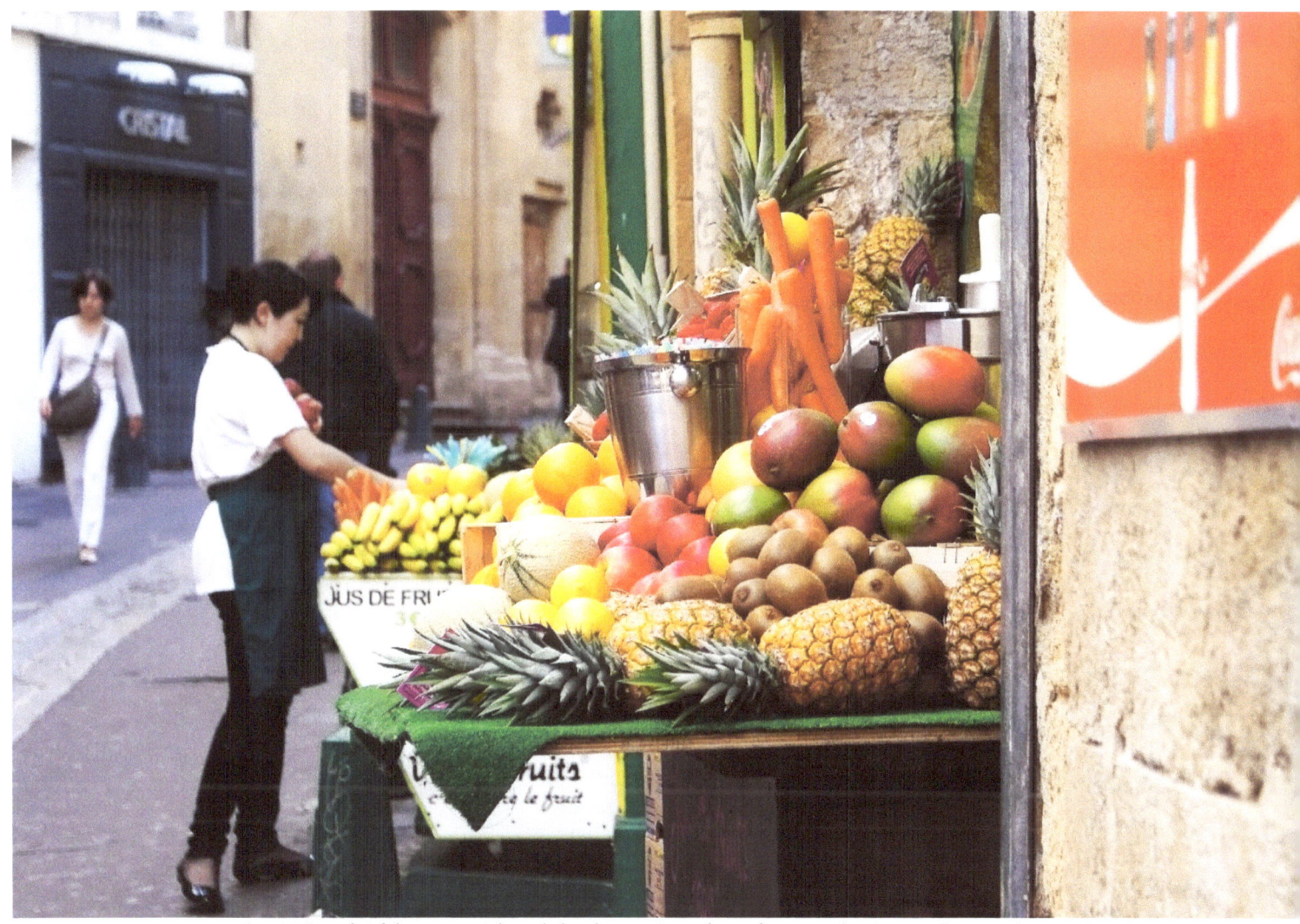

Vacation at last! I loved Afghanistan. I loved the desert. But after a few months, I missed some things: abundance, contrasting colors, the smell of moisture, greenery, the joy of hearing rain, the feeling of walking in peace, with hands that were practically empty and armed only with a camera.

Two weeks into my vacation, I was already bored. I needed to return to Kandahar's mountains and fields of grapes. I needed to return to my second home.

This is what is on the other side of the lens . . .

Experiencing the sound of battles on the horizon, the voices of children at play. At the top of the cross-hair of the lens of my weapon, the crescent crowning a mosque. One degree lower, a little girl helping her big brother push a cart like an ant pushing an enormous twig. Beneath the cloud of an explosion, the cooking smoke emerging from the chimney of a house. In the foreground of battalions combing through a village, a shepherd leaving for another day. In the background of a mechanized offensive, an ancient mountain hiding the first glows of the sunrise.

A photographer is like a magician. With a simple click, he can make ugliness disappear and stop time. He can isolate the beauty of a tiny flower and remove the heat of the desert. He can make a battle be forgotten to future generations. He can silence the ordeal of gunshots and explosions. With a simple activation of the lens, he can destroy a large army approaching on the side. He can freeze a joyful moment and make it continue for eternity. He can capture a soul that is imprisoned by war and place it in a book like a sacred work in the gallery of a magnificent museum. He can gather pieces of hell and assemble them into a mosaic that is worthy of paradise. He can recruit the image of several isolated orphans and raise an army resolved to conquer hearts the world over.

I have been told that in Hawaii it is possible to experience all four seasons in a single afternoon. In Afghanistan, it is possible to experience all the states of mind during a single patrol. One can see a child stand up in the waves of an ocean of wheat and, just a few moments later, a man work in the shade of a leaning tree. One can go from the whistling of bullets to the song of birds in the fields. From the corpse of a fighter to the guileless look of a parent. From the tears of a soldier to the charm of a river under a bridge of earth. From desert-colored camouflage to vineyards papered with green grapes. From blood to the red of the rising sun. From desperation to hope. From death to life. If I were to summarize my stay in this country, I would compare it to a long, light-filled journey interspersed with a few nights.

For Afghanistan is not just a war. Perhaps one day it will no longer be a war at all!

Under the constellation of a distant helicopter formation, night was falling. A day was drawing to a close, like the photographer's adventure.

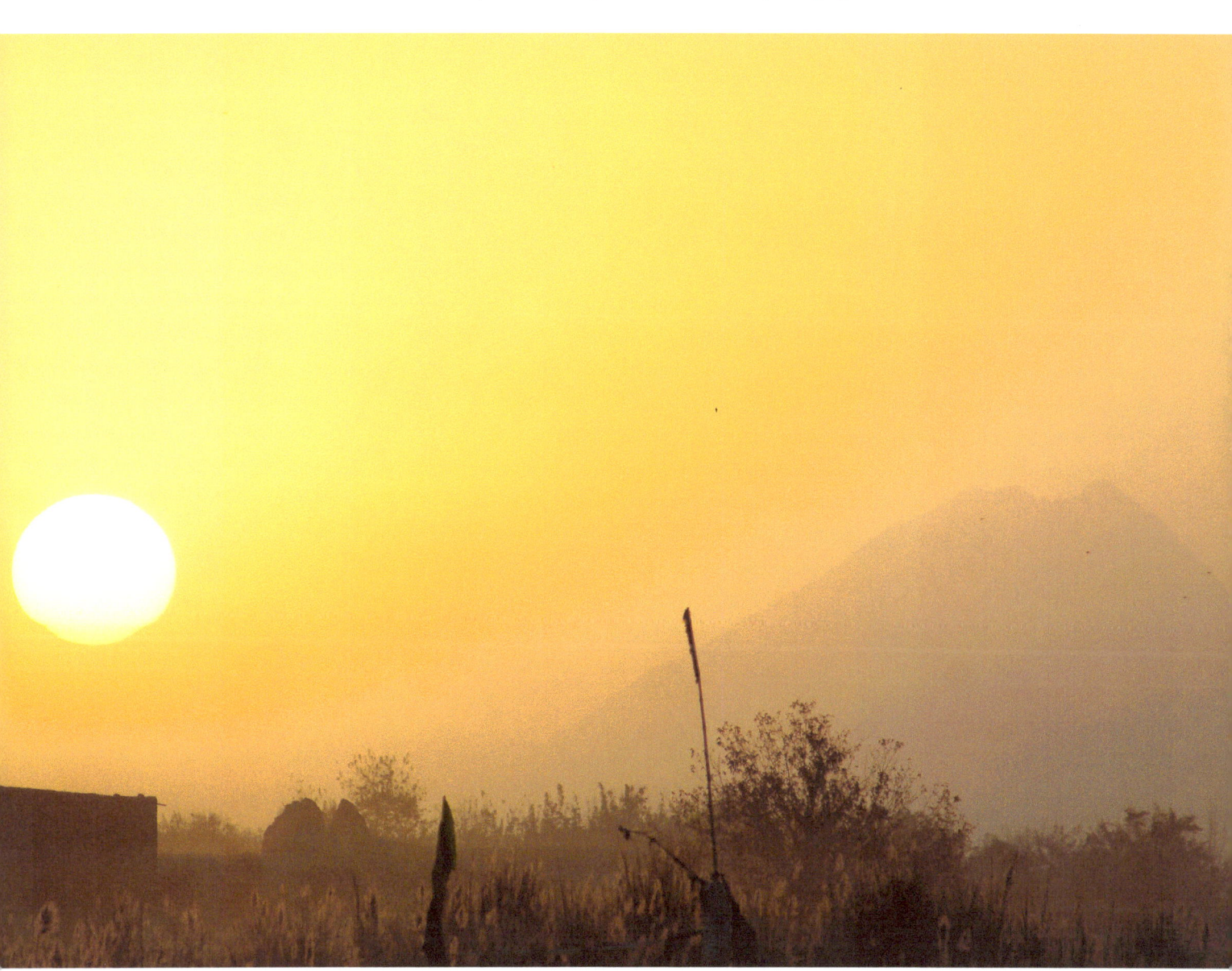

End of volume 1

www.ingramcontent.com/pod-product-compliance
Lightning Source LLC
Chambersburg PA
CBHW051909210526
45473CB00006B/1963